THE WORLD AND GOD ARE NOT-TWO

Comparative Theology / *Thinking Across Traditions*

SERIES EDITORS

Loye Ashton and John Thatamanil

This series invites books that engage in constructive comparative theological reflection that draws from the resources of more than one religious tradition. It offers a venue for constructive thinkers, from a variety of religious traditions (or thinkers belonging to more than one), who seek to advance theology understood as "deep learning" across religious traditions.

THE WORLD AND GOD ARE NOT-TWO

A Hindu–Christian Conversation

DANIEL SOARS

Fordham University Press NEW YORK 2023

Fordham University Press also publishes its books in a variety of electronic formats. Some content that appears in print may not be available in electronic books.

Visit us online at www.fordhampress.com.

Library of Congress Cataloging-in-Publication
Data available online at https://catalog.loc.gov.

Printed in the United States of America
25 24 23   5 4 3 2 1

First edition

CONTENTS

ABBREVIATIONS AND CONVENTIONS

Vedāntic Texts

BSBh	*Brahmasūtrabhāṣya*
US	*Upadeśasāhasrī*
VC	*Vivekacūḍāmaṇi*
BG	*Bhagavadgītā*
Ch.Up.	*Chāndogya Upaniṣad*
Br.Up.	*Bṛhadāraṇyaka Upaniṣad* (and so on for other Upaniṣads)
-Bh.	After any *Upaniṣad* signifies Śaṁkara's commentary (*bhāṣya*) on it

Thomas Aquinas

ST	*Summa Theologiae*
SCG	*Summa Contra Gentiles*
De pot.	*Quaestiones disputatae de potentia dei*
De ver.	*De veritate*
LdC	*Liber de Causis* (Aquinas's Commentary on the LdC)

Conventions

Throughout this book I use diacriticals (e.g., Śaṁkara, Vedānta) for the names of Sanskritic philosophical traditions, concepts, texts, and thinkers. The only exceptions are for South Asian names of figures from about 1800 on, where I use established roman renderings (e.g., Vivekananda, Abhishiktananda).

"The person who discriminates between the Real and the unreal, whose mind is turned away from the unreal, who possesses calmness and the allied virtues, and who is longing for liberation, is alone considered qualified to enquire after Brahman."

Vivekacūḍāmaṇi 17

My son, if you accept my words
and store up my commands within you,
turning your ear to wisdom
and applying your heart to understanding—
indeed, if you call out for insight
and cry aloud for understanding,
and if you look for it as for silver
and search for it as for hidden treasure,
then you will understand the fear of the Lord
and find the knowledge of God.

Proverbs 2:1–5

Introduction

The primary task of Christian theology is to clarify how the God we believe in is to be understood. He is not a part of the world, and yet the world has its being and definitive sense from him. What kind of existence does he enjoy and, consequently, what kind of being does the world enjoy in relation to him? Only when this issue is sufficiently clarified can we approach other things—like the history of salvation, the sacraments, Christian virtues, and the Christian moral life—in our theological reflection.[1]

Framing the Questions

This book is one particular way of tackling what Robert Sokolowski has identified as the primary and foundational task of Christian theology: to clarify how God is both *distinct from* and *related to* the world.[2] The reason this is such an important issue is because it is like the all-encompassing canvas on which the minutiae of one's theological worldview is meticulously painted. While all Christians might be working with broadly the same palette and brushes, the hues will come out very differently depending on the precise nature of what is underneath.

As a professional theologian, my approach to these issues is primarily an academic one: I engage with texts and philosophical arguments, and I write in a register that is scholarly and, at times, technical. My hope is that my work will be taken seriously by other laborers in the academic vineyard. A foreseeable but unintended consequence of such an approach, focused on textual details and conceptual refinements, however, is that this book is likely to be considered somewhat abstruse by many of those who inspired it. I am thinking of my father, who first showed me how to pray; I am thinking of some of my students who have given up on the idea of God because of a lack of evidence; and I am also thinking of the multitude of friends and acquaintances who are not hostile to religion but who live their lives quite happily "without God." In all of these cases, the question that seems to linger in the background—often answered before it has been carefully asked and systematically explored—is what or who we understand "God" to be in the first place.

I remember this question striking me with particular force at Mass one day. At the moment of the consecration, the priest explained to the congregation that this high point of the eucharistic rite was when "heaven came down to earth," when God "became really present in our midst." The language may have been consciously intended by this priest as metaphorical, and, of course, there are rich Roman Catholic patterns of symbolic articulations of the real presence. Nevertheless, I felt a deep sense of unease, and I realized that it was the same unease that had started to affect my prayer life; which irked me when students asked for empirically verifiable evidence of God; and which bemused me when friends said that they were happy "without" God. As a Roman Catholic, it wasn't that I disagreed with the priest's sacramental theology on the "micro"-level, but that I balked at the way God was being understood at the "macro"-level—for I couldn't help thinking (and feeling) that whatever might be going on in the Eucharist, the ritualized actions of one human being could not make the omnipresent God any more concretely present than God already (always) was. Whether or not the priest meant it this way, the implication of his words seemed to be that God was not *already* there—and language shapes our mental pictures, especially when it is language that is heard over and over again and shapes Christian living from the cradle to the grave.

The picture of God I was resisting was that of some sort of a thing that exists alongside of or parallel to the world. This is a god of whose existence one could justifiably ask for evidence; indeed, it is a god one could conceivably do without altogether. Picturing God this way inevitably colors one's understanding of other aspects of Christian existence—as Sokolowski says—like salvation and sacraments. It may not be a carefully worked out picture, but this makes it all the more pernicious: as with so many other "unconscious biases," it affects us almost in spite of ourselves.

I have become increasingly conscious of my own orientation—cognitive, experiential, and spiritual—toward an understanding of God as an *ever-present* reality and, consequently, an understanding of the world as always already suffused with the vital presence of God. The "evidence" is all around us, and we can no more do without God than we can do without the air we breathe. This too has implications for the rest of our theological terrain. A God who is ever-present is not a God who created the world at some time in the distant past, but a God who is *continually* creative at every moment in the here and now; a God who is ever-present is not a God who capriciously or occasionally intervenes in the world (as if God existed somehow "outside" of created reality), but a God who is *constantly* active in and through the world; and a God who holds me in being is not a God who looks at me from the other side of an altar, but a God in whose very life I share. There are confusing and potentially troubling doctrinal questions likely to be provoked by understanding God in this way—not least, why a God who is ever-present could become specifically incarnate in one man or how to understand the nature of salvation, if the world and God are always already "at-one" in the first place.

Of course, I do not claim to be the first or only Christian thinker to address these questions. The nature of the distinction and relation between the world and God has been explored by the greatest theologians and mystics in the tradition: from Augustine to Boethius, Eriugena to Anselm, Aquinas to Eckhart, and many more besides. Yet, it was a fairly chance encounter with the work of someone I had never heard of which led me to want to pursue these questions for myself. Sara Grant—a little known twentieth-century Roman Catholic who spent most of her life in India—wrote an autobiography entitled *Towards an Alternative Theology: Confessions of a Non-dualist Christian*.[3] She said there that she hoped her words

> might find an echo in the heart of at least a few other crypto non-dualists and so help them to recognize their own identity and come to terms with it, and also, especially if they were from a Christian background, help them to recognize and relate to the ultimate non-dualism of Christian revelation.[4]

For this "crypto non-dualist," her voice continues to reverberate through my spiritual and existential fabrics, and the years I have spent writing this book represent something like the extended conversation I would like to have had with Sister Sara in person, had we been able to meet before she died in 2000. I hope that you will enjoy taking part in this conversation too.

My Argument

The key conceptual argument that underpins each chapter is that God cannot be identified with any "thing" in (or out of) the world (because "God" does not refer to any kind of "thing" but to the originating source and sustaining ground of all that exists) and that there is nothing in (or out of) the world that is ontologically separate from God either. It is precisely *because* God is not-a-*thing* that can be conceptually contrasted with empirical things that there is *no*-thing that is ontologically constituted without relation to God. Indeed, certain Christian theologians have even dared to say that the world is *not-other* than God—such is the relation of radical intimacy entailed by creation—without wanting to suggest any straightforward identity between the finite contingent order and its eternal divine cause.[5] In seeking to navigate with these thinkers between the Scylla of an undifferentiated monism and the Charybdis of a detached deism, I point beyond the enumerative dualism of creature "and" Creator toward a non-dualism in which the world and God are neither "one" nor "two."

To make my case, I begin in the familiar waters of Christian theology with the work of the contemporary Thomist David Burrell. By exploring the ways in which Aquinas (1225–1274) was drawing on Jewish and Muslim interlocutors like Moses Maimonides (1135–1204) and Ibn Sina/Avicenna (ca. 980–1037), Burrell shows how Thomas's attempts to conceptualize the sui generis distinction-and-relation between the world and God are influenced by, at times differ from, and also converge with, certain ways of thinking through this distinction-and-relation in the other Abrahamic traditions. One of Aquinas's key concerns is to explicate the *asymmetrical* character of this world-God relation, for this is what "creation" means for Aquinas: not merely or primarily a temporal beginning, but an ongoing and nonreciprocal dependence of creature on Creator. In other words, what it means to be "world" does not and cannot exclude what it means to be "God" because the world is ontologically constituted by and through its existence-giving relation to the Creator, while God would be God even without the world. The particular argument of this book is that the language of "non-duality" can help us to articulate this unique relation in which the world and God are neither separate nor the same.

It is for this reason that I pick up on a tantalizing invitation in the footnotes and margins of many of Burrell's articles to explore the metaphysics of the "Christian" distinction in conversation with religious traditions beyond Abrahamic borders. Specifically, he directs Christian theologians to the work of Sara Grant. I set off from Christian shores, therefore, and journey out with Grant to the farther depths of Vedāntic Hinduism in order to see more clearly what it might mean to say that the world and God are "not two" (in Sanskrit, *advaita*). This exploration not only has the merit of helping Grant's own work to receive some of the attention that it richly deserves, but also shows how *inter*-religious dialogue (in this case, between Roman Catholic Christianity and Vedāntic Hinduism) holds the potential to inform, and even transform, the shape of *intra*-religious (Christian) theology as well.

Grant argues on the basis of a meticulous textual analysis that non-dualism (*advaita*) does not amount to ontological monism in Śaṁkara (ca. 700 CE)—the key systematizer of the Vedāntic tradition on whom she concentrates. It implies, rather, deep ontological inseparability in the sense that the world has its "self" in Brahman/God and exists only to the extent that it shares in the being of its divine source.[6] This existential "not-two-ness" of the world *in* the divine is expressed in Advaita by the notion that the ontological reality of an effect (in this case, the world) is ultimately rooted in the reality of its transcendent cause (*satkāryavāda*), and in Christian theology by the belief in a radical creation "from nothing" (ex nihilo) of the world. Both of these doctrines attempt in different ways to hold transcendence and immanence together in a creative tension and, in so doing, point not toward a total flattening out of any distinction between the world and God, but to a non-contrastive relation in which the creature is fundamentally not ontologically other (*advaita*) to the Creator.

The encounter with Advaita does not, therefore, push Christian theology toward monism (or pantheism), but it does offer a particularly arresting way of articulating what it means to see even mundane reality as radically *theo*centric. One can, of course, find clear expressions of such a theocentric and non-dualistic view of reality at the heart of the Christian tradition—not least in some of the imagery used by Jesus himself, especially in John's Gospel.[7] This work is an attempt to listen carefully to another tradition in order that we might hear this "alternative theology" in our own with fresh ears.[8] It is an exercise in interreligious learning that can help Christian theologians to rethink old problems in new ways, by highlighting a distinctive strand of non-dualism running through certain key figures and periods in the Christian tradition—from

Pseudo-Dionysius and John Scotus Eriugena to Meister Eckhart and Nicholas of Cusa, to name just a few. The reason why these resonant parallels can also be found in Aquinas, I argue, is because he shares a certain Platonic inheritance with these other thinkers—and it is particularly their *Platonism* influenced Christian doctrines that bring them close to Vedāntic non-dualism.[9]

As we will see, notwithstanding certain significant areas of conceptual convergence between Thomism and Advaita, there are also some distinctive differences. Even a non-dual Christianity has to affirm the value of embodied particularity, human corporeality, and ecclesial sociality to a greater extent than is common in mainstream Advaitic texts and thinkers, which is why Aquinas talks of "participation" and "similitude" rather than oneness and identity between creatures and their Creator. I do not attempt to resolve these differences or to explain them away because the kind of comparative theology I am engaged in here does not aim toward a Hegelian synthesis of opposites or an apologetic (whether Christian or Hindu) weighing of one tradition against another. Indeed, it is precisely in the areas of aporia where we see more clearly what distinguishes a Christian (Thomist) understanding of the distinction-and-relation between God and the world from an Advaitic (or Platonic) one.

Which "Non-dualism"?

The problem of how to articulate the character of the relation between the world and God is hardly a recent one. Some of the earliest Christian theologians tried to spell out how a changing finite order could be related to the one eternal God without making it sound as if they were two separate enumerable realities, on the one hand, or that there was no real distinction between them, on the other.[10] In thus seeking to avoid both ontological dualism and ontological monism, it could be said that a certain concept of *non*-dualism has always been at the heart of Christian theology. The explicit vocabulary of "non-dualism," however, only started to gain popular currency in the Christian tradition in the second half of the last century (partly through increasing contacts with Asian thought-worlds) and the term itself is used in a wide—and potentially confusing—range of ways in academic and popular spiritual literature. "Nondualism" is sometimes used, for example, to designate a certain manner of thinking that seeks to avoid disjunctive categorizations like "good versus evil," "life versus death," or even "Christianity versus Hinduism."[11] It can refer also, in a related sense, to a way of perceiving the world that accentuates from a scientific or philosophical point of view the (meta-)physical unity underlying the diverse empirical appearances of discrete subjects and objects.[12] In theological contexts, non-dualism is often employed to describe forms of prayer or mystical states that result in some sort of experiential union between the devotee and the object of devotion.[13] It also sometimes serves as a conceptual synonym for divine immanence or even as a term to foreground what immanence means in Indic contexts in contrast to Abrahamic ones.[14] An exhaustive inventory or genealogy of all of these distinctive, though often conceptually overlapping, usages of "nondualism" could occupy a study of its own and would be tangential to my aims and arguments here.[15] While I touch on some of the senses of the term mentioned previously, my own use of it is specifically drawn from Grant's work on Aquinas and Śaṁkara, whose conceptual systems she explains as follows:

> Both were non-dualists, understanding the relation of the universe, including individual selves, to uncreated Being in terms of a non-reciprocal relation of dependence which, far from diminishing the uniqueness and lawful autonomy of a created being within its own sphere, was their necessary Ground and condition . . . [16]

"Nondualism," in other words, is used by Grant—and will be used in this book—as a shorthand for the claim that the world is ontologically and inseparably related to God by virtue of its very existence.

Why Ask a Question About Non-dualism in Christianity at All and Why Ask It Now?

Sokolowski's contention that the God-world dialectic is the central issue around which Christian theology hinges is hardly idiosyncratic or confessionally biased to his Roman Catholic milieus. To mention another Christian theologian who espouses the same view, Kevin J. Vanhoozer asserts from his Reformed Evangelical location:

> Assumptions about the way in which God relates to the world lie behind every doctrine in systematic theology. The decision one makes as to how to conceive this relation is arguably the single most important factor in shaping one's theology.[17]

In one sense, then, there is perhaps little need to defend my focus on this question or to provide a case for its particular timeliness. There are several reasons, however, which led me to write a book about Christian non-dualism and why I think it is relevant *now*. First, and primarily, I think Grant was correct when she stated in her Teape Lectures in 1989 that contemporary Christians find it increasingly hard to relate to the traditional imagery of a God "up there" or "out there."[18] My sense is that this dislocation between inherited tradition and articulation of faith is no less severe thirty years later. Indeed, the disenchantment with Enlightenment rationalism and secular faith in progress (continuous in some ways with nineteenth-century Romantic movements, but with postwar, postcolonial, and postmodern contexts that have reinforced the disenchantment still further), and the decreasing hold of orthodox Christian religious beliefs and rituals mean that significant numbers of Christians in the twenty-first-century West have rejected belief in the God of classical theism conceived as a magnificently powerful but distantly inscrutable deity. Such broad sociological claims would, of course, require a much more careful and nuanced demonstration to be completely convincing, for traditional religious beliefs and imageries continue to flourish across vast spaces of the contemporary world, and it may be objected in any case that Grant is setting up a straw man (or god) that is too easy to attack. A critic could reasonably object that the great thinkers of the Christian tradition such as Augustine and Aquinas never *did* believe in a God "up there" or "out there" in the first place, so there is no need even to refute such a misplaced understanding.

My answer to this objection would be with a scholastic *sic et non*. Yes—it is, of course, true that Grant is not the first or the only Christian theologian to point out that it is a conceptual error to think of God as some kind of a "thing" like other finite things, which exists in some specific spatiotemporal location. In fact, part of her aim—and part of my own aim as well—is to demonstrate that the Christian tradition has consistently rejected such an idolatrous and anthropomorphic understanding of God. However, it is *not* true that such a pernicious view is nonexistent in the wider social milieus of Christian existence and, therefore, unnecessary to dismantle. If that were the case, there would be no need for Christian theologians to continue to respond to these ways of misconceiving God—whether in the pews of the Christian churches themselves or in the evidentialist critiques of contemporary New Atheism where God is misplaced as another object within the finite world.[19]

Along with the (perennial) theo*logical* timeliness of Grant's concerns, the second reason why I think that this study is relevant (now) is because no one has as yet responded to Burrell's invitation to explore Grant's work as a way of rethinking the "Christian" distinction between God and the world. This may well be because she was living in an Indian ashram rather than teaching in a Western university faculty and because her written works seem to belong primarily to a fairly small subdiscipline of Christian theology (i.e., Hindu-Christian comparative theology). Part of my aim here, however, is to show that her thought (and that of her intellectual predecessors like Georges Dandoy, Pierre Johanns, and Richard De Smet) deserves to be known and discussed more widely, since it makes noteworthy contributions to Thomist scholarship, broadly conceived, and also bears on questions at the very heart of Christian theology.

Third, a book on Christian non-dualism is relevant (now) because of the particular ways in which some variant on my central question (i.e., of precisely how the world is related to God) continue to preoccupy philosophers of religion and philosophical theologians, as evidenced by the steady flow of academic publications and conferences that seek to explore "alternative" models of God.[20] A good example of this ongoing interest (and disagreement) about the God-world dialectic is Philip Clayton's 1998 essay "The Christian Case for Panentheism" and, especially, the debates it generated.[21] The "panentheistic" concept of God that Clayton seeks to defend is that "the infinite God is ontologically *as close to finite things as can possibly be thought without dissolving the distinction of Creator and created altogether*."[22] With certain qualifications that will become clear in subsequent chapters, this outline could serve as my thesis statement as well, which is why I use the language of "pan-en-theism" in places. The conceptual temptation, however, is to dichotomize a relational complex into two essentially opposed categories that should not be seen—in the first place—in terms of an either/or binary. As such, I do not aim to defend an "alternative" model of God (as Clayton puts forward panentheism as a conceptual *competitor* to his depiction of "Classical Philosophical Theism" which he sees as dependent on a particular kind of substance metaphysics),[23] but rather to show, along with Grant, that "classical philosophical theism"—at least in Aquinas—*already* espouses a non-dualistic (and, in that particular sense and to that extent, pan-en-theistic) model of the God-world relation anyway. Far from requiring the conceptual minutiae of a Process metaphysics and the eschewal of the doctrine of creation ex nihilo, I seek to show that an Advaitic Christian theology can be found at, or unearthed from, the heart of Thomas's understanding of creation. Conversely, while it is therefore wrong to suggest that classical theism denies or ignores the immanence of God (Aquinas insists that "God exists in all things" and that "by a certain similitude to corporeal things, all things exist in God," and, before him, Augustine famously prayed to God as "*interior intimo meo*"),[24] it is equally unhelpful to dismiss allegedly panentheistic theologies for obliterating the God-creature distinction altogether.

Finally, while my focus in this book is on the metaphysics and spirituality of Christian nondualism, I am convinced that this "alternative theology" has profound *ethical* purchase and promise as well. I think the type of theology I develop—inspired by Grant—and the power of such theology to bring us into an imaginative engagement and experience of the truth is of value to all human beings, because having a right and creative relationship with God is a source of salvation in any situation. It seems especially pertinent, however, at a global moment of fragmentation and rootlessness in so many spheres—cultural, political, and environmental, among the most obvious. The ethical and theological value of human solidarity that emerges from the concept of non-duality could effect the kind of Copernican revolution in areas as diverse as race relations and green economics that Grant envisaged it would in the spiritual realm. Indeed, it may help us see how deeply interwoven the "practical" and the "spiritual" are anyway. I will sketch an outline of some of these ethical fruits of non-dualism in the conclusion to this book.

Comparative Theology: The Context

I see this study primarily as an exercise in (Roman Catholic) Christian philosophical theology (with a specific focus on Thomas Aquinas), which is carried out in conversation with Vedāntic Hinduism (specifically, Śaṁkara's Advaita). It thus straddles several research and methodological contexts. In terms of my "home tradition" (Roman Catholic Christianity), the book makes a contribution to the considerable literature on Thomas's metaphysics of creation and also to the slightly less voluminous work that has been done on Thomas's (Neo-)Platonism.[25] It adds an argumentative drop to the boundless ocean of Christian thinking on the distinction-and-relation between God and the world, and joins the modest but burgeoning literature on the idea of Christian non-dualism.[26] In its comparative aspect, the book is inspired primarily by the work of David Burrell and Francis X. Clooney. To zoom in further, the specifically "Hindu-Christian" comparative focus of my inquiries situates this study in a particular subdiscipline populated by some of the thinkers with whom I engage (like Dandoy, Johanns, De Smet, and Grant) and others from whom I have drawn less explicitly (such as Bede Griffiths, Henri Le Saux, and Raimon Panikkar).[27]

At the most conceptually magnified level, this book contributes to the scholarship on Roman Catholic Christian encounters with Vedāntic Hinduism. As I outline in Chapter 2, there are a number of works that offer excellent overviews of these engagements (e.g., K. P. Aleaz and B. Malkovsky),[28] detailed accounts of particular figures (e.g., R. Otto on Eckhart and Śaṁkara, W. Teasdale on Bede Griffiths, and S. Doyle on Pierre Johanns),[29] or their own reflections on particular texts and problems different from those that I address.[30] In its argument for a form of Christian non-dualism as found in certain (Neo-)Platonic themes in Thomas Aquinas, *combined* with its thematic focus on Śaṁkara's Advaita *and* the question of the God-world dialectic, especially *as addressed by Grant*, my book makes its distinctive scholarly contribution. There are, of course, works that focus on one or more of the elements that form the core of my study and also some that bring several of these elements together: J. Thatamanil's book on Vedāntic non-dualism and Christian panentheism focuses on soteriological and anthropological themes in Śaṁkara and Paul Tillich;[31] M. von Brück explores non-dualism in Vedānta and Trinitarian theology;[32] M. Ganeri examines the God-world dialectic in Aquinas and Rāmānuja;[33] and F. X. Clooney engages in a careful textual comparison of particular passages from Bādarāyaṇa's *Uttara Mīmāṃsā Sūtras* (and later Advaitic commentaries thereon) and Aquinas's *Summa Theologiae*.[34] Less well known but no less intriguing is the work of an anonymous French Cistercian who seeks to pave the way for a Christian nondualism by bringing Advaita into conversation with figures like Bernard of Clairvaux, Aquinas, and Nicolas of Cusa, as well as with more recent (twentieth-century) official Roman Catholic teaching.[35] I have been influenced by all of these works and have only been able to complete my own study by standing on the shoulders of these theological giants and walking further into unexplored territories. Nevertheless, in bringing together each of the elements enumerated previously, this book does offer something different from what has been envisioned by the giants of old.

I chose to focus on Grant, as I have explained, because I think her work deserves to be more widely known by Christian theologians,[36] and I was drawn to concentrate on Aquinas because of Grant's work and that of Burrell who is one of her contemporary Thomist admirers. Aquinas's metaphysics of creation thus came to form the natural parameters of my inquiry and explains why I look more toward some figures in Grant's intellectual hinterlands (i.e., those who also focused primarily on Aquinas and the God-world distinction-and-relation, such as Dandoy, Johanns, and De Smet) than others (like Griffiths, Le Saux, and Panikkar). The importance of the (Neo-)Platonic threads that help explain some of the deeper resonances, and also highlight some of the differences, between Aquinas and Advaita became clearer to me as my research progressed.

I would be happy for this book to be seen as an example of comparative theology as broadly conceived by Clooney, who frames it as a theological exercise of "deep learning across religious borders."[37] Similar to his work, this study is a theological exploration that sets out from within the matrices of a particular tradition (Roman Catholic Christianity) and crosses over into another one (Vedāntic Hinduism) in order to learn in a spirit of existential openness and epistemic humility, before *re*turning—changed by the journey—to a home that is now seen through fresh eyes. At the same time, it could be argued that Christians have been involved in this sort of interreligious and intercultural learning, albeit with varying degrees of enthusiasm and a whole range of complex motivations, ever since the Church Fathers began to engage with Greek philosophy.[38] In this sense, I do not see my work as belonging to a peculiar subdiscipline (i.e., Hindu-Christian comparative theology) which is substantively different from Christian philosophical theology as such. Whether it looks to a Plato or a Śaṁkara, such philosophical theology is always a case of *fides quaerens intellectum*.

Outline of Chapters

In Chapter 1, I focus on the work of David Burrell and his somewhat surprising invitation to Christian theologians to explore the distinction-and-relation between creature and Creator in conversation with Sara Grant and the Hindu tradition of Advaita Vedānta. The aim of the chapter is to establish a Christian theological context for the subsequent comparative inquiry by pointing to early and medieval figures like Pseudo-Dionysius and Meister Eckhart, as well as Renaissance and contemporary thinkers such as Nicholas of Cusa and Kathryn Tanner, and their ways of articulating the sui generis relation between the world and God. In so doing, I suggest that non-dualism has been latent—in spirit if not in letter—in certain Christian thinkers throughout the tradition. Perhaps somewhat unexpectedly, we see that this claim is also true of Thomas Aquinas: by paying close attention to his metaphysics of creation, Burrell shows how the notions of "distinction" and "relation" cannot be conceptually separated in Aquinas's understanding of the world-God dialectic. Finally, I examine how Thomas's own thinking through of these issues was carried out in engagement with voices from outside the Christian tradition and then elucidate the motivation in this study for extending the conversation beyond Abrahamic frontiers toward the nondualist (*advaita*) school of Vedāntic Hinduism.

In Chapter 2, I continue to set out the comparative and historical contexts required to understand Grant's own arguments by offering an outline of the metaphysics of Advaita Vedānta and an overview of Thomist-Vedāntic encounters. In particular, I examine the contributions of a number of key earlier figures in what became known as the "Calcutta School" of Indology, toward which Grant was pointed by her academic mentor in India, Richard De Smet. These Thomist theologians argued, somewhat remarkably, that Advaitic vocabularies, allegories, and imageries can be reworked and resituated within Christian doctrinal universes to explicate the distinctive relation between the world and God in such a way as to move beyond both monism and dualism. By focusing on the conceptual affinities between Aquinas and Śaṁkara, Grant's work builds on that of earlier scholars like Georges Dandoy, Pierre Johanns, and De Smet.

The main focus of Chapter 3 is a close reading of Grant's interpretation of Advaita Vedānta and her work on the concept of relation in Śaṁkara and Thomas, for it is here that she locates the possibility of moving beyond contrastive distinctions between God and world, and toward a "non-dualist" Christianity. As I have already indicated, my exploration of her work points not so much to a theological lacuna within Christianity, which can only be filled from without, as to deep resonances between the spiritualities of Grant's own Catholic tradition and the wisdom traditions of Vedāntic Hinduism. The exciting result of this Scholastic-Vedāntic comparative engagement is, according to Grant, the Copernican revolution that it could bring about in Christian theological understandings of God—not as a distant entity "out there" to whom many people find it increasingly hard to relate, but as the transcendent and yet immanent Self of our own self always already present in creation by the very fact of the world "being there" at all.

In Chapters 4 and 5, I seek to uncover some of the deeper conceptual resonances that explain why Thomism is particularly suitable for critical engagement with Vedānta on comparative registers. I build on the already well-established parallels between Neoplatonism and Indian thought to argue that the Neoplatonic aspects of Aquinas (i.e., themes and concepts taken from Plato and mediated via figures like Plotinus, Proclus, Augustine, and Pseudo-Dionysius) make him an interesting thinker to bring into conversation with a metaphysical non-dualist like Śaṁkara.[39] This conceptual connection between Thomas's Neoplatonism and Śaṁkara's nondualism is implicitly indicated by Grant and De Smet (i.e., they do draw on some specifically Platonic themes and concepts in Aquinas, even if they did not always foreground these motifs), but I argue that more of an explicit focus would be one fruitful way of continuing their legacy and developing the comparative engagement between Scholasticism and Vedānta.

In Chapter 4, I look at the ontological structure of the world-God relation and how the world comes to "be" at all. Christian theology understands creation as the bursting forth of something ontologically new "from nothing" (ex nihilo), while the Vedāntic doctrine of causality known as *satkāryavāda* suggests that the world, as an effect (*kārya*), always already implicitly exists (*sat*) in Brahman, its cause (i.e., that it is never really radically "created" at all). I argue that a comparative exploration of Aquinas's understanding of the nature of divine causation ex nihilo and Śaṁkara's causal conception of *satkāryavāda* shows that these *prima facie* conceptual differences can be resolved, or even *dissolved*, in terms of a more fundamental alignment in two styles of relational ontology.

In Chapter 5, I suggest, however, that there are also some limits to how far the case for an *advaitic* (non-dualist) Christianity can be pushed by examining what each tradition means by saying that the world—as effect—exists "in" God, its supreme cause. First, I show that Aquinas and Śaṁkara both have recourse to ostensibly similar metaphysical strategies to explain how the world is pre-contained in, "unfolds" out of, and continues to exist "in" God. They do this via the concepts of *nāmarūpa* (in Śaṁkara) and of divine ideas (in Thomas). In the second part of this chapter, I explore these issues from a slightly unusual perspective.

Rather than focusing explicitly on issues to do with pan(en)theism or onto-theology (which are much discussed in Christian philosophical theology), I allow the Vedāntic tradition to frame the question in the following way: how real is the world for Aquinas? This is a question not fully answered by Grant, for while I think that she is correct to conclude that Aquinas and Śaṁkara both see the world as "not-other" than God—if "not-other" implies an independently existing ontological category—the problem remains of what it means to say that the world "exists" at all. I thus explore the Neoplatonic concept of "participated being" in Aquinas, which is a logical extension of Grant's work on relation. While this doctrine means that the world exists only by participating in the unqualified existence of God, I argue that there is a greater emphasis in Aquinas and in Christian theology generally, than there is in Śaṁkara and Advaita, on the relative *reality* of the created order in all its fine-grained discrete particularities.

Notwithstanding important differences between Thomism and Vedānta, my leitmotif in this study is that an "Advaitic Christianity" offers a philosophically attractive and theologically defensible way of articulating the "non-dual relation" between the world and God. This is because it is a mistake *both* to conceive of God and creation merely as two separate and finitely enumerable entities, *and* to conceive of them as ontologically one and the same. Precisely the human inability to logically articulate and conceptually explicate the "broken middle" (i.e., of a "causal relation" unlike any other) is, I suggest, the non-dual mystery at the living heart of the relation between the world and God.

1 The Distinctive Relation between Creature and Creator in Christian Theology

NON-DUALISM FROM DAVID BURRELL, CSC, TO SARA GRANT, RSCJ

> For creation is not a change, but the very dependence of the created being upon the principle from which it is produced. And thus, creation is a kind of relation.[1]

The aim of this chapter is to draw attention to some of the ways in which certain Christian theologians have consciously sought to avoid dualistic conceptions of the world and God as two things determined in opposition to one another.[2] In different ways, these thinkers argue that the "two" should be understood *non-contrastively*, such that being a creature does not exclude, but entails, in a certain limited and partial sense, also sharing in the being of the Creator. This claim, I will suggest, is less daring and paradoxical than it first sounds when we remember that God is not a particular *kind of thing*, which exists here and not there, but is the enabling condition of the existence of anything at all. The world is saturated with the presence of God for, as Plotinus puts it, "Whatever is not somewhere has nowhere where it is not."[3] As such, I argue not that the world is straightforwardly reducible to God (pantheism) or that the world's existence is illusory, but that the world exists *in* (ontological dependence on) *God* (pan-en-theism) and that its very being, as Aquinas reminds us in his description of creation at the head of this chapter, is a kind of relation to its Creator. It is in this sense that there is a "non-dualism" between the world "and" God.

More specifically, I focus in this chapter on the work of the contemporary Thomist, David Burrell,[4] and his surprising invitation to Christian theologians to explore the distinctive relation between creature and Creator in conversation with Sara Grant[5] and the Hindu tradition of Advaita (non-dual) Vedānta.[6] I set the context for this comparative inquiry by pointing to early and medieval figures like Pseudo-Dionysius and Meister Eckhart, as well as Renaissance and contemporary thinkers such as Nicholas of Cusa and Kathryn Tanner, and their ways of articulating the sui generis relation between the world and God. I suggest here that metaphysical non-dualism (between creatures and their Creator) has been latent—in spirit if not in letter—in certain Christian thinkers throughout the tradition. Perhaps somewhat unexpectedly, we will see that this claim is also true of Thomas Aquinas: by paying close attention to his metaphysics of creation I will show how the notions of "distinction" and "relation" cannot be separated in his understanding of the world and God. Finally, I will examine how Thomas's own thinking through of these issues was carried out in engagement with voices from outside the Christian tradition and then elucidate the motivation for extending the conversation beyond Abrahamic frontiers toward the non-dualist (*advaita*) school of Vedāntic Hinduism.

David Burrell on the Distinction-and-Relation between the World and God

Burrell has made the task of spelling out the nature of the distinction-and-relation between the world and God central to his work.[7] It is a task that has been unhelpfully complicated, he thinks, by an overemphasis (especially in post-Reformation Christian theology) on the doctrine of redemption rather than the doctrine of creation. By focusing disproportionately on redemption as the conceptual framework that explains how and why the world is related to God (in response to the "gulf" brought about by sin), we risk losing sight of the *original relation* between creature and Creator involved in creation.[8] He thus calls for a "Keplerian revolution" in Christian theology in order to redress this imbalance and to restore a vivid sense of a world always already intimately connected to its Creator.[9] It is for this reason that Burrell has focused over the last thirty or so years on clarifying the theological ramifications of the Christian doctrine of creation as he finds it in the pages of St. Thomas Aquinas and, in the particular approach he has taken, he is widely recognized as a leader in the field.[10] Specifically, Burrell focuses on how this "central though often hidden element" in Aquinas's philosophy[11] (viz. the doctrine of creation) provides a context for understanding and speaking both of the relation and of the distinction between the world and God.

One of Burrell's most frequently acknowledged influences in this regard is Robert Sokolowski's *The God of Faith and Reason*.[12] When he first came across this book in the early 1980s, he was struck by Sokolowski's central argument: that Christian theology depends for its coherence on being able to explain how God is both *distinct from* but also *related to* what God creates—the world.[13] Whereas some Christians are wont to introduce concepts like incarnation and redemption to speak of this relation between the world and God, Burrell insists that these items of Christian belief should not "have to bear the burden of *establishing* a relationship, but rather of restoring one already embodied in an original order otherwise irremediably distorted by sin."[14] In other words, if God simply *is* the founding raison d'être for all else, then there must be some sort of ontological relation between the world and God,[15] just as truly as there must also be an ontological distinction between God and the world (since the world is not, after all, the raison d'être of God).[16]

Although it is necessary, therefore, to hold relation and distinction together, Sokolowski tends to focus on the latter—specifically, on

> the distinction between the world understood as possibly not having existed and God understood as possibly being all that there is, with no diminution of goodness or greatness. It is not the case that God and the world are each separately understood in this new way, and only subsequently related to each other; they are determined in the distinction, not each apart from the other.[17]

It is important to be clear about what Sokolowski is (not) saying here. In the first sentence cited previously, and throughout his work, his concern is to emphasize the radical contingency of all that exists and, thereby, the sheer gratuitousness of creation. This is the corollary of the traditional insistence of classical Christian theism that God is "that than which a greater cannot be thought,"[18] combined with an emphasis, drawn from scripture, on God's loving generosity. In other words, God chooses to create out of sheer goodness, not out of any necessity. There might, then, appear to be a slight air of contradiction between this affirmation in the first sentence of the giftedness of creation and the claim in the second sentence that God and the world cannot be understood apart from each other: surely, if God would still be God without the world, and the world need not "be" at all, it is precisely the case that *God* is *not* determined in this distinction-and-relation, but quite independently of it. Hence, Sokolowski can say a few pages later that "in the Christian distinction, God is understood as 'being' God entirely apart from any relation of otherness to the world or to the whole."[19] On the other hand, however, the *world* could *not* be understood as "world" *apart* from its relation to God, since without this relation established by and continually grounded in creation, it would not "be" at all. This is why Martin Poulsom is right to insist on precision and consistency in the *directionality* of our statements and prepositions when trying to speak of creature and Creator, for while there is indeed a distinction and a relation between the world and God, it is more difficult to speak of a distinction or a relation between God and the world.[20] Sokolowski's point, I think, is to emphasize that we cannot seek to understand the world and *then*, as some sort of afterthought, try to work out its ontological relation to God. Why not? Because "to be" simply *is-to-be-in-relation-to-God*. In other words, given that there *is* a created world (even though there need not be), we must picture its constitutive relation to God not as an "extrinsic" one—as if the two "things" (world + God) exist separately and only later, as it were, become "connected" (e.g., through a special act of grace like incarnation or redemption)—but as an originary relation that is inherent to the very meaning of what it is "to be" created.[21] As we will see, Burrell takes over and develops several themes from Sokolowski, albeit with different emphases. Above all, it is the *unique* nature of the "distinction" and its central *importance* to the "grammar" of theology that form the key pillars in both of their arguments.

A Distinction Unlike Any Other

The reason why the distinction-and-relation between the world and God is unlike any other can be stated quite simply—it comes down to the insistence of Burrell and Sokolowski (and Aquinas) that we will get our theology badly wrong if we imagine God as an extra "item" in a universal inventory or a cosmic catalogue; not being any kind of "thing" at all, God cannot be compared and contrasted to other things with the same logic of difference and sameness that applies in every case within the world. On this, Burrell is in agreement with Sokolowski:[22]

> In the distinctions that occur normally within the setting of the world, each term distinguished is what it is precisely by not being that which it is distinguishable from. Its being is established partially by its otherness, and therefore its being depends on its distinction from others. But in the Christian distinction . . . God could and would be God even if there were no world.[23]

In other words, something's being a pear, for example, "is established partially by its otherness" from, say, an apple or a peach. The reason it would sound odd (in ordinary language use) to try to compare or distinguish a pear and a book is because there is no obvious domain of comparison within which pears and books can be situated, similar to the way in which pears, apples, and peaches can be distinguished and located against a common background of being examples of fruit. As Thomas puts it, "things not in the same genus are not comparable; as, sweetness is not properly greater or less than a line."[24] The reason this sort of logic cannot apply in the case of God, however, is not just that "[t]hings not of the same genus are in no way comparable to each other" and that "we say that God is not in the same genus with other good things," but that, more fundamentally, God is not in *any* genus: "He is outside genus, and is the principle of every genus."[25] In other words, there is no common background or genus within which we can situate God because God, as Creator, is the *source* and the ontological *ground* of all that exists, so there cannot possibly be any antecedent category to which God belongs as one particular instance.[26] As such, even talking of a "distinction" or "relation" between the world and God is, Burrell admits, something of a "philosophical conceit" because there is no domain of comparison between the world and God within which distinctions and relations can be situated.[27]

It is for these reasons that Burrell insists on what Kathryn Tanner calls a "non-contrastive" mode of discourse when it comes to speaking about God and, in particular, when it comes to how we conceive of the nature of the "distinction" between creation and Creator.[28] In *God and Creation*, Tanner is concerned with how to reconcile traditional accounts of God's omnipotence as Creator with creaturely freedom, but in the background of this problematic is the broader one of how to speak coherently about the distinction-and-relation between the world and God in the first place.[29] Indeed, her primary focus is not so much on *what* theologians talk about, as on the *way* they talk about it, and it is her strategy for getting our theological grammar correct that interests Burrell. She compares the task she is attempting to Kantian "transcendental arguments," in the sense that she is concerned not to establish any one particular doctrine but to demonstrate the logically prior conditions of possibility for theological meaning.[30] The body of rules she lays out is adopted by Burrell to make sense of how to speak of creature and Creator. Their governing principle for Christian discourse is that "[a] God who genuinely transcends the world must not be characterized . . . by a direct contrast with it"[31] because there is no logical common background against which such a contrast could be made. The result of forgetting this key rule of theo-logic is that:

> Divinity characterized in terms of a direct contrast with certain sorts of being or with the world of non-divine being as a whole is brought down to the level of the world and the beings within it in virtue of that very opposition: God becomes one being among others within a single order.[32]

In other words, while Christian theology has historically been wary of *diminishing* the distinction between the world and God lest it end in pantheism or some sort of idolatry, a certain type of naïve emphasis on *exalting* this distinction can have almost the same consequence, albeit from the other end of the conceptual spectrum, of *finitizing* God. Indeed, turning God into one being among others is one of—perhaps *the*—major misunderstanding that Burrell (and Sokolowski) want to guard against. Tanner's first rule for coherent Christian theology, therefore, is to "avoid both a simple univocal attribution of predicates to God and world and a simple contrast of divine and non-divine predicates."[33] In this way, Christian theologians can navigate, she argues, between collapsing divine transcendence into *identity* with the world, on the one hand, and *opposing* it contrastively with the non-divine, on the other.[34]

As Tanner amply demonstrates, she is far from being the first Christian theologian to be alert to the need for non-contrastive language use when talking about God; nor is she the only contemporary voice emphasizing the importance of these "rules of grammar." Though not discussed by Burrell as extensively as Tanner is, Denys Turner is another important influence on Burrell,[35] and it is worth turning briefly to his work for a genealogy of "non-contrastive" ways of picturing the creature-Creator distinction-and-relation. Turner poses essentially the same question as the one Tanner and Burrell try to answer—namely, "What *is* the difference between God and creatures? How are we to talk about that difference? Does such talk have a 'grammar'?"[36] To take the last question first, Turner's answer is yes and although he does not actually use the term "non-contrastive," his conception of the rules of this grammar of God-talk is much the same as Tanner's. Where she talks of "non-contrastivity," Turner tends to talk of the logic or grammar of "sameness and otherness," and what he means by this dialectic is that "'otherness' and negation are inconceivable except in terms of 'sameness' and affirmation . . . the differences between one kind of otherness and others are themselves intelligible only against the background of sameness."[37] This is precisely the point we saw Thomas making in the language of species and genus in ST I.6.2, and Turner further elaborates it as follows:

> the less things differ, the easier it is to describe how they differ. It is easy to say how a cat and a mouse differ, because we can readily describe what they differ *as*; they belong, we might say, to a readily identifiable community of difference—that of animals. But how does this piece of Camembert cheese differ from 11.30 in the morning? Here, the community of difference is too diffuse, too indeterminate, for this difference, obviously bigger as it is than that of chalk and cheese, to be so easily described. In general, the bigger the difference, the harder, not easier, it is to describe the manner of its difference.[38]

Before we too quickly assume, however, that the reason it is difficult to spell out the precise nature of the distinction between the world and God is because the qualitative difference is too big, we must remind ourselves of the conceptual infelicities we are here trying to avoid.[39] It is not that there is a big, or even infinite, difference between creatures and Creator but that there simply is no overarching background against which such a difference could be drawn:

> the question of "sameness" and "distinction" can arise only as between creatures. If this is so, then clearly there can be no good sense, but only a misleading one, in any, even casual and metaphorical, calculation of the greater and lesser degrees of "distance" which lie between Creator and creatures as contrasted with that between one creature and another; for it is not on some common scale of difference that these differences differ. Indeed, that is precisely what is meant by saying that nothing can be predicated univocally of both God and creatures.[40]

In other words, if God's difference from creatures is categorically incomparable with any creaturely difference, "incomparable" does not mean enumeratively or qualitatively *greater*, or *peerless* against a backdrop of logically possible peers, but radically *incommensurable* because there simply is no common scale.[41] "[T]his difference [between God and creation]," Turner insists, in a clear echo of Tanner, "cannot be set in *any* form of contrast with sameness."[42]

This insight into the sui generis nature of the distinction-and-relation between the world and God—crucial as it is to all the thinkers I have discussed so far—from Turner to Tanner, Sokolowski to Burrell, and, not least, to Thomas himself—finds early and sophisticated expression in one of Thomas's greatest intellectual influences, and around whose formulation of this "grammar" Turner structures his own argument: namely, Dionysius, the pseudo-Areopagite (ca. fifth–sixth centuries CE). We will see in subsequent chapters—given the enormous influence he exerted on later figures in the mystical and theological traditions of the Christian West and East, both before, including, and after Thomas—that Dionysius will prove to be of more than merely peripheral interest to our broader argument.[43] In the conclusion to his essay *The Mystical Theology*, as the culmination of a series of apophatic denials of what God is, Dionysius insists that the Supreme Cause must be "beyond assertion and denial":[44]

> We make assertions and denials of what is next to it, but never of it, for it is both beyond every assertion, being the perfect and unique cause of all things, and, by virtue of its pre-eminently simple and absolute nature, free of every limitation, beyond every limitation; it is also beyond every denial.[45]

Here, Dionysius draws together two key notions: precisely because God's nature is unlike that of any created nature (because of God's "preeminent simplicity"), "God cannot be different from, nor therefore similar to, anything at all, at any rate in any of the ways in which we can conceive of similarity and difference; or else God would be just another, different, thing,"[46] and Dionysius, along with Aquinas, Turner, Tanner, Sokolowski, and Burrell, all deny—as we have seen—that there is any kind of thing that God is.[47] Later thinkers influenced by Dionysius, like John Scotus Eriugena (815–877), and Aquinas, develop this distinction "beyond sameness and otherness" into full-blown theologies of creation, and some even creatively exploit the Dionysian hyper-logic of negating (ordinary) negation itself to insist that "the distinction" between the world and God consists precisely in the *indistinction* that sets God "apart" from all else. In other words, we are unable to talk meaningfully of difference and sameness at all when it comes to God—because of the absence of common conceptual background necessary to make such comparisons coherent—and this indistinction *is* what uniquely distinguishes God from creation, but *not*, of course, in such a way that the one is contrasted with the other. Language cannot cope with this hyper-logical "difference" between God and creatures, other than to mutter the sort of paradoxical statements we find preeminently in Aquinas's near-contemporary, Meister Eckhart (1260–1327) and, later, Nicholas of Cusa (1401–1464)—God is distinct because of God's unique *indistinctness*:

> God is distinct from any creature in this alone, that if any creature is necessarily a distinct being, a *hoc aliquid*, God is not. A creature is, as he [Eckhart] puts it, an *unum distinctum*, distinct from another by means of its difference in respect of some background sameness which they share, whereas God is an *unum indistinctum*, that is to say, is distinct from any creature whatsoever in this, that, unlike any creature, God is not distinct in kind from anything created at all—for there is no background against which a distinction of kind can be set. Therefore, God is distinct because God alone is not distinct. "Indistinction", as he puts it, "belongs to God, distinction to creatures."[48]

Before discussing why the sui generis nature of the distinction-and-relation between the world and God is so significant to Christian theology, we must return to Burrell and Aquinas in order to spell out a little more clearly what exactly it is about God that renders contrastive ways of picturing the distinction-and-relation between creation and Creator incoherent. In other words, we ask: What is it about God's nature that makes God not only "other" in a unique way, but also, in fact, the *non-Aliud*—the one and only "*not-other*"?[49]

"Distinction," "Relation," and "Creation" in Aquinas and Burrell

The starting point for understanding what makes God uniquely (in)distinct from creatures, Aquinas insists, is to be clear from the outset about what God is not. This is why—having established the nature and the extent of *sacra doctrina* and discussed whether God exists at all in the first two questions of the *Summa Theologiae*—his next priority in that work is to establish what we should *not* say about God, and this he does by means of an investigation into divine simplicity.[50] Here, Aquinas means, above all, that what distinguishes God (non-contrastively) from everything else is that God is "non-composite," and, in this simplicity, God is unique. In other words, God is not composed, metaphysically, of matter and form, subject and accident, or essence and existence—which is both not to say very much at all and to say what is most important. It does not say much, in the sense that simplicity, ex hypothesi, cannot describe an "attribute" of God, but it gets to the heart of things by pointing to a formal feature of divinity that is intended to proscribe talking or thinking of God as if God were another one of the items in the world. For Burrell, this "formal feature of divine simpleness is intended to distinguish God from everything else,"[51] and must, therefore, be borne constantly in mind as guarding "the distinction" and preventing us from lapsing into the sorts of theological errors that result from forgetting it.[52] The reason Aquinas wants to insist on simplicity as the bedrock of our divine grammar is to underline the fact that "God" does not refer to a thing that may or may not exist, but to that which exists of its very nature:

> Aquinas proposes to identify the creator God uniquely as the One whose very essence is to-be. This succinct formula offers *simpleness* as the "formal feature" securing "the distinction" by singling out God in the only way possible—without turning God into god, the "biggest thing around" . . . [Aquinas] . . . does this by reversing the picture itself, proposing that the One whose essence is to-be (and so can cause all else to be) should not be conceived as "mere being" but as the fulness of being, so that *simpleness* here denotes plenitude rather than a lack.[53]

Sokolowski takes the same starting point of God as the "fulness of being" for his discussion of the "Christian distinction."[54] He takes his lead, however, from Anselm's famous "formal feature" of God as *id quo maius cogitari nequit* and, from here, goes on to emphasize the idea that God could and would be God even without the world. Although, as we have seen, Burrell agrees wholeheartedly with Sokolowski in the content of his arguments,[55] the differing emphases of their theses can be traced back, I would suggest, to this choice of preferred conversation partner—Anselm or Aquinas. William Hasker, indeed, questions whether "the distinction" requires a specifically Thomistic metaphysics (which he sees as emphasized more by Burrell than by Sokolowski) at all.[56] It may well be that Burrell could agree—in much the same way Tanner concedes in the case of her non-contrastive rules of grammar—that a Thomistic framework is sufficient rather than necessary for articulating the (Christian) distinction, and that it could be reached via alternative philosophical-theological routes.[57] Indeed, part of the question motivating this book is precisely whether the Thomistic distinction rearticulated by Burrell could be articulated also via the philosophical-theological resources of Advaita Vedānta. Showing that this distinction could be established with a *Christian* metaphysical paradigm other than a Thomistic one (which is presumably what Hasker has in mind) would not negatively impact my overall argument, though it might alter the ways in which parallels could (not) be drawn with the Hindu traditions. Nonetheless, the focus on Aquinas is far from arbitrary or idiosyncratic. Aquinas is a paradigmatic Christian figure, and as Simon Oliver points out, "[s]ubsequent theologies of creation, both Catholic *and Protestant*, are frequently interpretations, reformulations or rejections of Aquinas's position."[58]

The fact that Burrell does, in fact, choose Aquinas as his theological interlocutor, has important implications—both for his argument and for my own. Had Burrell chosen to focus on God, as does Sokolowski, in Anselmian terms as "that-than-which-a-greater-cannot-be-thought," we might suppose that the same logic would have led him, as it leads Sokolowski, to emphasize the *distinction* between God and the world more emphatically than the *relation*. This is because Anselm's formula strongly suggests that God would be God without creating: if God really is "that-than-which-a-greater-cannot-be-thought," then God does not become any "greater" by creating because the world does not "add" anything to God. Sokolowski makes this point repeatedly: "God + world" is not quantitatively or qualitatively greater than "God" alone.[59] A significant consequence of this emphasis is that the *distinction* between God and everything else is foregrounded, and the *relation* seems to hold less ontological priority. That said, if creation indeed "adds nothing" to God, then the world, a fortiori, cannot be separate or separable from God as an enumerable entity in some ontic space disconnected from God, but must be intimately related to God. In certain ways, this brings Anselm and Sokolowski closer than Aquinas and Burrell to traditional interpretations of Advaita, though the logic is followed in the Vedāntic tradition to a rather different (sounding) conclusion: namely, that if creation cannot add anything to God, all that exists, ultimately, *is* God, and the physical world only has a limited (and quasi-illusory) existence from a certain point of view.[60] As we will see in the next chapter, this is not quite the same as saying that the world *is* God (which would be pantheism), but that the reality of the world must be in some sense illusory, since nothing can be added to God's infinite being.

To be sure, there is nothing in what Sokolowski says here that Burrell would substantially disagree with, and Poulsom rightly notes that Burrell, too, *seems* to prioritize "distinction" over "relation"—at least in terms of the frequency with which he uses the terms.[61] A careful reading indicates, however, that working from within a Thomistic metaphysical paradigm, Burrell focuses on creation precisely as the simultaneous key to the "distinction" *and* the "relation" between the world and God—and he is led in this direction because of the central role that creation plays in Aquinas. It is the relation established by this founding and ongoing creative act that Burrell wants to emphasize in order to avoid speaking dualistically of God "and" the world. Indeed, it is the non-contrastive character of the "distinction" that "is intended to capture that singular *relation* of the created universe to its creator."[62] Thus, "distinction," "relation," and "creation" coalesce conceptually for Burrell: if we focus on the *distinction* between God and world without also attending to the relation, the risk is that we characterize them as two "entities" (God + world) alongside each other; whereas if we emphasize *relation* and lose sight of the all-important distinction, we veer toward pantheism; therefore, it is the manner in which we explain creation that will crucially shape the distinction-and-relation that results. This mutually informing constellation of the three concepts is evident throughout Burrell's work, but comes out particularly clearly in his article "Analogy, Creation, and Theological Language."[63] Here, he talks of how Aquinas factors into Aristotle's explorations of "being" "what Robert Sokolowski calls 'the distinction' of creator from creatures" and then, in the following line, of how "[i]njecting the creator/creature *relation* so directly into the argument at this point displays what Josef Pieper has so astutely noted: that *creation* is the 'hidden element' in the philosophy . . . of Aquinas."[64] The only way Burrell's argument can work here is if we assume that he is using the terms—"distinction," "relation," and "creation"—interchangeably. It is *creation* that "introduces" the all-important *distinction*,[65] but the fact that this introduction is not a temporal or sequential one allows us to say that creation simply *is* (constitutive of) the distinction, and that "[w]hat is at issue is the *relation* between creator and creation."[66] The concepts of "creation," "distinction," and "relation" form such a deeply interconnected semantic and theological matrix in Burrell's work that it is not possible to discuss one of these terms without entailing the others.[67] In sum, uniquely in the case of God, God's ontological *distinction* from the world is God's logical *relation* with the world, and vice versa.

The Theological Significance of This Distinctive Relation

Burrell's contention is that the way we articulate the precise nature of the distinction/relation between creatures and Creator will also establish the underlying grammar that governs and shapes the rest of our God-talk. As Aquinas noted in a slightly different context, this is a prime example of an area in which a small mistake in the beginning will lead to major ones in the end.[68] Sokolowski also agrees that creation "is not merely one teaching among many in Christian belief," but is *foundational* in opening up the logical and theological space for all other doctrines.[69] Articulating the distinction-and-relation implicates us, for example, in the sorts of "grace" versus "nature" debates that structure so much intramural Christian disagreement.[70] Protestant voices typically accuse Roman Catholic thinkers of reducing the "gap" (what I have been calling "the distinction") by means of an overarching ontology that includes God and the world, in order to accentuate human independence, in the style of a Pelagius; while Roman Catholics tend to reverse the charge and accuse Protestants of emphasizing divine sovereignty to the point of nullifying capacities inherent to human nature as a created gift, in the style of a Calvin.[71] Paradoxically, but perhaps unsurprisingly, opening up these intra-Christian conversations to voices that do not necessarily share the same sets of presuppositions—in this case, from the tradition of Advaita Vedānta—may yet enable us to see new ways of framing questions and disputes that seem intractable from within familiar sets of firmly established paradigms. As Tanner correctly points out: "A certain modern framework of discussion is disenchanted of its obviousness when an initially strange discourse is allowed to make a claim on it."[72]

As we have seen, the challenge can be posed as follows: how to *distinguish* God from the world in such a way as to avoid a pantheistic identification of creature and Creator, on the one hand, and how to *relate* God to the world in order to avoid conceptualizing them as two competing realities that exist in parallel, on the other.[73] Focusing on the *distinction* will tend toward emphasizing the *trans*cendence of God, while a focus on the *relation* will align with an emphasis on God's *im*manence in creation. The result is that Christian "[t]heologians of creation have all teetered on a thin line between monism [as a result of a one-sided emphasis on immanence/relation] and dualism [as a result of another one-sided emphasis on transcendence/distinction], each leaning towards one or the other of these poles."[74]

Poulsom provides a helpful survey of the different sorts of "big mistakes," which these initial choices of emphasis can lead to.[75] At one end of the spectrum is the Scylla of deism, that is, of a monarchical God who is conceived as so utterly transcendent that the "distinction" between creatures and Creator is turned into an ontological *separation*. This leads to "the blatantly dualist presentation of Christianity as a redemptive scheme" and of a God as a deus ex machina "out there," which is, as we will see, precisely the source of Sara Grant's unease with a certain type of Christianity.[76] We are left with a "transcendentally transcendent"[77] God who is either entirely unrelated to the world or who is so terrifyingly powerful that any creaturely freedom is completely swallowed up. Ironically, given the motivations behind such theologies to protect the otherness of God, the end result can be exactly the opposite—divine transcendence can become domesticated into a mundane sort of transcendence, where God is spatially contrasted with the universe in such a way that they become two separate objects. Throughout Burrell's work, this lament becomes his most consistent refrain: God is not any kind of *thing* in (or outside) the world at all (not even the "biggest" thing), and therefore must not be pictured in enumerative *contrast* to the world.[78] At the other end of the spectrum is the Charybdis of pantheism or, in other words, of a complete flattening out of divine transcendence altogether, leading to an "immanently immanent" God (or, in Advaita, of an illusionistic world).[79] In this case, distinction is dissolved into identity, and creation tends to be pictured as a sort of continuous God-world emanation.

Traditionally, Christian theology has seen both of these extreme positions as erroneous: that is, conceiving of God and world as two separate enumerable entities (God + world), on the one hand, and conceiving of them as one and the same reality (God = world) on the other.[80] It is hardly surprising, therefore, that it is often when thinkers—not just in Christianity, but also in all three Abrahamic traditions—have struggled to articulate the uniqueness of this distinction/relation between creatures and Creator (and, in particular, when they have ostensibly emphasized "relation" over "distinction") that they have tended to come under suspicion in their respective faith communities. Whether we think of an Eriugena or of an Eckhart, history testifies that "[v]ery frequently positions that are judged to be heretical are those that, by implication at least, blur the Christian distinction between God and the world."[81] This further suggests that Sokolowski and Burrell are correct in viewing the distinction/relation as a—perhaps, *the*—foundational issue in philosophical theology. It is not that disputed questions cannot be found in other areas of theology, but even these can invariably be traced back to an initially mistaken way of conceiving this distinction-and-relation. The way we understand this "creation relation"[82] between creature and Creator will structure everything else in our theology—from our understanding of incarnation and sacraments to redemption and human freedom.[83] Formulating this unique distinction in such a way as to respect the reality of both creature and Creator therefore becomes "the quintessential theological task,"[84] which is aptly summarized by Sokolowski:

> It is as though the Christian understanding of God and the world provides the setting that lets there be controversies about Christ, the church, and grace. However, it is also the case that various heresies concerning such issues are heretical because they would, by implication, obscure the Christian distinction between the world and God.[85]

As well as inviting us to see "relation" as correlative with "distinction," Burrell's emphasis on Aquinas's metaphysics also accounts for another major difference between his and Sokolowski's treatment of these issues—namely, that Burrell follows Aquinas's lead in approaching this as an interfaith inquiry and therefore sees "the distinction" as one that is at the heart of all three Abrahamic traditions.

Aquinas's Interfaith Achievement

Although we might not be surprised that a Roman Catholic priest and theologian like Burrell chooses to follow Thomist metaphysics in his discussions of creation, his consistent emphasis on the interfaith dimensions of Aquinas's project is more unusual. By exploring the ways in which Aquinas was drawing on Jewish and Muslim interlocutors like Moses Maimonides and Ibn Sina (Avicenna), Burrell aims to show how Thomas's attempts to conceptualize the distinctive relation between the world and God are influenced by, at times differ from, and also converge with, certain ways of thinking through this distinction-and-relation in the other Abrahamic traditions.[86]

Burrell characterizes the common challenge presented by their respective revealed scriptures to medieval theologians in the Jewish, Christian, and Islamic traditions as one of how to adapt the metaphysical resources they had at their disposal in such a way as to articulate the concept of a world that was both utterly dependent and entirely gratuitous.[87] For Aquinas, this meant explaining, on the one hand, the notion of a "created substance" (*pace* Aristotle), and, on the other, avoiding the sorts of implications of necessity associated with Neoplatonic emanation schemes.

Although Aristotle resolved the question of "what a thing is" into the question of particular *substance/form* as the "bedrock" that stood under the rest of the categories,[88] by taking substance to be "what subsists in itself," he failed to answer to the satisfaction of his medieval Muslim readers the question of why there was any "being" (substance) at all.[89] Burrell suggests that a concern for ultimate origins was never a major focus of the Greek metaphysical traditions, given the widespread assumption that the universe was eternal.[90] It was not until one of Aristotle's most famously persistent students—determined to understand precisely this question of "why anything at all"—introduced a key distinction between essence (*mahiyya*) and existence (*wujūd*) that the foundations started to be laid for Thomas's own analysis of "Being." This crucial link in the chain between Aristotle and Aquinas was Ibn Sina/Avicenna (ca. 980–1037 CE).[91] Avicenna's essence/existence distinction allowed Aristotle's understanding of substance (*ousia*) as "self-sufficient" to continue to distinguish substance from accident but was motivated by Avicenna's conviction that the being (*wujūd*) inherent to these worldly substances (*mahiyya*) proceeded from another. In other words, given Qur'anic insistence on a Creator, Avicenna had to show that substances did *not* "subsist in themselves," but owed their existence to a divine source. This led him to argue that the existence of anything in the world was only ever merely *possible*, while the existence of God was, uniquely, *necessary*, and he took over Al-Farabi's (ca. 875–930 CE) metaphor of emanation (which itself can be traced back to Plotinus) to depict how all things could share in the being of the one God.[92] This transformation of the Greek philosophical paradigm in which "Being" was identified with Form, Substance, or Essence (as in, for example, Plato and Aristotle), to an identification of "Being" with *existence* (*esse*) and a consequent relegation in ontological priority of Form/Substance/Essence would have far-reaching effects on Aquinas's metaphysics.

Avicenna's influence on Aquinas is such that an authority as revered as Étienne Gilson can say that "[b]etween the metaphysics of Aristotle and that of Thomas Aquinas, the metaphysics of Avicenna acts as a kind of filter."[93] However, Burrell identifies two aspects of Avicenna's characterization of "the distinction" that troubled Thomas. The first was the possible implications of "emanation" as a model for creation, which had concerned other thinkers even within the Islamic tradition. Most notably, Al-Ghazali (ca. 1058–1111 CE) objected to the enthusiastic appropriations of Greek philosophy by his predecessors—primarily Al-Kindi (ca. 801–873 CE),[94] Al-Farabi, and Ibn Sina—to explicate the Qur'an; not least their use of emanationist schemes to explain creation.[95] The problem, as Al-Ghazali saw it, was that emanation involved intermediaries between God and creatures, on the one hand, and implied a sort of logical necessity to creation, on the other—on both counts, divine power and freedom seemed to be compromised. Although Thomas had no direct access to the works of Al-Ghazali, he learned of these debates via his Jewish interlocutor, Moses Maimonides (1135–1204 CE), whose stated aim in the *Guide of the Perplexed* was to reconcile the Torah with the Neoplatonism that he knew (especially as mediated through Avicenna). In this way, Aquinas

> profited from al-Ghazali's critique of Ibn Sina, as he had learned it through Moses Maimonides, to the point where he refused to picture creation as an orderly logic-like progression from "the First" (as al-Farabi always characterized the creator). He objected primarily, of course, to the logical necessity that model presumed, but Aquinas also chafed at the need for intermediaries to effect the activity.[96]

Notwithstanding these objections to intermediaries between God and creatures, as well as any hint of necessity, we will see in Chapter 4 that Aquinas did not dispense altogether with the Neoplatonic notion of creation as emanation.[97] The second aspect of Avicenna's metaphysics that Aquinas would go on to revise was the distinction between "necessary" and "possible" existence as a way to characterize the distinction between God and creatures. The worry was that talking of essences as "possibly existing" seems to suggest that an "essence" is some*thing* that *receives* existence as an "accident." Aquinas wanted to insist more firmly that if creation is a genuinely free gift, there cannot *be* anything "already there" to claim existence and, in any case, it is misleading to think of "existence" as an accidental attribute of a substance—"[f]or as Aquinas had to remind Avicenna, the only possibility there can be prior to creation ex nihilo lies not 'in the passive potentiality of matter,' but [in] the active power of God" to create without presupposing anything at all (ST 1.46.1.1).[98]

So, Aquinas would accept Avicenna's key distinction between "existence" and "essence," as well as his argument that this distinction was the characteristic mark of a creature. He also took over Avicenna's manner of distinguishing God as the only One whose essence simply is "to-be."[99] However, by reintroducing Aristotle's language of act (*energeia*) and potency (*dunamis*) to understand existence (*esse*) and essence (*essentia*), rather than Avicenna's necessary/possible hermeneutic, Aquinas was able to creatively combine and transform his Greek-Arabic sources in such a way that they could be used to explain the radical notion of creation ex nihilo found in the Jewish-Christian and Muslim scriptures.[100] Rather than substances "existing in themselves," Aquinas argued that, on the contrary, substances are *created*, in the sense that they are composed of essence "in potency" (which does not, *pace* Avicenna, mean the same as "possibly existing" because there *is* no essence without existence) to an act(ivity) of existence (*actus essendi*)—and that pure act(ivity) of existence simply *is* the essence of what we call God (*ipsum esse per se subsistens*).[101] By "participating" in this divine pure act of existence, creatures are most intimately and profoundly related to *esse* (that is, to God), since this *is* the creature's very "be-ing," without which it simply would not *be* at all.[102]

Crucially, then, we can see why Burrell identifies *creation* as the very foundation of the distinction *and* the relation between God and creatures. By the very fact of its existence, every creature shows a *relation* of "towardness" to the Creator who, in turn, is really present "in" each existing thing by virtue of its ontological constitution (as composed of essence/potency and existence/act)—existence is not something that "happens to" or befalls a creature but is that to which essence must be related for there to "be" a creature at all.[103] In continuously giving each individual thing its sheer existence, God may be said always to be intimately present in the world. At the same time, God is distinct from creatures in virtue of God's simplicity (i.e.. God's *not* being composed of essence and existence), which makes the relation an asymmetrical one—creatures are *really* related to God, because they would not "be" otherwise, but God is not really related to creatures because God would be God even without them.[104] Creating, therefore, belongs to God alone because creation simply is the "emanation of all *esse* from universal being"[105] and God is *esse* itself. The radical contingency of the world, for Aquinas, does not lie in the fact that it could have been otherwise, but that it is there at all, for creation ex nihilo simply means that each thing receives its existence directly from the Creator. Thus, to the famous question later put by Leibniz, "Why is there some-*thing* rather than utter nothingness?" Thomas's response in a word would be: "Creation."

On one level, Burrell's own project has been about putting Aquinas into an interfaith perspective—especially clarifying the influences of Maimonides and Avicenna, whom Thomas himself so often cites. In this way, Burrell has demonstrated throughout his work "that Aquinas's classic synthesis of Christian understanding by way of Hellenic philosophy was in fact already an interfaith, intercultural achievement,"[106] and so we have good grounds for hoping that Thomas would be delighted by the prospect of further extending his interfaith inquiries beyond Abrahamic frontiers. O'Meara is surely right that "[b]ecause Aquinas' thinking was a tireless dialogue with the largest number of resources, he would be awed and stimulated by today's possibilities for preaching, holiness, insight, and ministry in a world growing closer and a church growing larger."[107]

From David Burrell to Sara Grant

Given the increasing recognition of the significance of global horizons for Christian theology, we will surely see more Thomist scholars joining Burrell in emphasizing Aquinas's openness to interreligious dialogue in the pursuit of "faith seeking understanding."[108] However, one of Burrell's more startling claims seems to have gone largely unnoticed. In speculating in the margins of his work on how these medieval Christian-Jewish-Islamic conversations in philosophical theology could benefit from an engagement with non-Abrahamic traditions, Burrell has suggested (somewhat to his own surprise) that his "struggles to understand the utter uniqueness of that relation [viz. between creature and Creator] could find expression in a conceptuality at the heart of Hindu thought."[109] The "conceptuality" he is talking about is "non-dualism" (*advaita*).

Burrell first encountered the Hindu tradition of Advaita (non-dual) Vedānta via his colleague, Bradley Malkovsky,[110] but only appreciated the possible significance of this worldview for Christian theology when he read *Toward an Alternative Theology: Confessions of a Non-Dualist Christian*—a largely autobiographical work written by a Roman Catholic sister of the Sacred Heart congregation, Sara Grant.[111] Grant claims, somewhat controversially, that the metaphysical "non-dualism" between the world and God, which she came across in Advaita Vedānta, also lies at the heart of Christianity, and she argues that the language of non-dualism provides a particularly useful way of balancing a number of oppositional tendencies in Christian thinking about creation and of avoiding conceptual errors in Christian talk about God. She thus offers a way of opening up an avenue of *inter*-theological engagement with a non-Abrahamic faith tradition that has the intriguing possibility of informing *intra*-Christian theological reflections as well. This dialogical exchange brings challenges as well as opportunities, but Burrell's central argument is that:

> *Nondualism* [*advaita*] mediates two proclivities: on the one hand, the tendency to treat the relation of the universe to its origin as one between two distinct entities—if not on the same plane at least comparable in ordinary discourse (dualism); on the other hand, considering the universe merely as expression of its originative source, so that there is no *relation* between them (monism).[112]

In particular, he notes how the work of Sara Grant—regarding the "non-dual" Christianity she claims to find (via the Hindu Advaitin, Śaṁkara) in Aquinas—could help Christian theologians to "think Creator and creature together."[113] An "advaitic" Thomas would be one way of moving beyond the conceptual impasse that often results from seeing the available options as either a dissolving of the difference between the world and God into some sort of pantheistic (at least, from a Christian point of view) monism or the maintaining of such a clear enumerative distinction that the two "things" appear to exist in splendid dualistic isolation from each other.

I have already suggested that it is Burrell's choice of Aquinas (and, specifically, his doctrine of creation) over Anselm that leads him to see relation as correlative with distinction, and of equal ontological and theological import.[114] This will become crucial to my overall argument, since Grant does not really talk about the "distinction" at all; rather, it is her work on relation in Śaṁkara and the suggestive parallels she draws between the non-dualism she finds in Advaita Vedānta and Aquinas's way of conceiving the relation between the world and God that first brought her to Burrell's attention. Relation even in an everyday sense between two things is, as Aristotle recognized, a peculiar sort of category, standing as it does "between" things, rather than being identifiable as an accident of a single substance, as with all the rest of the categories.[115] As Burrell rightly points out, this difference is a crucial one:

> The strains emerge whenever we overlook the difference between relations and accidents, so can be tempted to reduce relations to accidents.

> For then the radical dependency of substances on their creator, in such a way that being related to the creator is part of their very being, could be construed as making the entire universe an accident of divinity. That way of thinking leads, of course, to some form of pantheism. On the other hand, to try to resist that move by re-asserting Aristotle's dictum that substances are what exist "in themselves" (and not in relation to anything else) is to render the creator as separate from creatures as creatures are from one another, and so to deny the pervasive dependency that creation entails.[116]

Grant's presentation of non-dualism in an Indian context invites us to a way of thinking about this relation that avoids both of the errors outlined previously, precisely because it resists contrasting God and world as if they were two enumerable entities. Burrell says that it dawned on him when listening to Malkovsky's delineation of Vedāntic teaching on the relation of the world to its origin that "Nondualism is an attempt to state positively what Kathryn Tanner puts negatively."[117] More specifically, "pondering the manner in which Aquinas characterizes creation in things as a *relation* to their source, she [Grant] observes how malleable is this maverick Aristotelian category of *relation*" and, as we will see, she is able to utilize the Vedāntic concept of *advaita* to stress the ontological dependence of creatures on their Creator, and thus the asymmetric nature of this relation:

> Her prolonged study of Shankara, with the subtle language he introduces of "nonduality," helps her to see what many commentators on Aquinas have missed: the way his insistence that the *esse* of creatures is an *esse-ad-creatorem* (their to-be is to-be-towards-the-creator) utterly transforms Aristotle's world, where the hallmark of *substance* is to "exist in itself."[118]

Conclusion

I develop the case in the following chapters that the connecting thread between figures as diverse in time as Pseudo-Dionysius, Thomas Aquinas, and Sara Grant may be found in a certain concept of non-duality (*advaita*). This means that we must picture the distinction-and-relation between the world and God as a non-contrastive one: they are neither separate nor yet the same. The reasons for this statement, unpacked by Tanner and Turner, as well as a host of thinkers from Meister Eckhart to

Nicholas of Cusa, boil down to there being no common genus within which we can situate God and creatures, such as to be able to spell out the "difference" between them: God is "distinct" precisely in virtue of indistinctness. In Aquinas, this (in)distinction comes to the fore in the doctrine of creation, understood as the free bestowal of existence to all beings that participate in the act of unqualified existence (*esse*) we call God. This in turn shows why we can only talk of a "distinction" between God and what is not God if we also keep in mind the "relation" between them—namely, that the very being of creatures is an *esse-ad-creatorem*.

Burrell emphasizes not only the uniqueness of this relation but also its Abrahamic moorings as arising out of concerns common to Judaism, Christianity, and Islam. Lest he be accused, however, of evacuating theology in this regard of specifically Christian (i.e., Christological) content, it should be noted that Burrell and Sokolowski agree that with the theological inheritance of centuries of thinking through the "micro" problem of the distinction-and-relation between the human and the divine natures of Christ, Christian theologians have an especially nuanced conceptual framework for addressing the "macro" problem of the distinction-and-relation between the world and God.[119] Indeed, Burrell also puts it the other way around—that Chalcedonian Christology only makes sense in light of a non-contrastive (or *non-dualistic*) understanding of how creatures relate to God. As Turner reminds us:

> It is only because of the incommensurability between Creator and creature that the predicates ". . . is human" and ". . . is God", do not, and cannot, refer to natures standing in relations of mutual exclusion. For it is just on account of their incommensurability—on account, that is to say, of their not occupying common logical ground—that exclusion cannot come into it.[120]

We can, I think, borrow the "microcosmic" language of Chalcedon to articulate its "macrocosmic" iteration: God is (at least logically) related to the world "without confusion, without change, without division, and without separation" analogously to the way in which divine and creaturely natures are uniquely related in the one divine person of Jesus Christ.[121]

While a certain concept of "non-duality" is not, therefore, entirely unknown in the Christian tradition (as I have suggested throughout this chapter), I think that Burrell is right to encourage Christian theologians to explore more deeply Sara Grant's presentation of Śaṁkara's Advaita Vedānta to rethink old problems in new ways. Specifically, Burrell suggests three key motivations for doing so. First of all, there is the mandate handed down to us by Aquinas to work out Christian metaphysics in active conversations with thinkers from outside the tradition, to say nothing of the increasingly global horizons within which theology and philosophy must in any case be carried out.[122] Second, by confronting the language of "non-duality" which is uncommon for Christians, we are reminded of the uniqueness of the distinction between creature and Creator, and encouraged to articulate this in ways that avoid picturing God as "just another thing" existing alongside the world.[123] Finally, and, perhaps, primarily, the startling possibility of describing creature and Creator as "not-two" (*a-dvaita*) is one way of reasserting the true meaning of divine transcendence in Christian theology—not, as is too often the case, as a spatial metaphor *opposed* to metaphors of closeness and intimacy, but as precisely the unique sort of indistinctness that allows God to be, in the words of St. Augustine, *interior intimo meo* (closer to me than I am to myself).

Burrell's first allusion to Grant and the possibilities of a "non-dual" understanding of the relation between the world and God goes back more than twenty years. Here, he suggested that "the affinities between Sokolowski's *distinction* and a recent presentation of *nonduality* by a Christian writer [i.e., Grant's 1989 Teape Lectures] are so startling as to merit at least extensive notice."[124] This was followed a year later by Burrell's most detailed treatment of Grant in his chapter "The Creator and Creation" in a shared volume with Elena Malits.[125] Since then, he has consistently reissued this invitation to Christian theologians to look to Grant and Śaṁkara's non-dualism as a way of articulating the God-world distinction-and-relation in nearly all of his major published articles, chapters, and monographs, right up to the present day. The "at least extensive notice" of Grant's work, which Burrell called for in 1996, is surely long overdue.[126]

2 Roman Catholic Encounters with Advaita Vedānta

BETWEEN TRANSCENDENTAL ILLUSION AND RADICAL CONTINGENCY

> No concept is more important in Asian philosophical and religious thought than *nonduality* . . . and none is more ambiguous.[1]

In Chapter 1, I sought to contextualize David Burrell's intriguing invitation to Christian theologians to explore the unique nature of the distinction-and-relation between creature and Creator by way of an engagement with the Hindu tradition of Advaita Vedānta. Burrell directs us toward the work of Sara Grant and her attempts to show that the distinction-and-relation between the world and God in Christian theology involves neither a dualistic separation nor a monistic identity (and, as we shall see, that the distinction-and-relation between the world and Brahman in Advaita does not have to entail an illusionistic monism that denies the existence of the world altogether). In this way, Grant issues a challenge similar to the one that we have seen in Sokolowski and Tanner—to move beyond binary oppositions between the world and God to a 'non-dualism" (*a-dvaita*), which means neither "one" (i.e., God = world, or, in more Advaitic terms, God / Brahman alone minus—the world) nor "two" (i.e., God + world). Although her Christian framework is influenced, like Burrell's, by the metaphysics of creation found in Aquinas, she makes her case on a comparative horizon by turning to the non-dual philosophical-theological school of Advaita Vedānta.

Grant's work is not as idiosyncratic as it might first sound to theologians unacquainted with the histories of interaction between Christianity and Hinduism. She is, in fact, in good company because the most systematic Christian attempts to engage philosophically and theologically with Advaita Vedānta have been carried out by Roman Catholic scholars operating from within the frameworks of Scholastic metaphysics, often those of Aquinas, in particular. These theologians have argued, to differing extents, that Advaitic vocabularies, allegories, and imageries can be reworked and resituated within Christian doctrinal universes to explicate the distinctive relation between the world and God in such a way as to move beyond both monism and dualism. The world really exists; the world is not God, but the world is not straightforwardly other than God either.

In this chapter, I set out the context required to understand Grant's own arguments by offering an outline of the metaphysics of Advaita Vedānta and an overview of (Roman Catholic) Christian-Vedāntic encounters. In particular, I examine the contributions of a number of key earlier figures in what became known as the "Calcutta School" of Indology, to which Grant was pointed by her academic mentor in India, Fr. Richard De Smet, SJ (1916–1997).

An Outline of Advaita Vedānta

Martin Ganeri describes Vedānta as

> a tradition of textual exegesis and commentary, as well as philosophical reflection, which has been of immense importance in Brahmanical Hindu religious thought and practice, becoming the central ideology of the Hindu Renaissance in the nineteenth and early twentieth centuries.[2]

The texts to be explained and commented upon are the *Upaniṣads*—seen as the "end" (*-anta*) of the Vedic revelation, both in a chronological and in a teleological sense, as that toward which the Vedas point—as well as the *Bhagavadgītā* (ca. 200 BCE) and the *Brahma-Sūtras* of Bādarāyaṇa (ca. second–fifth centuries CE).[3] Vedāntic texts, therefore, are either "exegesis, commentary, and philosophical reflection" on one of the previously mentioned threefold canon (*prasthānatraya*) or self-standing "manuals" (*prakaraṇa*), which outline the important tenets of Vedānta in aphoristic prose or verse form.[4]

Several different Vedāntic schools developed during the long medieval period (ca. 900–1600 CE), offering distinctive accounts of the fundamental metaphysical worldview of the foundational texts. Each school claimed its doctrines as an authentic reading of *śruti* (revelation) and *smṛti* (tradition), and thereby asserted the Brahmanical orthodoxy of their own tradition.[5] The key feature that distinguishes different Vedāntic schools is how they interpret the distinctive ontological relation between the world and Brahman (with their differing interpretations indicated in the nomenclature that has become attached to them). The dominant interpretation of Vedānta (in the sense that it became the archetype against which doctrinal opponents would, explicitly or implicitly, set their own arguments) was the non-dual or "*advaita*" form as found in its most celebrated exponent, Śaṁkara (ca. 788–820 CE),[6] and, with significant developments and occasionally even divergences, in disciples like Sureśvara (ca. eighth century CE), Prakāśātman (ca. 1300 CE), and Sadānanda (ca. fifteenth century CE).[7] It was Advaita Vedānta that became "the central ideology of the Hindu Renaissance in the nineteenth and early twentieth centuries" in the writings and lectures of figures like Brahmabandhab Upadhyay (1861–1907) and Swami Vivekananda (1863–1902). The intellectual and cultural preeminence it was afforded by indigenous commentators and Western Indologists helps to explain, at least in part, why most of the twentieth-century European Roman Catholic theologians on whom we will concentrate chose to focus predominantly on Advaita rather than on other forms of Vedānta.[8]

In terms of its metaphysics, however, Advaita Vedānta might seem like a strange choice of conversation partner for a Christian tradition that typically wants to emphasize the "ontological distinction" between creatures and Creator. Advaitic exegetes insist on a non-dualistic interpretation of the *Upaniṣads*—arguing that there is, transcendentally speaking, only *one* changeless ground of being (*Brahman*) and that what a Christian would call the "created order" is (from an ultimate perspective) a less-than-fully-real "appearance" of this simple and undivided Reality. According to Śaṁkara and his followers, the world does not *really* exist independently (*a-dvaita*) of God (*Brahman*).[9] This is often pithily summarized as follows: "Brahman is real, the world is an illusory appearance; the individual soul is Brahman alone, not other,"[10] which can lead to the common (though, according to Grant, erroneous) interpretation of *advaita* as a form of acosmist monism.[11] Only ignorance (*avidyā*) is responsible for the illusion (*māyā*) of a "second" independent reality (viz. "the world") and it is this same ignorance that leads the individual self to misidentify with a particular body-mind complex (*jīva*), as if it were metaphysically separate from the rest of Reality. This "superimposition" (*adhyāsa*) of what is not real onto Reality prevents us from seeing our own true nature as the Self (*ātman*), which is ontologically non-different from the Absolute (*Brahman*), and it is this ignorance—both metaphysically and spiritually erroneous—which causes human suffering. The goal of the Advaitin, therefore, is to awaken to our true non-dual nature by removing this false view of the way things are—in other words, to come to realize the non-duality (*a-dvaita*) of the "relation" between the world / individual self and Brahman.[12]

Non-dualism and the Reality of the World: Different Readings of Advaita Vedānta

Interpreted as a form of illusionistic monism in which Brahman (God) alone exists, Advaita Vedānta would clearly seem like a step too far for a Christian theologian who wants to affirm the fundamental goodness and the reality of the created order. According to the eminent nineteenth-century German Indologist Paul Deussen (1845–1919), Śaṁkara's Advaita entails "the identity of the soul with Brahman, and denies all plurality, and therefore the validity of the ideas of the creation and existence of the world."[13] Indeed, such an illusionistic reading of Advaita is the one found in probably the majority of commentators in India and Europe.[14] Malkovsky highlights descriptions similar to Deussen's in indigenous figures of unquestioned academic authority such as M. Hiriyanna (1871–1950), S. Dasgupta (1887–1952), and T. M. P. Mahadevan (1911–1983).[15] The influential twentieth-century Indologist Paul Hacker summarizes the tradition tersely: "Advaita Vedānta holds that only pure spirit or consciousness—called Ātman, Brahman, the Highest Ātman, the Highest Brahman, even the Highest Lord—truly exists. The plurality of individual souls is illusory; only the universal Self is real,"[16] and the contemporary scholar C. Ram-Prasad summarizes Advaita as holding that "there is only a state of universal being, called *brahman*, to which all other states of existence—mental and physical—are reducible" and "that state of being, i.e., *brahman*, is said to be, in some ultimate way, the state of human beings too . . . and the realisation of that identity would mean the cessation of the problems that beset human consciousness."[17]

Examples could be multiplied, and it is not difficult to see where this characterization of Advaita comes from. Although the Viśiṣṭādvaita of an exegetical theologian like Rāmānuja will emphasize the ontological dependence of the world on Brahman, and the Dvaita Vedānta of Madhva will accentuate even more firmly the difference (*bheda*) between them, Advaita focuses resolutely on Brahman as the single substrative reality of the world. Thus, a typical manual of Advaita can say analogously that "A jar, though a modification of clay, is not different from it as it is essentially all clay. There is no separate entity of the form of the jar apart from the clay. Why, then, call it a jar? It is merely a false imagined name."[18] The implications of this lack of substantial reality of the jar are spelled out a few verses later: "Whatever is made of clay, like a pot and so on, is only and always entirely nothing but clay. Similarly, all this [the phenomenal world] that is the effect of the Real, *is the Real itself*, and entirely nothing but the Real. Because nothing exists, anywhere, anytime, other than the Real."[19] It seems, then, that in order to hold on to the primacy of Brahman as the unlimited plenitude of Being, Advaita dissolves the world into a series of convenient verbal and conceptual fictions—it suits us empirically for practical purposes to refer to jars, pots, and people as really demarcated entities, but ultimately, we are only ever referring to one and the same ground: "All that is, being the effect of the Existent Absolute (*brahmakāryam*), can be nothing but the Existent. It is pure Existence. Nothing exists other than it. If anyone says there is, their delusion has not vanished and they babble like one in sleep."[20] From here, it is a short step to saying that any talk of the "reality" of the world is merely the product of ignorance.

There are, however, other scholars (albeit in the minority) who emphasize a different reading of Śaṁkara's Advaita, as the secondary literature testifies.[21] One need only consider the title of a recent volume by Uma Pandey, an Indian Advaitin—*Śankara: A Realist Philosopher*, or the strongly "pro-world" interpretation of Advaita expounded by Anantanand Rambachan.[22] Indeed, Hacker points out that the issues are far more fine-grained than his initial summary might suggest: "If only the One Consciousness is real, it is argued, then everything in our experience that is multiple, changing and material—the entirety of phenomenal experience—is not truly real. Unreal, however, does not mean *non-existent*."[23] At the very least, it would seem implausible that an early Advaitin[24] like Śaṁkara would accept that the world is unreal if this means that its perceived externality is illusory, because he explicitly rejects this kind of subjective idealism as found in Buddhist *vijñānavāda*.[25] His argument, as we shall see, is that if "all that is made of clay" is really "just clay," the empirical world cannot be *entirely* unreal, or a metaphysical nullity, because the "clay" is not totally unreal.

This leads to the characteristically Advaitic conclusion that the empirical world is "neither real nor unreal" and, as we will see in the remainder of this chapter, a small but steady stream of Christian theologians have claimed that this seemingly paradoxical turn of phrase can be used to illuminate the God-world relation also in a Christian context. If the Real is defined as that which is unqualifiedly, immutably, and necessarily existent as it is in Advaita (and, for that matter, in classical Christian theology, such as that of Augustine and Anselm, and Aquinas's Five Ways), then the world is not Real, but the world is not utterly unreal either since it is perceived. Śaṁkara accepts both that the world is more than the mere perception of it[26] and (on the basis of *Upaniṣadic* testimony) that the world has an ontological foundation in that which is Real (Brahman). In this sense, the world is neither Real nor utterly unreal, but it is real in and through its *relation* to God. It is, in other words, only *relatively* real. The Roman Catholic theologians I will explore seek to show that there is no conflict here between Advaita and Thomist teaching on creation.

Christian doctrine and Advaita do, however, crucially differ in their varying accents on the two words in the phrase "relatively real" in the statement that "the world is relatively real with respect to the divine reality." For the former, the world is "relatively *real*"—though it exists only in and through its relationality to the divine, it *really* does exist. This, in turn, leads to a greater emphasis on the (relative) *reality* of the world as *distinct* from God. For the latter, in contrast, the world is "*relatively* real," so that whatever reality it has is only *relative* to Brahman, and its reality apart from Brahman cannot even be conceptualized, let alone materialized. Thus, Advaita leads us away from the idea of any ultimate distinction between the world and God because there are, in the final analysis, not *really* "two" to be distinguished. According to Advaita, the theistic claim that God and the world are *co*-real already postulates, to speak crudely in arithmetic terms, one thing too many in the metaphysical inventory. This subtle difference, as we will see, shapes the exegetical and conceptual engagements of these Roman Catholic theologians with Advaita, as they seek to answer, from within their distinctively Thomist perspectives, the momentous question: "in precisely what sense or senses is God *other* to the world?"[27]

An Overview of Some Encounters between Roman Catholicism and Advaita Vedānta

Several detailed critical histories of different facets of the encounters between Christian thought and Vedānta already exist.[28] K. P. Aleaz, an Indian Christian (Syrian Orthodox) theologian, focuses on Christian engagement with Advaita Vedānta, in particular;[29] Martin Ganeri, an English Roman Catholic (Dominican) theologian, focuses on Christian *Scholastic* engagement with different Vedāntic schools (though with a special emphasis on the Viśiṣṭādvaita of Rāmānuja);[30] and Francis X. Clooney, an American Roman Catholic (Jesuit) theologian concentrates on the history of *Jesuit* encounters with Vedānta and other Hindu traditions.[31] I do not intend to repeat these histories, but, rather, to focus on a particular fine-grained strand of these engagements in which Roman Catholic (often Jesuit) theologians have explored in meticulous detail the question that David Burrell—via Sara Grant—invites us to explore: namely, whether and how a Thomist account of creation can be reconciled with the non-dualist metaphysical picture of an Advaitin like Śaṁkara.

The idea that Christian faith and doctrine could be articulated on Indian soil using the conceptual categories of (Advaita) Vedāntic metaphysics was taken up in earnest in the second half of the nineteenth century by the Bengali Hindu-turned-Catholic, Brahmabandhab Upadhyay.[32] His arguments for convergence between Śaṁkara's notion of *māyā* (usually translated as "illusion") and Aquinas's understanding of creaturely dependence were both novel and pioneering. After all, according to influential interpretations of Śaṁkara as an ontological monist, the whole point of Advaita Vedānta is to stress that nothing other than God really exists anyway. Upadhyay's argument that the "illusory" nature of the world in Advaita could be harmonized with Thomas's insistence on the "contingency" of creation went on to influence an entire generation of Roman Catholic Indologists in the twentieth century who responded to and creatively reconfigured Upadhyay's pioneering exegetical attempts. Beginning with William Wallace (1863–1922), this galaxy of mainly Belgian Jesuits became known as the "Calcutta School," and included Georges Dandoy, SJ (1882–1962), Pierre Johanns, SJ (1885–1955), Robert Antoine, SJ (1914–81), Pierre Fallon, SJ (1912–85), and Richard De Smet, SJ (1916–98).

Given his foundational significance, I will look first of all at Upadhyay's arguments for significant parallels between Śaṁkara and Thomas in their understandings of the ontological status of the world and of its (non-)relation to the Absolute. We will then move on to Dandoy, Johanns, and De Smet, in whose work we find three of the most distinctive, detailed, and systematic treatments of the problematic running throughout this chapter—namely, how to reconcile Thomist teaching on creation with the Advaitic insistence on the metaphysical non-difference between the world and God. In seeking to draw out the continuities and the divergences across their work, we need to be alert to (at least) two variables. Although it is in their interpretations of *Advaita* that Upadhyay, Dandoy, Johanns, and De Smet differ explicitly, these differences can be appreciated more fully when we look carefully at the particular *Thomist* themes and thinkers who are (often more implicitly) motivating their engagements. The Thomism in the background of Upadhyay's work in the 1890s, for example, was rather different from that which was formative on De Smet in the 1960s and 1970s.

Brahmabandhab Upadhyay (1861–1907)

The canonical status afforded to a certain form of Thomism in Catholic theology at the time (Pope Leo XIII's 1879 encyclical *Aeterni Patris* was subtitled: "On the Restoration of Christian Philosophy in Catholic Schools in the Spirit of the Angelic Doctor, St. Thomas Aquinas")[33] and the valorization of Advaita Vedānta by Western Indologists and prominent Indian figures in the Hindu Renaissance,[34] perhaps makes it unsurprising that Upadhyay, a Brahmin convert to Roman Catholicism, took Thomas Aquinas and Śaṁkara as his key conversation partners.[35] Yet this comparison, unsurprising as it might be for these historical reasons, initially seemed far from obvious on doctrinal grounds to Upadhyay. Although Śaṁkara's Advaita was being propounded as the intellectual and the spiritual apex of Hinduism by contemporaneous Western orientalists like G. Thibaut (1848–1914)[36] and P. Deussen (1845–1919),[37] as well as by certain indigenous figures like Rammohan Roy (1774–1833) and Swami Vivekananda (1863–1902), Upadhyay was concerned, understandably enough, that many of the basic tenets of Śaṁkara's system, as it was generally understood in traditional exegetical streams, were incompatible with his new-found Roman Catholic faith. Advaita seemed to entail the nonpersonal and the non-dual nature of the Absolute Reality (or, at least, the provisional and somewhat illusory nature of a personal god, and an empirical world that is not fully real). This understanding of Advaita, which Upadhyay thought was being put forward by contemporary Vedāntins like Vivekananda, seemed to him to be a long way, doctrinally speaking, from his Catholic belief in creaturely humility before the Creator and the related doctrines of sin, contrition, forgiveness, and the like. As such, Upadhyay's first thought had been to turn to ancient Vedic theism as the "natural" platform for the "supernatural" revelation of Christ (as understood in Catholic doctrine), and *not* to Advaita Vedānta.

In spite of this initial opposition to Advaita, however, (or, to be more precise, to the particular kind of modernist Vedānta being promulgated by Vivekananda and others), Lipner argues that Upadhyay eventually had little hermeneutic choice but to reevaluate Advaita due to the intellectual prestige it was enjoying at home and abroad. As a result, by 1897 (when Vivekananda returned to India after appearing in 1893 at the Conference of World Religions in Chicago) "Upadhyay was faced with the *fait accompli* of Advaita being regarded as a chief, if not the chief, religious instrument of personal and collective *svaraj*."[38] His project from then on to resituate Advaita within Catholic doctrinal forms led to a series of important articles, which appeared in *Sophia*—the monthly Catholic journal that he had started in 1894 and aimed at a Hindu readership. In "An Exposition of Catholic Belief as Compared with the Vedānta" (January 1898), for example, Upadhyay famously argues that the Vedāntic conception of Brahman as Being, Consciousness, and Unlimited Bliss (*sat, cit, ānanda*) corresponds to the understanding of the nature of God found in Roman Catholic "natural theology" (i.e., Thomism). Even more interestingly for our purposes, Upadhyay puts forward a novel interpretation of "The true doctrine of Maya" (February–March 1899) in which he claims that *māyā* (commonly translated in Vedāntic contexts as "illusion") is what Aquinas calls "*creatio passiva*" (i.e., creaturely existential dependence or continuous receiving of being). Lipner summarizes Upadhyay's argument in the following terms:

> Since created being has no right to existence in itself, since of itself it is "darkness, falsity and nothingness" (or *tenebrae, falsitas et nihil*, says Upadhyay, quoting St Thomas), it is an illusion to regard finite being as existing in any way apart from the divine being. Creatures "exist by *maya*, i.e., by the habit of participating in the divine being and springing from the divine act" . . . The conclusion of this point is put in a mixture of Advaitic-Thomistic terminology. "*Maya* is neither real nor necessary, nor unreal, but contingent."[39]

Somewhat ingeniously, Upadhyay thus dissolves any apparent doctrinal conflict between Thomistic and Advaitic doctrines of originative causality by equating the "unreality" of the world in Advaita with the "contingency" of the world in orthodox Christian theology of creation.

On this account, a Catholic and a Vedāntin could agree that it would be a misconception or a transcendental "illusion" to regard the world as a self-sufficient and existentially autonomous reality, which stands apart from its sustaining ontological Cause.[40] There is, thus, *some* truth captured by the stock Vedāntic comparisons of the world to a subjective delusion, like a mirage in the desert or a rope confused for a snake; just as there is *some* truth captured by comparing the world to an objective illusion like a reflection in water; and, finally, there is *some* truth captured in comparing the (non-)relation of the world to God to the (non-)relation between waves and the ocean. In each case, the truth is that the finite realm has no *necessary* or *independent* reality—that is, it has no aseity. Timothy Tennent suggests (and Upadhyay would agree) that the underlying theme of these Advaitic metaphors taken together is not that the world is a purely subjective hallucination, but rather that ontological unity and ontic multiplicity, and the immeasurable infinite and the measurable finite, cannot be *equally* real; indeed, that the one (multiplicity and finitude) only exists in virtue of its grounding in the other (unity and infinitude).[41] It is in this sense that Ultimate Reality can be described as *a-dvaita* ("not-two").

> *Avidya* or *maya*, then, is not "illusion", it is the principle of creation . . . *maya* is simply made out to be the principle of divine creation, which itself is "the communication of being". And being, "divorced" from its "substratum" is, to use Thomas' own phrase in Latin, *nihil* (nothing), *falsitas* (falsity), *tenebrae* (darkness). Thus, Shankara becomes a crypto-Thomist; indeed, he is the Indian precursor of St Thomas (since he lived centuries before the latter), had he but known it![42]

As we have already noted, this "contingency" (and "realist") reading of Śaṁkara's Advaita ran counter to the prevailing ways in which Vedāntic non-dualism was usually understood both by Indian and by Western interpreters. The Jesuit Indologist, A. Hegglin, for example, maintained that Upadhyay's reading was incorrect, and that the Vedāntic concept of *māyā* was irreconcilable with orthodox Christian understandings of creation.[43] With the benefit of hindsight, Lipner, too, is skeptical about Upadhyay's strategy and of the degree of genuine convergence between these two medieval Scholasticisms (viz. Thomism and Advaita Vedānta). The problem, according to Lipner, is that Upadhyay's comparative project was predetermined by his acceptance of certain key Neo-Thomist theological frameworks (e.g., the distinction between the "natural" and the "supernatural"), on the one hand, and by his socio-historically shaped push toward Advaita Vedānta, on the other. As a result, he criticizes Upadhyay for attempting to make Christianity more appealing to Hindus

> not by seeking to implant Christian concepts in Vedantic soil so as to arrive at a genuine first-order indigenization of the Christian faith, but rather by constructing more or less exact correspondences between Vedantic ideas and Thomistic ones so that Vedanta in some respects may be seen as a form of crypto-(neo-)Thomism and Shankara as St Thomas in disguise.[44]

Although Lipner sees Upadhyay's project in this regard as a somewhat misleading attempt to "Christianize" Vedānta, Aleaz is much more positive in his assessment. He commends Upadhyay precisely for what he sees as his acceptance of Vedānta on its own terms and rejects any notion that Upadhyay was reinterpreting Śaṁkara's doctrines in order to align them with a predecided Christian theology.[45] The only misgiving expressed by Aleaz is that Upadhyay's focus on the concept of *māyā* risks distorting Śaṁkara's thought, as this particular term is used far less by Śaṁkara than it was by later Advaitins:

> We gladly accept in principle Upadhyaya's formulation of the Indian Christian doctrine of creation as *Māyā*, but we suggest that it would be better for avoiding misunderstandings if, instead of *Māyā*, we put forward Śaṅkara's theory of causation to explain the Indian Christian doctrine of creation.[46]

As we will see, this shift in emphasis from *māyā* (~ illusion) to causation is apparent in some of the later figures who followed in Upadhyay's footsteps. Śaṁkara's theory of causation is put under a conceptual microscope by Dandoy and De Smet, in particular, but they come to two somewhat differing conclusions about its suitability for articulating a Christian understanding of creation.

Georges Dandoy, SJ (1882–1962) and Pierre Johanns, SJ (1885–1955)[47]

Upadhyay's attempts to formulate a distinctively "Indian" Christian theology via the combined resources of Scholastic and Advaitic metaphysics became influential for a number of Belgian Jesuits centered in Calcutta during the first half of the twentieth century, who sought to develop what Upadhyay had begun.[48] Among these, two of the most prolific and influential were Georges Dandoy, SJ, and Pierre Johanns, SJ.[49] Both Oxford-educated Orientalists, Dandoy and Johanns were convinced that a creative synthesis of the different Vedāntic traditions would result in a metaphysical system akin to Thomism, and argued their case in regular articles written for *The Light of the East*, the monthly periodical they established. Indeed, they were encouraged to begin this journal (which was started in 1922 and remained in publication until 1934) by Brahmachari Animananda, a disciple of Upadhyay, which is why Doyle can point to "an unbroken line of influence from Upādhyāy and Animananda to the Jesuit William Wallace and on to Johanns and his Belgian associates."[50] As Doyle mentions, a crucial influence on Dandoy and Johanns was the Anglican missionary-turned-Jesuit, William Wallace (1863–1922), who can be seen as the doctrinal link between Upadhyay and the later "Calcutta School" of Jesuit Indologists.[51] Dandoy and Johanns are particularly important for our purposes because of their explicit Christian moorings in Aquinas. Along with Upadhyay, and other later figures like De Smet, Henri Le Saux, OSB, Bede Griffiths, OSB Cam, Raimon Panikkar, and Sara Grant, there is a strong argument for agreeing with R. Boyd that "Thomism has been the theological point of departure for some of the most important Catholic missionary-scholars in India."[52]

GEORGES DANDOY, SJ

Dandoy's views on Advaita can be found in a treatise he wrote in the decade after Upadhyay's death, "The Doctrine of the Unreality of the World in the Advaita."[53] He makes no explicit reference to Upadhyay in this essay, though he draws similar connections between "illusion" or "unreality" in Advaita and "contingency" in Thomism. In the final analysis, however, he is less convinced than Upadhyay had been that the two systems are really converging on the same concept because, he argues, of their quite different conceptions of causality.

Dandoy sees Advaita as the "Monistic" school of Vedānta, and explains the precise nature of the "non-duality" taught by Advaitins as meaning that "there is only one Reality."[54] He points out that the reason a Thomist is unlikely to use this sort of language or come to this sort of metaphysical conclusion, is because the reality of the empirical world is taken as the unquestioned starting point of their system. From this premise, the

Scholastic philosopher ascends conceptually to the idea of the First Cause or the necessary Being, which alone can provide the sufficient reason for contingent, finite existence:

> God, for our philosophy, is essentially and primarily the First Cause and the Prime Mover. Our reason for supposing His existence, our motive for predicating of Him certain attributes, is that this existence and these attributes follow as mediate or immediate conclusions from the existence of our starting-point: the world.[55]

In other words, Scholastic arguments do not, according to Dandoy, begin with the First Principle and then seek to explain the world (*demonstratio propter quid*), but instead they begin with the world (whose reality is pre-reflectively granted) and then seek to show that it is only intelligible in light of a Creator (*demonstratio quia*). As such,

> We Schoolmen are never tempted to deny the existence of the world of sense. It is the very basis of our system . . . [w]aive the reality of the world we cannot, because that is the corner stone, and, if we remove it, our whole edifice crumbles.[56]

Vedānta, on the other hand, is quite different in its argumentative orientation. The starting point here is the scriptural datum of Brahman, the supreme, unrelated, self-sufficient Absolute, the one-without-a-second, and the finite world can only be explained (if it is to be explained at all) as a function of this ontological foundation. Both systems (Vedānta and Thomism) face the same philosophical-theological problem of how to explain the relation between an eternal, unchanging, and simple First Principle that is absolute fullness of Being and a temporal, transient, and differentiated empirical realm. Dandoy affirms that "there is hardly anything *positive* that [Vedānta] says about God that we may dare to reject."[57] The key differences between (Advaita) Vedānta and Christian Scholasticism, however, emerge as a result of the different starting points, which determine the shape of their arguments:

> for Vedāntism God's self-sufficiency and His unrelated eternity is the thesis; this world of ours is the objection—whereas for Scholastic philosophy the existence of the world is the primary assertion and God's unconnected essence is the difficulty to be solved.[58]

Dandoy's analysis helps to explain why the sort of monism toward which certain Christian thinkers have been drawn—in a determined effort to avoid any hint of dualism between the world and God—has been a *pantheistic* monism in which the whole world is seen as divine, while the sort of monism toward which certain Advaitic thinkers have been drawn has been of an *illusionistic* sort (because their starting point is not the unquestioned reality of the world). In other words, there is not just one form of monism at play here: pantheism is a distinctively *Christian* "solution" to the problem of the world-God dialectic, whereas illusionism has been the characteristically *Advaitic* response—and neither tradition has much of a history of contemplating the problematic in the other's terms (i.e., Christian theology has not tended to concern itself with whether or not the world really exists—even though, as we will see, this language can be found in seminal figures like Augustine, Anselm, and Aquinas—and Advaita Vedānta has not really articulated itself in terms of pantheism).

Dandoy summarizes *Upaniṣadic* teaching on the nature of Brahman with four key doctrines:[59] Brahman is Being, Consciousness, and Joy (*sat-cit-ānanda*); immaterial, simple, infinite, and unchanging; one only without a second (*ekam eva advitiyam*), which he explains as meaning that "there is nothing *beside* Brahman,"[60] and identical with the "self" (*ātman*) of all living creatures. Although he is not prepared to equate this doctrinal set wholesale with the Christian conception of God, Dandoy is willing to say that it is "at least partly true":[61]

> For, if we say: the Absolute is the *ātman*—the Unconditioned at the back of the universe is the Unconditioned at the back of *me*, we have but repeated that the cause of the universe is also He *in quo vivimus movemur et sumus*. The only Being which can be said so to exist in itself that it needs for its existence no other being [is] the Absolute Brahman or God.[62]

The problem, then, is how to explain the fact that we experience an empirical world that seems manifestly different from the unchanging Absolute that constitutes, according to the *Upaniṣads*, "all that there really is." As Dandoy puts it, "Śaṁkara's idea seems to be . . . that the world is neither to be explained as distinct nor non-distinct from Brahman."[63] The world seems to hover in some sort of indeterminate ontological limbo—insofar as it exists, it must exist "in" Brahman, the unlimited fulness of Being, and yet the world "adds" nothing to Brahman, and so does not seem to be fully real.

The metaphysical premise in the background of the Vedāntic worldview becomes crucial here: if Brahman is the sole first Principle, one only without a second, then the world can only be understood in relation to (and not independently of) Brahman. That is, the world must be, in some sense, a dependent "effect" of Brahman, because otherwise it would constitute a second Absolute, which is conceptually incoherent as Brahman is the unlimited fullness of Being. When seen in this light, it becomes clearer why the Vedāntin struggles to articulate the precise ontological status of the effect because, as depicted in Dandoy's exposition of the common Vedāntic simile of clay and a clay pot, "[t]he effect is and is not identical with its cause: in itself it can neither be called being nor not being."[64] In other words, there would simply be no "pot" without the substrate of the clay, and the pot does not "add" anything, in a deep ontological sense, to what was already there before it came into existence. It is no more helpful to talk of the clay being *transformed* into the pot because, ontologically, no change has occurred at the bedrock of reality—which is precisely why Vedāntins (and Thomists) would strongly resist any notion of the immutable Brahman/God undergoing any real change (*pariṇāma*) in order to explain the existence of the world. As Dandoy puts it, "[t]he question of the reality of the world thus reduce[s] itself to the question of the reality of any effect."[65]

To the extent that Christian traditions struggle with these same metaphysical challenges and, up to a point, have to concede that there is a certain unavoidable "mystery" (*māyā*) to how creation is somehow other than God, Dandoy recognizes that a Christian Thomist would be willing to accept many of the Vedāntin's conclusions:

> The world has not the reality of its cause. Compared to God, the world that we are, touch, and see is only "analogously". Something infinitely below the fulness of existence which God is, it is something more than the pure vacuity of a hare's horn. And the *materia prima* from which the material world derives its multiplicity, is, as St. Augustine remarked long ago (*Conf.* xii.4.8) a very unintelligible something which might as well be called a magic or a mystery, something between being and non-being.[66]

The challenge, then, is how to account metaphysically for the relation between the "pot" and the "clay" (i.e., between the temporal world and the eternal God) and (at least for a Christian like Dandoy) how to account for the reality of the "pot"/world as ontologically distinct from the "clay"/God (though an Advaitin might well object that framing the difficulty in these disjunctive terms is question begging and gets things wrong from the outset). Dandoy summarizes this thicket of problems as follows:

> First it [the pot or jar] has the reality of the clay that goes to constitute it, and still remains in it as its substratum. Thus, the world has the reality of Brahman, its cause—it is real in its substance or essence, since that essence is Brahman, which, as cause, remains immanent in its effect. But what is the reality of the jar *formaliter considerata* in so far as it is a jar and not mere clay . . . Similarly what is the reality of the world *as such*, as distinct from Brahman its cause?[67]

The problem, he concedes, in somewhat understated language, "is a difficult one . . . [which] has perplexed the philosophers of ancient and modern times."[68] Once the existential contingency of the world is put in terms of an effect of its (substrative) cause (*upādānakārana*), the Advaitin reasons that the ontological nature or essence (*svabhāva* or *svarūpa*) of the effect must be "not-other" than the ontological nature or essence of its cause. In other words, the world cannot have an independent nature separate from the nature of God.[69] Yet, at the same time, God cannot be ontologically identified with the change, multiplicity, and finitude that (seem to) characterize the material world. To identify these features with the essence of God would be to commit the error of superimposing (*adhyāsa*) one thing onto another and thereby ignorantly confusing the two (*avidyā*), or, in the language of Christian theology, to fall into the trap of onto-theological idolatry—confusing beings with Being, creatures with Creator. It seems, then, that while the ostensible fact of a transient and contingent empirical realm tells us something about how that reality must be related to God (i.e., it depends entirely on God for whatever degree of reality it enjoys), it does not tell us anything positive at all about how God must be related to it. Indeed, it seems to entail no real relation at all of God *to* the world—which is precisely the conclusion reached by Dandoy (and Śaṁkara and Thomas):

> If we call Brahman a Creator, it is therefore an *adhyasa*, a superimposition on Brahman's nature of what does not pertain to that nature . . . because in its essence, in what it is in itself, Brahman is no support of multiplicity, no cause, no creator, but only pure, unbroken light. All this is due to our mixing in one notion Brahman and World.[70]

Dandoy recognizes "the great truth embodied in these statements," which agree with Aquinas's own teaching about God as Creator:

> "Creator" is no essential name of God—it is a *denominatio extrinsica* (cf. I. q.XIII, a.7). The being a Creator is not an attribute of God's nature;

it implies a relation of the universe to God, not a relation of God to the Universe.[71]

Similarly, Dandoy sees no reason to object to the Advaitic teaching that the world "is neither [absolute] being nor [absolute] non-being," for this "admirable doctrine" is "the nearest approach I have seen to the Schoolmen's doctrine of Analogy."[72] As he explains, much depends on the "vantage point" from which one is speaking:

> If we take God's being as standard, we are not; if we take our being as standard, God is not. Only this neither proves that God *IS* not, nor that we *are* not. And, unfortunately, it was to the last conclusion that the Advaita was led by the very logic of its principle, that all effect is only a material cause modified, that therefore, the First Cause in order to act must change, and by the assumption that all that is, is ever fully actualised, that all potential, all power to do or to become is a mere illusion.[73]

So, herein lies the rub. While Dandoy admires the determination in Advaita to maintain the simplicity and the immutability of the Absolute (even at the cost of denying the reality of the world), and agrees that one is forced inexorably to the conclusion that the world of change and multiplicity cannot really exist if it is seen as ontologically non-different from its cause, he thinks that the very basis of the system is weak (i.e., "its conception of causality").[74] He explains his reservations in a passage that is worth quoting at some length:

> let us notice it at once, if we wish to know what Samkara is leading us to: in his system this evident truth [viz. that being a Creator is not an attribute of God's nature] implies a conclusion from which St. Thomas would have recoiled. It is this: that the multiplicity of the world has no substratum, no essence. Why will you ask? Because we had proved that the essence of the world must be Brahman—that Brahman is the only essence, and we have now seen that Brahman could not possibly be the essence of a multiplicity. The multiplicity is an unsupported accident! Alice in Wonderland saw a cat's grin without a cat. But such things are seen in Wonderland, and we are now in search of realities. An accident is not without support.[75]

Advaita, Dandoy claims, cannot help but arrive at the antinomy "that God *must* be and yet *cannot* be the cause of the multiplicity that we call the world,"[76] and it can only "solve" this antinomy by denying the metaphysical reality of the latter. Dandoy sees this move as an evasion of the difficulty and rejects it as "a solution of despair . . . and the end of all philosophy."[77]

The real solution, according to Dandoy, is to deny the antinomy (viz. "that God *must* be and yet *cannot* be the cause of the multiplicity that we call the world") by rejecting the Advaitic notion of causality itself. The confusion arises, he argues, because of the types of causality analyzed by the Advaitin, such as threads transformed into cloth, clay assuming the form of a pot, or curds produced from milk.[78] In these sorts of examples, the most obvious form of causality is, to speak in Aristotelian terms, material or, more specifically, "the accidental [in philosophical terms] transmutation of material substances, the transmutation which leaves the substance intact and only changes its modalities."[79] The problem, Dandoy thinks, is that

> if we take this kind of causation as typical, and assimilate to it all causation, we must come to the conclusion that everywhere and always the cause is the permanent, the real, the *sattva*, the *atman*, the *svarupa*, the essence, the substance; the effect is the mode, the form, the accidental; the cause is the existent, the effect is the transitory, the apparent. Consequently, the Supreme Cause is the universal substance, permanent under all its effects, and the latter are simply its modifications, its accidents, its transitory appearances.[80]

Dandoy seeks to move away from the category of material causation by suggesting alternative examples, such as a child and its parents, in which the "effect" (the child) is clearly more than simply a transformation of its "cause" (the parents); indeed, where the essence of the effect is *not* the same as the essence of the cause, but is clearly distinct from it.[81] This child-parent analogy is more like the relation between the world and God, he argues, than are the Vedāntic similes (of clay pots, etc.), for the child-parent example suggests "not that [God] is *separated* from us, but that He is *distinct* from us."[82]

I am not convinced, however, that there is a substantive disagreement between Advaita and Thomism on this point. The causal analogies of threads and cloths, of clay and pots, and such like are misleading only if they are taken too literally (as Dandoy seems to be doing) and as suggesting, which no Advaitin would, that Brahman is the material cause in exactly the same sense as clay is the "stuff" out of which the pot is made. If "material cause" is instead understood as the "reality-giving" Cause on which all things depend in order to "be" at all, a Thomist would surely agree that God is indeed "everywhere and always . . . the permanent, the real, the *sattva*, the *atman*, the *svarupa*, the essence, the substance."[83] Perhaps Dandoy's child-parent example reveals the real crux of the issue at stake between Advaita and Christianity. When he says that this analogy suggests that God is not separate, but, nevertheless, *distinct* from us, the critical question is: "distinct from whose perspective"? An Advaitin could agree that there is a (provisional) distinction if we are speaking empirically but would disagree if we are speaking metaphysically from a transcendental standpoint. Advaita was never meant to be an empirical discussion of what things look like from the point of view of the creature, but is a metaphysical exposition of the fabric of reality from the perspective of Brahman. Of course, a child can be clearly distinct from its parents in terms of personality and physical features, but these empirical distinctions do not necessarily indicate or map onto a metaphysical distinction; to think that empirical features are isomorphic with deep reality is precisely a form of spiritual ignorance. Dandoy would perhaps want to argue, from a Christian realist standpoint, which for him is a foundational presupposition, that there is both an obviously empirical *and* a deeper ontological distinction between the child and its parent, a distinction that is reflective of, and underpinned by, the more profound ontological distinction between the world and God. My objection, however, to Dandoy's example is that analogizing the relation between the world and God to that between a child and her parent is to set up the two in terms of a mutually exclusive contrast. It is not possible simultaneously to be both a child and the parent of that same child because being the one conceptually excludes being the other—and this is because "child" and "parent" are two different tokens of the same (empirical) type of human being. As I argued throughout Chapter 1, however, this is a misleading way of conceiving the distinction-and-relation between the world and God because the "two" here do not belong to the same order of reality. Indeed, God does not belong to any antecedent order of reality at all as one of its constituents. This is why it is not only *conceptually possible* but also *metaphysically necessary* that the world is not *other* than God. Thus, *pace* Dandoy, I would argue that the analogies found in Vedānta of clay and pots, threads and cloth, etc. are to be properly understood as non-contrastive articulations, and in this respect they *are* helpful reminders to the Christian theologian steeped in the metaphorical language of God as parent that the distinctive relation between creature and Creator is an *advaitic* one.

PIERRE JOHANNS, SJ

The particular approach of Dandoy's Jesuit confrère, Pierre Johanns, can be understood in the light of two major influences. First, in his desire to synthesize thinkers like Śaṁkara, Rāmānuja, and Vallabha, he was following the systematizing tendencies of late nineteenth and early twentieth century Neo-Thomism, especially of the school associated with Louvain (where he had studied) and key figures such as Pierre Scheuer and Joseph Maréchal (1878–1944).[84] Johanns's self-professed goal was to harmonize what he saw as the disconnected and partially correct doctrines found in the different Vedāntic schools into a single system that would resemble Thomism.[85] Second, he also found inspiration in the irenic attitude toward non-Christian thought of Church Fathers like Justin (100–165) and Clement (150–215). In particular, he saw in their understanding of Greek philosophy as a *praeparatio evangelica* a fruitful way of incorporating Vedānta into Christian theology. He was convinced, as Upadhyay had been, that Vedānta could serve as the metaphysical framework of an enculturated Indian Christianity in the ways that Greek philosophy had been utilized to formulate early Christian doctrinal statements.[86] As Doyle puts it, "Johanns was attempting to do with the *Vedānta* what his neo-Thomist colleagues were doing with contemporary Continental philosophies, integrating their various perspectives into a *philosophia perennis*."[87]

When it comes to Śaṁkara, Johanns followed Dandoy (and scholars like P. Deussen, F. Max-Müller, and G. Thibaut) in interpreting Advaita as a form of philosophical monism that emphasizes the "illusion" of the reality of the world.[88] In places, Johanns is prepared to affirm—in somewhat remarkable language for a Christian theologian—that as far as "there is [the] question of what the world is by itself, in itself, and for itself, the answer must always be that it is nothing, thorough unreality,"[89] but his objection is that Śaṁkara does not do enough to underline the *relative* value and reality of the contingent world. Indeed, it is this lack of balance in Śaṁkara's language that has historically led to the impression that (Advaita) Vedānta is a form of illusionistic monism.[90] The key doctrine that needs to be developed in Advaita, according to Johanns, is that of creation ex nihilo, since this allows Christian theology to emphasize the utter dependence of the created order and, at the same time, to preserve its relative *reality* as distinct from God.[91] Thus, "from Śaṅkara's [alleged] acosmism, Johanns developed the idea that the world does not have necessary or absolute being in itself. And from Śaṅkara's pristine view of an unrelated God, Johanns argued that God cannot be dependent upon the world in any way or necessarily related to it."[92] Johanns, in other words, did not think that the Thomist emphasis on dependency or contingency was precisely what Śaṁkara himself would have meant by the "unreality" of the world. However, this translation of Advaitic terminologies into Thomist registers is defensible because in Thomist theology as much as in Vedānta:

> The world's status is such that if God would remove His sustaining creativity, the world would vanish into nothingness. Of itself, the world is absolute void. But due to God's continual act of conferring being into the void, the world does have a contingent reality, not of itself but of God.[93]

Once brought into existence, the world, according to Johanns, is an "image" of God (i.e., not utterly unreal, but completely dependent on divine Reality) and he insists that the world is, therefore, related to God in a modality of nonreciprocal dependence (i.e., it is not the case that God depends on the world).[94] As well as this affirmation of the relative *reality* of contingent existence, Johanns emphasizes—in ways not quite found in Śaṁkara—the "self-giving" nature of a supremely personal God, and prefers the "positive" image of a willed creation ex nihilo to the language of *māyā*, *avidyā*, and *vivartavāda*. Doyle sums up this difference as follows:

> For Johanns, a metaphysic of *creatio ex nihilo* indicates not only that God is self-conscious but also that God is self-giving. God has need of nothing . . . God is not "related" to the world in the sense that He is dependent in any way upon the world-reality; it is the world that is related to God in that it depends upon Him for every moment of its contingent being.[95]

Like Dandoy, Johanns saw the Advaitic doctrine of causation and its inability to allow for the possibility of something coming from nothing (*nihil*) as the key obstacle to reconciling Śaṁkara with Aquinas. Johanns agrees that the effect must exist preeminently in the cause, but argues that God's ability to create ex nihilo means precisely that God can produce a distinct effect without simply becoming that effect.[96] I will address these concerns in detail in Chapter 4.

Richard De Smet, SJ (1916–1997)

An intellectual heir of Upadhyay, Wallace, Dandoy, and Johanns,[97] De Smet was another member of the "Calcutta School" of Belgian Jesuits who continued to explore the relations between Scholasticism and Vedānta.[98] He came to reject an illusionistic reading of Śaṁkara, and argued for an interpretation of Thomas's account of creative causality, which goes beyond any straightforward dualism between creature and Creator.[99] Indeed, having arrived in India in 1946, one of De Smet's earliest articles was an appraisal of Upadhyay's interpretation of Śaṁkara, and the seeds of many of the ideas crucial to his later work can be found in nuce in this short piece.[100] He agrees with Upadhyay that when Śaṁkara talks in terms of the unreality of the world, he intends to stress not the "absurd conception of the absolute unreality of all creatures, so often attributed to him,"[101] but, in ways similar to the "Schoolmen," "the transcendental relation of the creature to the Creator."[102] De Smet's careful wording here is important for, as with Thomas, it is not the Creator who is related to the creature, but vice versa, and it is precisely the sui generis nature of this asymmetrical causal relation that accounts for both the distinction *and* the non-separateness between them. As De Smet puts it:

> Being (*sattā*) is indeed the one characteristic feature of the world as well as of Brahman (*B.S.Bh.* 2,1,6), but they are irremediably distinct and different because existence in the creatures cannot receive the attributes of absolute substantiality and infinity as in Brahman. Created existence is only an image, a reflection of the absolute existence, and as such a dependent participation, not an existence by right.[103]

By introducing the language of "dependent participation," De Smet is already moving toward the sort of interpretation of Śaṁkara that he develops in his subsequent work. To rebut the charges that Advaita has to mean acosmist monism, De Smet affirms that Śaṁkara never intended to claim that the world was "unreal" in a Berkeleyean idealist sense, but that any reality it has is owed entirely to the constitutive causal relation that Christian theology refers to simply as "creation." The fact that the world is sustained in existence by this relation of ontological dependence on God is what leads an Advaitin like Śaṁkara to stress that there are "not two" (*a-dvaita*) metaphysically separate realities; effect and cause are ultimately non-different. De Smet is more willing than Dandoy to maintain that there is no fundamental disagreement between Christian and Vedāntic conceptions of originative causality or of the relation between creature and Creator. De Smet even provocatively suggests that God *can* be thought of as a "material cause," in the following, carefully qualified, sense. God is

> the Being of whose substance the effect—i.e. both the potency and its act in their substantial union—is made . . . He [God] can very well, by communicating Himself, be the very stuff His creatures are made of. As His reflections they *have* in their finite way a share in that being which He alone *Is*. Our doctrine of analogical participation does not teach anything else.[104]

De Smet is at pains, in other words, to emphasize the simultaneous reality of both dependency *and* distinction, and he seems happy to go further, on his theological pilgrimage of faith seeking understanding, into Advaitic territory than Dandoy or Johanns. He explicitly argues, for example, that the common Vedāntic similes rejected by Dandoy are misleading only if we take them too literally as suggesting that God is a material "thing" out of which the world is made—and that, therefore, "the effect is a part, an emanation, or a self-evolution of Brahman and that there is univocity and continuity (*pariṇāmavāda*) between God and the world."[105] Seeing the world in this way, as some sort of outgrowth or transformation out of God is rejected just as forcefully by Śaṁkara as it is by Thomas. As De Smet puts it,

> Śaṅkara holds *vivaṛtavāda* [causality which implies no change in the cause] asserting simultaneously the ontological identity and the absolute discontinuity of Cause and effect. The springing into existence of the effect does not bring about any change, increase or decrease in the infinite Cause. Such a mode of causing is of course beyond the range of our imagination, although within the suggestion of well-chosen analogies.[106]

This is perhaps why De Smet is wary, in this early work, of the language of emanation. He explains that

> creatures, while being identical to God in so far as being is common to both, are also radically different from Him because the same attributes of perfection can never be predicated in the same way of both; that creatures therefore cannot be parts of, or emanations from, God, but only reflections or participations, at the same time identical with, and different from, Him (BSBh 3,2,5).[107]

If Upadhyay could have been accused of "Christianizing" Vedānta, we might ask whether De Smet is traveling too far in the reverse direction of "Vedānticizing" Christianity. At least two serious objections could be raised against him by a Christian theologian: First, it is surely misleading to talk of creatures as identical to God "*in so far as being is common to both.*" Being cannot be a common ontological category in which God and creatures share if God is the originative source of—and, in that sense, is "beyond"—being. Second, in the section of Śaṁkara's commentary (*bhāṣya*) on the *Brahmasūtra*, which De Smet references in support of this argument (BSBh 3.2.5), the aphorism in question runs as follows:

> By meditation on the supreme Lord, that which is obscured (becomes manifest); for from Him (are derived) its (the soul's) bondage and its opposite.
>
> *parābhidhyānāttu tirohitam tato hyasya bandhaviparyayau*[108]

Śaṁkara explains that the similarity between the individual self and God is obscured by ignorance, and that meditation can remove this ignorance. The difficulty that might arise for a Christian theologian is that the focus on ignorance seems to suggest that the (non-)distinction between creature and Creator is merely linguistic or epistemic, and is a chimera that, far from indicating the sort of ontological distinction implied by a Scholastic metaphysics of participation, suggests precisely the opposite—that the distinction itself is based on a false way of seeing things because nothing "new" has really been produced by God in "creating."

If Christian and Vedāntic understandings of the causality involved in creation really are reconcilable, De Smet crucially needs to demonstrate that Śaṁkara means the following: when the ignorance of seeing my-self as separate from God is removed, I clearly see not that I am *identical* to God (for such undifferentiated unity cannot be accommodated within mainstream Christian orthodoxy), but that I and God are ontologically *a-dvaita*, distinct but not separate in our being (which is consonant with Thomism). This, indeed, is precisely how De Smet interprets Śaṁkara's use of the notion of *māyā*:

> by using it Śaṅkara wishes to stigmatize our congenital error of believing ourselves and the world to be self-sufficient beings, while compared with the Infinite Being, the only adequate measuring-rod of all beings, we are like nothing. Hence to say that the world is *Māyā* means that the

world has no right to exist; it is not absolute but contingent being and entirely dependent on the Supreme.[109]

According to De Smet, then, Advaita does not have to imply illusionistic monism (still less, pantheism), but is the denial of the existence of anything *apart from* or *independent of* God/Brahman, and in this sense, he argues that there is nothing for a Christian theologian to disagree with. Śaṁkara uses his own homespun analogies to reinforce this point, but De Smet turns to Platonic and Pythagorean similes rather than the more exotic-sounding imageries of snakes, mirages, and mother-of-pearl common in Vedāntic texts. He conducts a thought experiment in which the idea of a circle is endowed with self-consciousness and comes to believe itself to exist independently of the mind of the mathematician on which it depends.[110] Seeing its mistake, De Smet explains, the circle would recognize its own existential contingency and, eventually perhaps, discover

> the higher Self completely immanent to, but absolutely transcendent to, its own little self, and which alone could be the explanatory cause of its own springing into existence. That, it would say, is my own higher Self, not my own in the sense of my individual self, but my true Self in the sense of the type, of the original of which I am only a reflection, of the being of which I am a participation different and non-different, real and not absolutely real. Such is our own situation with regard to God. We exist in Him from all eternity like the potential contingent products of His mind. At His wish, out of no necessity in Him but by a kind of sportfulness (*B.S.Bh.*2,1,33) we come to be real in time.[111]

De Smet never went on to develop in detail the metaphysics of Divine Ideas ("We exist in Him from all eternity like the potential contingent products of His mind") as a way of articulating the ontological relation between the world and God, but his analogy of the circle in the mind of the mathematician is an apt one—precisely because the "expressed" circle and the "inner" idea of it are not mutually exclusive, it is coherent to say that the circle is *not-other-than* the mind of the mathematician. To what extent it is possible for a Christian theologian to agree, analogously, that the world is not-other-than the mind of God, is a question I will address in Chapter 5.

In an article on Śaṁkara's doctrine of creation, written in the same year as his appraisal of Upadhyay, De Smet focuses on the kind of causality that can be attributed to Brahman.[112] As the efficient cause of the world, Brahman is intelligent and free: "he therefore creates not on account of any inner necessity but merely at his wish (*saṅkalpa*) and by a kind of sportfulness (*līlārūpaḥ*) (BSBh 2,1,33) . . . having no need of any instrument or pre-existing matter."[113] De Smet goes on to clarify that the metaphor of sportfulness (as he translates *līlā*, rather than "play") is used to avoid two mistaken conceptions of divine activity:

> First, concerning His action *ad extra* as springing from inner necessity; second, conceiving it as orderless, merely fanciful, illogical and absurd . . . The notion of sport is most adequate to characterise such a causality.[114]

Līlā is a particularly useful image, in other words, because it highlights a form of structured creativity, rather than an arbitrary act of will, as constituting the nature of God, but also resists any implications of necessity, constraint, or lack. This Vedāntic metaphor could surely also have a place in Christian thinking about creation, but Śaṁkara complicates the picture in a terse concluding statement to his commentary on this *Sūtra*, when he says:

> And yet the Vedic statement of creation [viz. that it is a mere pastime] does not relate to any reality, for it must not be forgotten that such a text is valid within the range of activities concerned with name and form called up by ignorance, and it is meant for propounding the fact that everything has Brahman as its Self.[115]

Thus, we return again to Dandoy's sense of disquiet with Advaita—for what it seems to give with one hand, it takes away with the other. We can indeed talk about the divine "play" of creation from a creaturely standpoint, but Śaṁkara seems to be insisting that from an ultimate, transcendental vantage point, there is nothing *really* other than Brahman. However, while it might sound more jarring in a Christian church than in an Advaita ashram to hear that creation ultimately "does not relate to any reality," De Smet yet maintains that there is nothing here that explicitly *contradicts* Christian teaching on creation, for the ignorance of taking "name and form" to be realities that exist independently of God as their ontologically sustaining Self is seen as erroneous by both Christians and Vedāntins. I could no more exist separately from God than the pot can exist separately from its causal substratum of the clay. According to De Smet, Śaṁkara is asserting, as we saw earlier, "simultaneously the ontological identity and the absolute discontinuity of Cause and effect."[116] We are starting to see, then, that asking whether (and how) the world is different from God is somewhat akin to asking whether a reflection of a mountain in a lake is different from the mountain itself: the answer in both cases must surely be yes and no. The world is neither straightforwardly the same as God nor is the world utterly different from God because we are talking here about two different orders of reality (like the mountain and its reflection), which do not stand in a contrastive relation to each other.

While this might sound like a sophistical attempt to eat one's cake and have it too, Thomas wrestles in similar paradoxical terms with the sui generis nature of the divine causality, which is called creation. In Q.45 of the *Prima Pars* of the ST, Aquinas is clear that there is nothing that is not, in the entirety of its being, caused directly by God.[117] He is clear, moreover, that this existence is not merely a question about temporal origins, since no creature exists independently of the Creator at any time:

> Therefore, as the becoming of a thing cannot continue when that action of the agent ceases which causes the "becoming" of the effect: so, neither can the "being" of a thing continue after that action of the agent has ceased, which is the cause of the effect not only in "becoming" but also in "being" . . . Now every creature may be compared to God, as the air is to the sun which enlightens it. For as the sun possesses light by its nature, and as the air is enlightened by sharing the sun's nature; so, God alone is Being in virtue of His own Essence, since His Essence is His existence; whereas every creature has being by participation, so that its essence is not its existence. Therefore, as Augustine says (Gen. ad lit. iv, 12): "If the ruling power of God were withdrawn from His creatures, their nature would at once cease, and all nature would collapse."[118]

We can see from this passage why De Smet was convinced that Thomas's understanding of the relation between the world and God could accurately be described as an *advaitic* (non-dual) one. In the same vein as Śaṁkara, Thomas insists that creation brings about no change in God because "creation in the creature is only a certain *relation* to the Creator *as to the principle of its being*"[119]—but there simply would not be a created order without God. In other words, it is the creature that is constituted by its causal relation of dependence on God, not vice versa. We can assuage Christian fears of pantheism because although it is true to say that the proverbial pot is clay (i.e., the pot would not *be* without the clay), it is not true to say that the clay is the pot.[120] Aquinas, therefore, has to navigate the thin conceptual line between metaphysical monism and metaphysical dualism in ways very similar to Śaṁkara. This conceptual resonance can be clearly discerned in his response to the objection that God cannot be *in* all things because God is *above* all things—for Thomas, as for Śaṁkara, it is both/and: "God is above all things by the excellence of His nature; nevertheless, He is in all things as the cause of the being of all things."[121] In the preceding article, Aquinas explains this at length:

> I answer that, God is in all things; not, indeed, as part of their essence, nor as an accident, but as an agent is present to that upon which it works. For an agent must be joined to that wherein it acts immediately and touch it by its power . . . Now since God is very being by His own essence, *created being must be His proper effect*; as to ignite is the proper effect of fire. Now God causes this effect in things not only when they first begin to be, but as long as they are preserved in being; as light is caused in the air by the sun as long as the air remains illuminated. Therefore, as long as a thing has being, God must be present to it, according to its mode of being. But being is innermost in each thing and most fundamentally inherent in all things since it is formal in respect of everything found in a thing. . . . Hence it must be that God is in all things, and innermostly.[122]

Pace Dandoy, then, it seems a Thomist *can* conceive of creation as the "effect" of God, who is its sustaining and substrative Cause. By the 1960s–1970s, De Smet is more explicit about these conceptual convergences between Śaṁkara and Aquinas on creation,[123] and becomes more comfortable even with the language of emanation, which is, of course, used by Thomas himself.[124] De Smet becomes convinced that it is the precise nature of the *relation* between creature and Creator, established by the divine originative causality that Christians call "creation," which is the key to understanding both Thomas and Śaṁkara. This is a relation that implies asymmetry, dependence, indwelling, non-separateness, and distinction—summed up for Śaṁkara in the Sanskrit term *tādātmya*, literally "having that as one's self."[125] Unlike "identity," which is a perfectly reciprocal notion (and effaces distinction), this term, De Smet insists, "does not eliminate distinction but stresses the ontological character of the creature's dependence as well as the Creator's transcendence."[126] As we will see, it is precisely by focusing on "relation" that Sara Grant develops the work of Upadhyay and the Calcutta School.

Conclusion

No worldview seems prima facie more diametrically opposed to orthodox Christian teaching on creation than one that claims a metaphysical non-difference between creature and Creator. Christian doctrine is pivoted around the claim that the contingent order of the finite world is brought into being out of sheer nothingness by the providential God (God + world), whereas Advaita Vedānta claims that, in the ultimate analysis, there *cannot* be two ontologically separate realities (~~God~~ + ~~world~~). Given the theological premise taken as foundational by Advaita, that Brahman is unlimited fullness of Being, the only philosophical option seems to be to deny the separate reality of all that is not Brahman, namely, "the world" (God + ~~world~~). We have seen that some Roman Catholic theologians have viewed this denial (or, at the very least, downplaying) of the fundamental ontological reality of the created order as a theological Rubicon that they have not dared—or wanted—to cross. In this vein, Dandoy's conclusion is that Advaita fails as a philosophy because of what he sees as conceptual weaknesses in its notion of causality. In particular, the problem seems to be that Advaita is unable to countenance the appearance or production of anything genuinely "new" because all effects are always already metaphysically contained in their cause. This critique is taken on and developed by Dandoy's Jesuit contemporary, Pierre Johanns. Even these friendly critics are willing to admit, however, that the world is not *as* unequivocally real as God in Christian theology either. Richard De Smet argued somewhat more boldly that there is, indeed, no disagreement at the level of metaphysics here between Thomist and Vedāntic Scholasticisms, and that the language of "unreality" and "illusion" used in Advaitic universes is conceptually equivalent to the emphasis on contingency and finitude in a Christian thinker like Aquinas. We will see in the next chapter that Sara Grant picks up this baton from De Smet and makes her case for a "non-dualist" Christianity through a careful examination of the concept of "relation."

3 The Relation between the World and God in Śaṁkara and Thomas

SARA GRANT'S CASE FOR A FORM OF CHRISTIAN NON-DUALISM

> Imagine a man standing in a field, only the man and his shadow. If you asked a group of people how many things were in the field, some might say one, some might say two—only the man, or the man and his shadow. The non-dualists would argue for the reality of the shadow, but they could not deny its dependence on the man. The crux of the question is the nature of the relation between man and shadow.[1]

Introduction

In Chapter 1, I set out the key conceptual argument that runs throughout this book: namely, that the distinction-and-relation between the world and God in Christian theology is properly understood as a non-dualistic one. The "two" (God + world) cannot be added up as separate, enumerable realities or contrasted with each other against some common ontic or noetic background, since God does not belong in any category, while the creature is ontologically constituted by its relation to the Creator.[2] According to this relational ontology, what it means to be "world" does not and cannot exclude what it means to be "God" since the very being of the finite order always stands God-ward as, in Burrell's apposite phrase, an *esse-ad-creatorem*.[3] In Chapter 2, I then focused on this non-contrastive dialectic between the concepts of distinction and relation as it has been explored by certain twentieth-century Roman Catholic theologians in conversation with the Hindu tradition of Advaita Vedānta. Specifically, I looked there at Brahmabandhab Upadhyay, Georges Dandoy, Pierre Johanns, and Richard De Smet and their efforts to bring Aquinas's doctrine of creation into critical conversation with Śaṁkara's non-dualism. In this chapter, I want to show why

David Burrell is correct to urge Christian theologians to look to Sara Grant's work on Śaṁkara, building as it does on that of the earlier Calcutta School. Through a careful textual examination of his concept of relation, Grant argues that Śaṁkara never intended to propound a philosophy of illusionistic monism, but, rather, a sophisticated and nuanced articulation of the sui generis distinction between the world and Brahman, based on the nonreciprocal relation of ontological dependence between them. Returning home to her Christian roots, Grant finds that this reading of Śaṁkara has striking parallels in Thomas's metaphysics of creation. As Ganeri puts it,

> If we read Shankara this way [i.e., in the way De Smet and Grant do], he and Aquinas are fundamentally in agreement. They both reject the idea that the world has any independence of being or, in more Advaitic terms, would state the non-being of anything that does not depend on God . . . the world is not other than God. It is not separate from God.[4]

In spite of the seeming opposition between a Hindu tradition that asserts the metaphysical non-difference of the physical world from Brahman, the ultimate Reality, and a Christian imperative to preserve the ontological distinction between creation and Creator, Grant and De Smet claim to find deep conceptual affinities between the systematic philosophical theology of Advaita Vedānta and the Scholastic tradition in which they were trained.[5]

I will introduce Grant and identify some of her early theological and spiritual influences in order to situate her life and work on the broader canvas of (Roman Catholic) Christian–(Vedāntic)Hindu encounters. The main focus of this chapter, however, will be a close reading of Grant's interpretation of Advaita Vedānta and of her work on the concept of "relation" in Śaṁkara and Thomas, for it is here that she locates the possibility of moving beyond contrastive distinctions between God and world, and toward a "non-dualist" Christianity. Her argument partly is that reading Śaṁkara's attribution of "identity" between God and world in a simplistically monistic way would be an exegetical mistake. At the same time, he cannot be suggesting that the relationship involves a parity of two distinct ontological equals either because this claim would immediately entail a duality between two enumerable beings. Paradoxically, therefore, the relation seems to require that entities that are conceptually distinct are also metaphysically non-separate in the sense of *a-dvaita*, so that what is empirically a relation is not so transcendentally. The key to this argument is, once again, the sui generis relation-and-distinction between God/Brahman and the world.

Our exploration of Grant's work will suggest that it is not so much that there is a theological lacuna within Christianity that can only be filled from without from the East, but that it is precisely the deep resonances that she perceives between the spiritualities of her own Catholic tradition and the wisdom traditions of Vedāntic Hinduism, which attract her toward certain Indic styles of thought.[6] At least, there is not a lacuna in the Christian theological tradition as such, for we have seen in Chapter 1 that thinkers like Pseudo-Dionysius, Meister Eckhart, and Nicholas of Cusa (as well as Aquinas) are well aware of the mutually constitutive nature of divine transcendence and immanence, and of difference and sameness (between creature and Creator). Arguably, however, in wider social milieus (both among theists and atheists) there is a theological lacuna or misconception about the God-world dialectic that non-duality can correct—not least when it comes to how to understand creation.[7]

This will bring us back full circle—to the Thomist metaphysics of creation that Burrell finds so helpful in articulating how God can be *both* distinct from *and* related to the world and, in particular, to the insistence we have seen in figures ranging from Pseudo-Denys to Nicholas of Cusa, and from David Burrell to Kathryn Tanner, that these categories of distinction and relation must be seen not as contrastive, but as mutually constitutive. The exciting suggestion made by Grant is that Śaṁkara's concept of *advaita*, when understood correctly, can be an even more effective way for Christian theology to express this non-contrastive distinction-and-relation between God and world than that offered by Aquinas.[8]

Sara Grant, RSCJ (1922–2000)

EARLY INFLUENCES (1922–1956)

In his editor's introduction to Grant's *Towards an Alternative Theology*, Malkovsky notes that the nineteenth and the twentieth centuries saw a number of important works on Hinduism written by Christian scholars.[9] At first, these were predominantly concerned with themes related to Indology and mission,[10] but the latter part of the twentieth century started to see an increasing turn toward Christian theological and spiritual studies that were more genuinely comparative and open to the possible enrichment offered to Christianity by Hinduism. Particularly since the 1960s (thanks in part, no doubt, to the impetus provided by the positive approach to other religious traditions taken by Vatican II), Malkovsky identifies the emergence of a new literary genre among European Roman Catholic theologians who spent considerable periods of time in India—namely, a "blending of Christian theological reflection with first-hand experience of living Hinduism"[11]—and it is within this matrix that he situates Sara Grant, suggesting, in fact, that her *Towards an Alternative Theology* is the twentieth century's last example of such a work.[12]

Born in 1922 into a traditional Christian family in Scotland, Grant recounts early on in *Towards an Alternative Theology* how she gradually came to realize that she "had been a non-dualist from birth."[13] She describes this realization, in broad terms, as a "nameless discomfort" with "the at least apparently dualistic vision of the Bible" and the presentation of Christianity she received from an early age:[14]

> As far as I remember, much stress was put on the "first coming of Jesus into my soul," [at her first sacramental communion] but it was all expressed in rather concrete and "solid" terms without, I think, sufficient advertence to the very strong sense of the mystery and omnipresence of God which I am convinced is the birthright of all young children in their natural state, and no reference whatever—again, so far as I remember—to the fact that God was *already* in my soul.[15]

This unease continued to bedevil the "questing beast" during her formation in the Society of the Sacred Heart of Jesus, which she joined in 1941 at the age of nineteen. With the exception of her novice mistress, Margaret Shepherd, Grant found little sympathy for her dissatisfaction with a spirituality and an ecclesiastical discipline that seemed to run counter to her "profound metaphysical impulse for a depth of union which transcends all subject-object dichotomy, and yet is emphatically not pantheistic."[16] Indeed, the atmosphere she found so alienating within her own congregation was reflective of a broader culture of a "prevailing fear in the Catholic Church of mysticism."[17] As such, she gradually became aware of

> a sense of somehow living in two dimensions of consciousness, that of the visible world of everyday life, and that of another, mysterious world, least inadequately described as the sense of a presence which was also

> an absence, a rather crude way of expressing the transcendence-in-immanence which characterizes the non-dualist position as distinct from that of the absolute monist, who makes no real distinction between the Eternal and its created manifestation.[18]

The spiritual and theological tension she describes—between her felt intuition of the inner unity of all things, on the one hand, and the carefully regimented traditional Christian languages and imageries of a monarchical God "out there," on the other hand—would stay with her during her student years at Oxford and her time as a novice: it was this tension that would motivate her academic and spiritual journey throughout life. It was only when she answered an unexpected invitation to go to India that she encountered the tradition of Advaita Vedānta and found in Śaṁkara the conceptual and experiential avenue along which to pursue the connection she had been looking for between the standard templates of Thomistic Christianity with which she was familiar and the nondual understanding of it which she had long been implicitly striving to articulate.

Before she ever dreamed of going to India, however, Grant had already discerned intimations of this "transcendence-in-immanence" in certain corners of the Christian tradition. Specifically, she refers to her early attraction to St. John of the Cross and his *Ascent of Mount Carmel*[19] and, perhaps more surprisingly (but importantly for my argument), to Aquinas. Although she found aspects of Thomas's theology "oddly disappointing,"[20] when she first came across "his apophatic theology in the commentaries on the Pseudo-Denys . . . [she] . . . fell upon them ravenously."[21] More broadly, she started to have the first inklings of what she would later develop into a powerful interpretation of the Dominican master's vision of the creature-Creator relation:

> The *Summa Theologica* may not be everyone's idea of the perfect handbook of non-dualist theology, but even then, I dimly apprehended the non-dual intuition underlying the immense and orderly detail of Thomas's exposition of Christian theology.[22]

Like many of her predecessors, Grant's eventual move to India would only come after a considerable period of formation within her own Roman Catholic context—in her case, in 1956, some fifteen years after she had originally joined the novitiate of the Sisters of the Sacred Heart.[23]

DEPARTURE FOR INDIA AND THE CHALLENGE OF ADVAITA

Notwithstanding these early leanings toward a non-dualist Christian spirituality, which she would also later find in Vedāntic Hinduism, Grant's departure for India was the entirely unexpected outcome of her response to an appeal for volunteers to go to Brazil, where her Society had existed for over a century. Her initial reaction to being asked to go to the subcontinent rather than to South America was overwhelmingly negative even though she knew very little about either place.[24] Be that as it may, she found that she could not resist the call, and, given the intellectual acumen she had already displayed as a student of classics at Oxford,[25] Grant was immediately put in charge of the philosophy department at Sophia College, a constituent of the University of Bombay. Her first impressions of being asked to teach Vedānta as part of the BA in Indian Philosophy merit attention as they set the trajectory for the rest of her research and writing—and, indeed, for my own argument:

> It was an exhilarating but baffling experience. Both I and my students found Śaṅkara's thought as there presented [i.e., in the textbooks prescribed as set reading for the course] thoroughly mystifying, but it was clear that there was here some very profound and exciting intuition. This was most frustrating, and when a few years later I was asked to work for a doctorate in any field of Indian philosophy I chose, I knew at once what I must do: learn Sanskrit, go back to the original texts, and find out what Śaṅkara was really saying.[26]

It was this seemingly inauspicious set of circumstances that led to what would become the academic and spiritual focus of Grant's life in India—namely, an effort to "promote the significance of the experience and concept of non-duality (Sanskrit: *advaita*) for Christian faith and praxis."[27] In doing this, she became a leading voice in the Indian Christian Church and an enthusiastic supporter of the liturgical and spiritual initiatives of inculturation and renewal inspired by the Second Vatican Council (1962–1965).[28]

Grant's Encounters with Advaita Vedānta

By her own admission, Grant did not know what had and had not been done by way of research in this field,[29] so she sought advice from De Smet, who was already recognized throughout India as an authority on Advaita Vedānta, and who had done his own doctoral research on Śaṁkara.[30] He was convinced, as later Grant would also be, that Śaṁkara had been the victim both of a long indigenous commentarial tradition and of a more recent idealism-influenced European reading that had tended to distort what Śaṁkara really meant by *advaita*. Both argue that going back to Śaṁkara's original texts shows that his reputation as a "world-negating monist" is an error arising in large part from misunderstanding the philosophical language that Śaṁkara had at his disposal to express his exegetical-experiential insights.[31]

As we saw in the previous chapter, the majority of interpreters both in India and in the West have tended to characterize Śaṁkara's Advaita as a form of illusionistic monism, but Grant suggests that this reading may well be the result of intellectual biases reflective of certain dominant philosophical trends at a particular time in history. She argues that this way of looking at Advaita was partly shaped by the "spontaneous sense of affinity" aroused in nineteenth-century European (especially German) Idealist philosophers with a system seemingly based on a metaphysical oneness that is grounded in the fundamentally spiritual nature of reality.[32] She also points to the overreliance of many of these nineteenth- to twentieth-century interpretations on Śaṁkara's commentary on the *Māṇḍūkya Upaniṣad*, which is more uncompromising in its idealism than many of the other major *Upaniṣads*.[33] J. Clarke summarizes the nature of this Indo-Germanic engagement as follows:

> The Germans were greatly attracted to the Upanishadic teaching (as they understood it) that the world as we know it through our ordinary senses is not the "real" world, but only appearance, even an illusion (*māyā*), and that the goal of life was the realisation of the self—*ātman*—through its identification with the absolute—*brahman*.[34]

In other words, the ontological monism ostensibly at the heart of the *Upaniṣads* resonated with the post-Kantian idealist tendencies of certain nineteenth-century European thinkers.[35] This perceived resonance helped to compound a particular way of viewing Advaita, especially because the writings of some of these German thinkers were entering into Bengal and elsewhere into British India via the movements of peoples and ideas made possible by the colonial context. Thus, Western curricula in universities in India such as those in Calcutta and Madras during the century before Grant allowed for spirals of complex feedback loops between indigenous interpreters of the Vedāntic sources (such as Vivekananda and Radhakrishnan) and European philosophers, British colonial administrators, and orientalists.[36] The upshot of this intellectual synergy, in Grant's view, was a misunderstanding of "what Śaṅkara really thought about the nature of the world of our *vyāvahārika* [empirical] experience and its relation to ultimate Reality."[37]

Part of her academic project, therefore, became an effort to elucidate Śaṁkara's thought via a return to his original texts, rather than reading him through nineteenth- and twentieth-century European and Indian philosophical lenses or, indeed, through the dense strata of the commentarial traditions that had propounded Advaita Vedānta down the centuries after Śaṁkara.[38] In particular, she was convinced that if she could show that Śaṁkara was not a "world-negating pessimist" who regarded the physical world as somehow "not really there," his concept of relation could be the metaphysical key to "unite science, philosophy and religion in a mutually complementary and harmonious whole."[39] This was precisely the hermeneutic task she set for herself in her doctoral research on Śaṁkara's concept of relation.

If De Smet can be seen as Grant's academic and intellectual mentor, she also acknowledges the influence of the French Benedictine, Henri Le Saux, (1910–1973) on her understanding and appreciation of Advaita. Le Saux had already been in India for some eight years before Grant arrived, and he had, along with Fr. Jules Monchanin, founded the Shantivanam ashram in Tamil Nadu, which would later be taken over by Dom Bede Griffiths.[40] Known in India as Abhishiktananda (which literally means "the bliss of the Anointed One"), Grant describes her first meeting with Le Saux as "epoch-making."[41] She recognized a kindred spirit in Abhishiktananda's lifelong struggles to reconcile *advaita* with his Christian faith, and she was particularly drawn to his work *Sagesse Hindoue, Mystique Chrétienne*.[42] However, Grant says that it was not so much Abhishiktananda's attempted theological synthesis of the two traditions, as his fully immersive personal quest to embrace *advaita* directly into the very sinews of his inner being, which "hit her like a bomb."[43] His refusal to treat the question of "Christian advaita" merely as a metaphysical exercise, and his direct encounters with the contemporary Advaitin Ramana Maharshi (1879–1950), would have a lasting influence on Grant's own conception of theology and her approach to Śaṁkara and Thomas.[44] Ganeri and Malkovsky both argue that Grant was ultimately more successful than Le Saux in integrating theory and praxis on her journeys into the relatively uncharted waters of Christian non-dualism, holding on to the regulative value of theology while recognizing that such theology must always also be a lived—and not a merely cerebral—discipline.[45] To see how she attempted this dynamic synthesis, I will now turn to a close reading of Grant's work on relation, for it is here that she can help us understand the meaning of *advaita* as (in Abhishiktananda's words) "neither God alone, nor the creature alone, nor God plus the creature, but an indefinable non-duality which transcends at once all separation and all confusion."[46]

Grant on "Relation"

It is interesting that Grant, like Burrell, refers to Josef Pieper's work, *The Silence of St. Thomas* as key to her own philosophical approach.[47] Although Burrell credits Pieper with helping him to see that "creation" is the key that provides unity and intelligibility to Aquinas's understanding of the creature-Creator distinction-and-relation,[48] Grant is more concerned to unearth the unexpressed metaphysical option that permeates the holistic vision offered by Śaṁkara. In this case, she argues that the "hidden thread which holds together the entire fabric" is Śaṁkara's insistence on an intuitive-experiential (*anubhava*), and not merely propositional, knowledge of reality.[49] Grant sees Śaṁkara's most illuminating insight as his conviction that knowledge of Brahman is to be reached not through the senses (because this rests on the mistaken assumption that Brahman is some sort of "object" distinct from the knower) but by a withdrawal from sense-impressions to a supra-conceptual recognition of absolute Being as the very root and source of our own empirical self-awareness—in other words, a re-cognition of God/Brahman as the radically non-transitive and pure subjectivity *by which* we exist and know at all.[50] This claim is strikingly reminiscent of the repeated insistence we have seen in figures ranging from Pseudo-Denys, via Aquinas, to David Burrell, that God is not one or another kind of "thing." The question of how exactly "I" am related to God, however, remains, and Grant points out, in a passage often cited by Burrell, that any purely epistemological solution to this problem cannot stand secure without a metaphysical explanation to support it:

> In India as in Greece, the ultimate question must always be that of the relation between Reality and appearance, *pāramārthika* and *vyāvahārika*, Self and what appears as non-Self.[51]

She explains that, for Śaṁkara, the manifold objects of the empirical world (i.e., what a Christian would regard as the "created order," which includes the sense of an individual "self") are merely "names and forms" (*nāmarūpa*) that are superimposed (*adhyāsa*) through ignorance upon the one impartite reality that is Brahman.[52] These "limiting adjuncts" (*upādhis*) of the supreme self (viz. the objects of the *vyāvahārika* level of experience) metaphysically preexist in Brahman "prior" to their empirical manifestation (or, in Christian terms, "creation") and their coming into and passing out of existence no more affects Brahman than the sun is changed whether its rays happen to be illumining objects or not.[53] Numerous passages in Śaṁkara could be used to illustrate these ideas, but one of the clearest is in his commentary on the *Chāndogya Upaniṣad*, which is worth citing at some length:

> The universe with all it contains has its root in Being (*sanmūlāḥ: satkāraṇāḥ*). This Being is one only, without a second, supremely and absolutely real (*ekamevādvitīyam paramārthasatyam*); all the universe is a mere name, superimposed by nescience upon the said Being in the same manner as the serpent and other imaginary things are superimposed upon the rope: therefore, this Being is the root of the universe. Hence, my dear, all the creatures in the shape of animate and inanimate things have their root-cause in Being. It is not only that they have their root in Being—even now during the time of their existence they reside in Being—subsisting in Being itself; as for example, without subsisting in clay, the jar has no existence or continuance; hence, as Being is the root of all creatures, like the clay of the jar, etc. these creatures reside in Being and at the end they rest in Being: that is, they have their rest, they become merged and have their end in the same said Being.[54]

The echoes we can hear of Christian voices like Sokolowski and Burrell in Śaṁkara's emphasis on the ontological "rootedness" of beings in Being are clear; indeed, Grant claims on more than one occasion that Śaṁkara is making the same point as Aquinas—that "after" creation there were indeed more beings but not more Being (*plura entia sed non plus esse*).[55] Nevertheless, it is wrong, she argues, to read Śaṁkara as some kind of an acosmist idealist who denies the objective existence itself of the phenomenal world, because liberation does not consist in any metaphysical annihilation of these "limiting adjuncts," but in the epistemological dissolution of the *illusion* that the world of *nāmarūpa* is real in the sense of "ultimate" reality.[56]

The difference that Grant is trying to tease out, I think, is that certain forms of philosophical idealism amount to recognizing the phenomenal world as *merely* a construct of, and "internal" to, the mind's categorizing activity, while Śaṁkara wants to maintain some objective reality (albeit a "lesser" one) for the world of "phenomena" as distinct from the "noumenal" realm (though, as we shall see, the phenomenal could not exist without its rootedness in the noumenal because then we would not have *a-dvaita* at all). As Grant repeatedly affirms, "Śaṅkara in no way minimizes the lawful claim to objective existence of the phenomenal world . . . for him the 'non-being' of the phenomenal existence offered in empirical reality is relative, not absolute."[57] In a similar way, she argues that Śaṁkara's distinction between *saguṇa brahman* (possessing characteristics like creatorship, lordship, etc.) and *nirguṇa brahman* (ultimate reality in itself) is conceptual, and not metaphysical. In other words, Vedānta only speaks of one indivisible Brahman, but under two aspects—when Śaṁkara denies the transcendental reality of *saguṇa brahman*, he is simply emphasizing the utter simplicity and immutability of Being/ Brahman in itself in which *saguṇa brahman* is rooted. As Grant herself recognizes:

> It seemed necessary to clear up the foregoing points before making any attempt to discuss the conception of relation implicit or explicit in Śaṅkara's thought, in view of the frequently-heard objection that, since for Śaṅkara there exists nothing but the Absolute, One-without-a-second, and since *"Ātman Brahman, jīva brahman, jagat mithyā,"* the only relation that could reasonably be conceived relevant would be that of a monolithic identity.[58]

So, since he is neither an ontological dualist nor a world-negating monist, how exactly should we understand Śaṁkara's conception of a nondual relation between *Brahman* (ultimate Reality) and *Ātman* (the individual self) or, roughly translated into Christian terms, between God and world? Up to a point, the relation is one of *identity*; identity, that is, in the sense that the real or essential nature (*svarūpa*) of all creatures is metaphysically not-other than (i.e., has no existence apart from) the real or essential nature of the whole of existence.[59] Paradoxically, as we have already indicated, this relation seems to require identity *and* distinction, and much will depend on the perspective from which we are speaking.

> The truth of the matter seems to be that we are *not* here dealing with a normal case of identity, if we take "normal" to mean "conforming to the criteria of daily experience," because *ex hypothesi* one of the terms completely transcends the limits of that experience.[60]

Again, the echoes here of the emphasis that we have already seen in Christian thinkers like Pseudo-Denys, Eckhart, and Sokolowski—that "one of the terms (i.e., God) completely transcends the limits of experience"—are striking.

KEY RELATIONAL TERMS IN ŚAṀKARA

Grant makes her case for a realist reading of Śaṁkara through a fine-grained analysis of the different relational terminologies he uses in three key texts: his commentaries on the *Bhagavadgītā* (*Bhagavadgītābhāṣya*) and the *Brahma-Sūtras* (*Brahmasūtrabhāṣya*) and his independent treatise, "The Thousand Teachings" (*Upadeśasāhasrī*).[61] She limits her investigation to the philosophical implications in Śaṁkara's works of the generic Sanskrit term "*sambandha*," and the three other relational words that are listed in Monier-Williams's 1899 Oxford *Sanskrit-English Dictionary* as "philosophical"—namely, *saṃyoga*, *samavāya*, and *svarūpa*.[62] It is not surprising that the first of these terms, *sambandha*, occurs more frequently than any of the other three, given that it is the most generic, with wide-ranging connotations that embrace the more specific nuances of the others, and encompassing, as it does, a range of meanings from binding or joining together, to a close connection or relation.[63] Taken on their own, the many examples that Grant examines of Śaṁkara's use of *sambandha* leave an impression of "uncertainty, not to say confusion, concerning the propriety of attributing or not attributing relation [*sambandha*] to *Ātman-Brahman*."[64] Again, to be clear, it seems, prima facie, that there can be no real relation (or, indeed, distinction) unless there are two (or more) *relata*—and, given Śaṁkara's insistence that the Absolute is *a-dvaita*, One-without-a-second, we can see why scholars like Radhakrishnan have concluded that the question of "relation," when it comes to Advaita, is an "inadmissible one."[65]

Occurring only about a third as frequently as *sambandha*, *saṃyoga* tends to be used to describe the union or, more literally, "con-junction" of physical objects (e.g., a thorn with skin), though Śaṁkara also uses it for the relation between body and soul, and meditation and its aim, among other instances.[66] Grant concludes that while Śaṁkara "fully accepts the *saṃyoga* relation within the sphere of *vyāvahārika* or phenomenal experience," he is critical of attempts to use it to "explain the causal relationship between the created universe and its Creator."[67] Going by frequency of usage, *samavāya* seems even less appropriate for what Śaṁkara wants to express when he is writing about the type of relation that exists between ultimate reality and the changing physical world:

> A Lord distinct from the *pradhāna* [the root cause of matter] and the souls cannot be the ruler of the latter, without being connected with them in a certain way. But of what nature is that connection? It cannot be conjunction (*saṃyoga*), because the Lord . . . is of infinite extent and devoid of parts. Nor can it be inherence (*samavāya*), since it would be impossible to define who should be the abode and who the abiding thing . . . How then, it may be asked, do you, the Vedāntins, establish the relation of cause and effect (between the Lord and the world)?[68]

To answer that question, Grant turns to a detailed analysis of the more specific relational term *svarūpa*, which Śaṁkara uses almost as frequently as the generic *sambandha*. Literally meaning "own form or shape," *svarūpa* tends to be translated in philosophical contexts as the "real" or "essential" nature of a thing or, sometimes, even as "identity," as in the following examples from Śaṁkara's BSBh:[69]

> Scriptural passages such as "He is gone to his Self" (Chānd.U.VI.viii.1) declare that *the connection* (of the soul with the highest Self) *is one of "essential nature"—iti hi svarūpasambandhamenamāmananti.*[70]
>
> By Self we understand *a being's "own nature"—ātmā hi nāma svarūpam.*[71]

This theme of the supreme self/reality (*Ātman-Brahman*) as the *svarūpa* of all beings also dominates Śaṁkara's commentary on the *Bhagavadgītā.*[72] The question remains, however, what it exactly means to say that the essential nature of the one, unchanging, impartite ultimate reality is also *my* real nature. If "God's ground" really is "my ground," it would seem that we are, indeed, talking about ontological *identity* here, and not merely some kind of mystical communion-in-difference, but Grant insists that this unity should not be understood as a form of monistic idealism, given Śaṁkara's clear conviction that the question of relation is a legitimate one:[73]

> Granted that the ultimate reality realized in the depths of one's own being is identical with the ultimate reality underlying the phenomenal universe, it remains true that it would be a clear betrayal of Śaṅkara's thought to make him interpret the *mahāvākyas* [the "great sayings" of the *Upaniṣads*] "*tattvamasi*" ["you are that"], "*sarvam idam brahma*" ["all this is Brahman"] and "*aham brahmāsmi*" ["I am Brahman"] in a simplistically monist or monolithic fashion: the identity he predicates between *Ātman-Brahman* and *sarvam idam* does not involve the metaphysical destruction of either side of the equation. Yet neither can we interpret this "identity" as a simple parity of equals, in the sense in which we speak of identical twins or architectural plans or teapots. This would immediately entail duality.[74]

To sum up so far, we can see why Grant wants to resist interpreting Śaṁkara's attribution of a relation of "identity" between the phenomenal universe and ultimate reality (the world and God, in analogous Christian terms) in "a simplistically monist" fashion because Śaṁkara explicitly rejects the subjective idealist position put forward by some of his (Buddhist) interlocutors that the external world is "unreal" in the sense of being entirely subjectively constructed. However, he rejects just as firmly the idea that Brahman and the *jīva* (individual self) constitute two independent ontological realities. The key to the relation-and-distinction between them can be found, Grant argues, in Śaṁkara's use of the term *tādātmya*,[75] though attempts to understand what Śaṁkara meant by it have been hampered, she warns, "by the 'normal' connotations of such words as "identity" in English and *tādātmya* in Sanskrit to such an extent that its extreme individuality has been completely missed."[76]

> The relation of the Ātman to the *jīva qua jīva* and of Brahman to *jagat* is not a relation of identity in any obvious sense of the word: it connotes a radical unity of being, but at the same time does not exclude—indeed seems to demand, paradoxical as it may sound—an area of difference.[77]

Literally meaning something like [having] "that"/*tat* [as one's] "self/nature/*ātmā*," *tādātmya* is used by Śaṁkara to express the relation of *a-dvaita* between the supreme self (*Ātman-Brahman*) and the individual self, or between "creature and Creator," as a Christian might be more inclined to put it.

> *The relation we* (the Vedāntins) *assume* (between the Lord and the world) *is that of identity* (Thibaut's translation)—*tasya tādātmyalakṣaṇasamba ndhopapatteḥ.*[78]

The problem here is how there can possibly be a relation of identity between the immutable witness Self, which is pure consciousness (what a Christian might think of as the divine Ground of being), and an individual (transient and temporal) creature, given the prima facie difference between them. Śaṁkara seems to be suggesting that, in fact, there is both a phenomenologically undeniable awareness of an *empirical* distinction between the world and God *and* a deeply counterintuitive (non-)relation of *metaphysical non-difference* between them. In other words, if there were identity of a "simplistically monist or monolithic" kind, it would be cognitively unrecognizable as such because there would not even be an "I" to realize its identity with *brahman*. Non-duality requires, as it were, at least an "appearance" or a semblance of duality:

> If there were no awareness of difference, predication of identity would be impossible. (Thus, the predication of the absolute unity of *Ātman-Brahman* could not be made in the total absence of *upādhis*—it is only in terms of an at least apparent duality that the affirmation of ultimate non-duality can take place).[79]

Grant explains this subtle point in the case of the "*tattvamasi*" saying via the Sanskritic grammatical principle of *bhāgalakṣaṇā*, where one or both terms in a comparison are understood indirectly.[80] That is, while the "thou" in "that art thou" refers directly to the individual self or creature, it *indirectly* indicates the witness Self, which is reflected in the individual consciousness. In other words, it is not Śaṁkara who is identical with Brahman, or Thomas who is identical with God, if by that claim we comprehend all the individuating *nāmarūpa* features such as age, personality, and so on, that empirically characterize Śaṁkara and Thomas in an "everyday" sense, but it is the "real self" or the "essential nature" (*svarūpa*) of Śaṁkara and Thomas that is non-different from the supreme self:

> This means that in the *tattvamasi mahāvākya* all that belongs to the *upādhis* is dropped from the direct meaning of both "Thou" and "That," resulting in the predication of the absolute *identity of "nature"* or *svarūpa* of *Ātman-Brahman* without reference to their limiting conditions.[81]

The conclusion that Grant draws from these observations is that in spite of our empirical perceptions of the duality between creatures / the empirical manifold (*upādhis*) and ultimate reality, we can be led to recognize, through *Upaniṣadic* revelation, the essential ontological non-difference of the two—or, in other words, we come to see that the physical world exists only in virtue of having its "real Self" *in* the one, unchanging, impartite reality that is *Ātman-Brahman*. It is in this sense, then, that there is a *tādātmya* (non-)relation between the individual being and absolute Being—it is not that the physical world is nonexistent, but that it only exists by "sharing in" pure existence. Finally, it is crucial to Grant's systematic argument (and to our own) to notice that this relation is an asymmetrical one: the *upādhis* depend on *Ātman-Brahman*, but *Ātman-Brahman* does not depend on the *upādhis*. This is because there cannot be any "real relation" on the part of *Ātman-Brahman* (since there *is* only One-without-a-second) "with" or "alongside" the world, but there is a real relation of dependence of creatures on *Ātman-Brahman*. Grant expresses this point as follows, in a manner redolent of Sokolowski's way of parsing "the distinction":[82]

> *Ātman-Brahman—jīva/jagat* [the individual self / the physical world] = *Ātman-Brahman*
>
> Jīva-jagat—Ātman-Brahman = 0
>
> In other words,
>
> Somehow, in a way not fully specified, *Ātman-Brahman* gives being to and sustains the phenomenal universe in its wholly relative existence, yet without in any way being affected by this exercise of creative power.[83]

Grant's interpretation is also based on Śaṁkara's frequent use of the terms *vyatireka* (distinction, difference, separateness) and *apekṣā* in the BSBh. The former appears some seventy times and is always used with careful attention to the sort of directionality issues we have already stressed. Difference or separability (or, perhaps, "distinction") is only ever predicated of *Ātman-Brahman* in relation to the *upādhis*, and never the other way around, while *ananyatva* ("non-difference" or "not-otherness") is only ever used by Śaṁkara of the world in relation to *Ātman-Brahman* and not vice versa.[84] Three examples should suffice to highlight this ontological and conceptual asymmetry:

> As the world springs from Brahman it cannot be separate from Brahman—*prapañcasya brahma-prabhavatvātkāryakāraṇā-nanyatvanyāyena brahmāvyatireka ityevamjātīyakaḥ.*[85]
>
> The effect has no existence apart from the cause—kāraṇāt paramarthato 'nanyatvam vyatirekeṇābhāvaḥ kāryasyāva-gamyate (II.i.14)—so this manifold world has no existence apart from Brahman—prapañcajātasya brahmavyatirekeṇābhāva iti draṣṭavyam.[86]
>
> "For in the same way as scripture speaks of the origin of the world from Brahman it also speaks of Brahman as subsisting apart from its effects—*yathaiva hi brahmaṇo jagadutpattiḥ śrūyate, evam vikāra-vyatirekeṇāpi brahmano 'vasthānam śrūyate.*[87]

This is clearly reminiscent of the asymmetrical dialectic of distinction-and-relation that we saw in Chapter 1 being stressed by figures like Sokolowski, Burrell, and Poulsom. The empirical world is metaphysically *not-other* than its divine source because it simply could not exist separately from its ontological ground, while the claim of metaphysical dependence is not true in the other direction—God would be God even without the world. There is, in Advaita, a *conceptual* (and linguistic) distinction between effect and cause, but no ultimate *ontological difference* because, fundamentally, there are *not* two mutually independent "reals" to be compared and contrasted:

> The "not-otherness" is clearly non-reciprocal, and in a passage in the Brahmasūtrabhāṣya which frequently seems to have been overlooked, Śaṅkara gives the clue to his usage: *ananyatva*, he says, means "not existing apart from." In other words, the [ontological] identity is an identity with a [conceptual] difference—again an exact parallel to "He is thy Being, thou art not his Being.[88]

The *advaitic* "identity," then, between Brahman and the world in Śaṁkara is, Grant insists, neither a form of pantheistic monism, compromising divine transcendence, nor an illusionistic monism that denies any sort or measure of reality to the physical world.[89] There is, rather, an ontological dependence of creation on Creator (to use Christian terms), which is so radical and thoroughgoing that it is possible to say, in an ultimate sense, that they are "not two."

Returning to Aquinas

> In reality advaita is already present at the root of Christian experience. It is simply the mystery that God and the world are not two.[90]

Both in her doctoral work and in her Teape Lectures, Grant finds her way back to where she (and we) began—namely, the Thomist metaphysics she had been attracted to as a novice and the non-dualist intuition she had sensed beneath the doctrinal surfaces of her Catholicism because, she realized, "St Thomas Aquinas found himself confronted by exactly the same problem as Śaṅkara and arrived at a similar solution:"[91]

> For both, the chief relational problem arose from the dependence of the phenomenal universe on the infinite and unchanging Reality which is at once the Source and sustainer of its limited being and the end to which it ceaselessly tends.[92]

Although Śaṁkara's solution was to stress, through the language of "identity" (*tādātmya*), the ultimate ontological (if not, empirical) unreality of the world (in the sense that it has no independent existence "other-than" Brahman), Aquinas, as we saw in Chapter 1, emphasizes the dependent nature of created substance—"being" *is* a "being-toward" the Creator (*esse-ad-creatorem*) through the language of relation. Indeed, Grant notes the role that *relation* plays in the metaphysical theology of Aquinas is analogous to that of *distinction* or discrimination (*viveka*) between ultimate reality and conventional reality in Śaṁkara.[93] Just as there is a distinction at a conventional level between the physical world (*upādhis*) and *Ātman-Brahman*, but, ultimately, there is no ontological difference in the essential nature of the "two" (since the world is metaphysically "not-other" than Brahman), so for Aquinas, too, the creature is "not-other" than the Creator in its innermost being (because it could not exist separately without the divine ground).

For her understanding of Thomas's treatment of relation, Grant is indebted to A. Krempel's extensive study *La doctrine de la relation chez saint Thomas*.[94] Krempel explains how Aquinas distinguishes between "real" relations that inhere in things themselves[95] and "logical" relations that exist only in the mind of the perceiver.[96] Aquinas agrees with Aristotle that "relation" is not a thing in itself but simply refers two entities to each other and, as such, must inhere in some subject.[97] If a relation is "real," it is found within the subject (i.e., that of which the relation is predicated) and exists in the very being of that subject (what Krempel calls a *fundamentum immediatum*). If, however, a relation is "logical," it does not "inhere" in the subject but "exists" only in the principle by virtue of which it is predicated (in Krempel's terms, a *fundamentum mediatum*). Such "logical" relations come about when reason attributes order and relation to things (e.g., when we classify things into a particular species or genus) even though this relationality is not *really* part of the thing itself.[98] Through his analysis of the relation between a knower and a known object, Aquinas was led to formulate a third class of relation that was a mixture of the first two ("real" and "logical"). In such a "mixed relation," the relation between two *relata* is nonreciprocal.[99] In other words, although there is no "immediate foundation" for the relation of "being known" in an object known (on its side, the relation remains purely logical), there *is* a real foundation for the relation in the knower. A tree in a forest, for example, undergoes no change when it is seen by a walker, just as an algebraic symbol is not affected when it is grasped by a student—but the walker and the student *are* really related to the tree and the symbol because a change occurs in them.[100]

When it comes to the relation between the world and God, therefore, Aquinas crucially argues that no "real" relation can inhere in God because this inherence would make creatorship constitutive of what it means to be God.[101] As we have seen—in Anselm and Aquinas, and reiterated by Sokolowski and Burrell—God cannot be defined *in relation to* the world since the world is not a part of God or a necessary emanation from God. God could and would be God even without the world. On the other hand, the world simply could not exist without God as its sustaining ontological cause: creatures are radically dependent on God, but not vice versa. Thus, "It follows that there is in [God] no real relation to the creature, though there is a real relation of the creature to [God] as of effect to cause."[102] As Grant puts it, the "creation relation" is a necessary constituent of every creature because the foundation of the relation is an integral part of the subject and its relational "term" (that to which it, as the subject, is related)—that is, God—must necessarily coexist with the subject.[103]

As M. McWhorter has shown, Aquinas's teaching on relation here not only draws on Aristotle, but is also consistent with Augustine and, more proximately, with Peter Lombard,[104] as seen in Aquinas's references to the "Philosopher" (i.e., Aristotle) and the "Master" (i.e., Lombard) in the following passage:

in all things which are referred to one another in some respect, of which one depends upon another and not the converse, in the one which depends upon the other there is found a real relation, but in the other there is a relation according to reason only, as is clear from knowledge and the knowable, as the Philosopher says. A creature, moreover, is referred according to name to the Creator. The creature depends upon the Creator, yet not the converse. Thus, it is proper that the relation by which the creature is referred to the Creator be real, but in God there is a relation according to reason only. And this the Master expressly says in the first book of the Sentences, distinction thirty.[105]

This agreement is not surprising, since the impossibility of a real relation in God is an entailment of God's simplicity and immutability—doctrines held as axiomatic by all exponents of "perfect being" theology such as Augustine, Anselm, and Aquinas.[106] The emergence of a finite order in time cannot add to, improve, or change God in any way, which is why Aquinas insists that the relation that ensues must only be "logical" (i.e., seen to exist from our vantage point) and is not "real" in God. McWhorter is nevertheless right to point out that an "unreal" relation is not the same as a "false" one:

> Importantly, Aquinas teaches in this passage [*SCG* II.XIII et XIV, §919] that while rational relations exist in human intelligence only, this does not mean that these relations are falsely ascribed to God. He argues that such rational relations are truly able to be attributed to God in light of how God's effects relate to God and terminate in God.[107]

In other words, there is indeed a relation in the God-world dialectic because creatures are *related-to-God* by their very be-ing.[108]

Even though Śaṁkara does not offer such an explicit treatment of relation, his ideas emerge in discussions of theories of world production other than his own (e.g., the Vaiśeṣika categories).[109] Grant argues that he was trying to articulate the same concept of a "non-reciprocal relation of dependence" that Aquinas does through his doctrine of mixed relations.[110] On the one hand, there cannot be any "real" relation on the part of *Ātman-Brahman* (since there is only "One-without-a-second" and, therefore, nothing to enter into relation with) but on the other, there is a real relation of dependence on the part of creatures vis-à-vis *Ātman-Brahman*.[111] In other words, "dependence" rather than "identity" (monism) would be, according to Grant's reading, a better way of expressing what Śaṁkara meant by nondualism. The relation of Brahman/God to the world is only "logical" as opposed to "real" on the part of God (in the way a mountain is not "really" related to its reflection in a lake) but is "real" on the part of the world (just as the reflection is "really" related to the mountain) since the foundation of the relation actually inheres *in* every contingent being that exists only in virtue of this very relationship.[112] This concept of a nonreciprocal and asymmetric relation of radical dependence seems to preserve both the transcendence and simplicity of God/Brahman and the *relative absoluteness* of the world. That is, the world neither independently exists in and through itself, which would imply dualism, nor does it not really exist at all as a pure *nihil*, which would imply monism:

> Since the foundation of this relation of real dependence lies in the *upādhi*, neither its coming to be nor its passing away affects *Ātman-Brahman*, any more than the sun is affected by the appearance or disappearance of its reflection in a pool of water.[113]

In his work, *The Unknown Christ of Hinduism*, Raimon Panikkar makes fundamentally the same point—that is, this understanding of divine causation as a "mixed relation" of one-sided dependence is common to both Christian and Vedāntic theology. Indeed, he goes so far as to say that "this theory [i.e., of an asymmetrical relation of dependence] already transcends dualism and opens the door to an Advaitic answer; it is therefore the least vulnerable philosophical attempt [to navigate between monism and dualism in our understanding of how God is both distinct from and related to the world]."[114] It must also be conceded, however, that even this attempt to explain the sui generis relation between creature and Creator does not, in Panikkar's view, "entirely resolve the difficulty."[115]

Whose Śaṁkara? Which Aquinas?

The "relation" between creature and Creator is, then, *asymmetrical*—one depends on the other, but not vice versa, which is why Grant can claim that

> Both [Śaṁkara and Aquinas] were non-dualists, understanding the relation of the universe, including individual selves, to uncreated Being in terms of a non-reciprocal relation of dependence.[116]

It is important at this stage, however, to address one pressing concern—if there really is such profound agreement between Śaṁkara and Thomas, is there any need for a Christian theologian to turn at all to the Indian tradition of Advaita Vedānta? Less provocatively, "must its significance for us be reduced to a simple exhortation to return to the study of St Thomas with a greater alertness to the apophatic dimension of his theology?"[117] There is a risk that the more Grant succeeds in demonstrating deep resonances between the two traditions (Advaita and Thomism), *the less convincing* the case for any Christian engagement with Śaṁkara's Vedānta becomes, rather than simply with (more of) Aquinas or, say, a Pseudo-Denys or a Nicholas of Cusa. Grant is aware of this hermeneutic dilemma, and does insist on considerable agreement between Śaṁkara and Thomas and their wider respective contexts of non-dualist Vedānta and Scholastic Christianity:

> Both are intensely aware of the dependence of creation on the Mystery beyond name and form without which it would simply not exist at all: both are nevertheless keenly aware that the creation is very much "there"—relative, indeed, but ineluctably to be reckoned with.[118]

Any form of comparative theology is vulnerable to the challenge that the distinctive particularity of one or both of the systems, thinkers, or doctrines compared has not been fully recognized, foregrounded, and appreciated. In the cases we have been examining, this would amount to the challenge that Christianity has been "Vedānticized" or that Vedānta has been "Christianized"; that Aquinas is being made to look like Śaṁkara or that Śaṁkara is being made to look like Aquinas; that creation ex nihilo has become production *ex deo* or that *māyā* has become contingency, and so on. None of the key figures we have explored, however, could be accused of these failings on account of a lack of understanding of, or empathy for, either of the traditions compared—whether their "home" tradition of Thomist Christianity (in which Dandoy, Johanns, De Smet, and Grant were rooted) or the "foreign" tradition of Advaita Vedānta, which they were prepared, in varying degrees, to indwell at different intellectual, social, and spiritual levels.[119] Nor, it seems to me, are any of them guilty of willful misreadings of Thomas or Śaṁkara; as we have seen, they each proceed carefully through a close analysis of particular texts and are charitable when they see genuine convergences, and critical when they perceive significant differences.

Nevertheless, no theological engagement is carried out in an intellectual, institutional, or spiritual vacuum, and the particular ways in which Upadhyay, Dandoy, Johanns, De Smet, and Grant interrogate and critique

Advaita Vedānta are shaped and informed by their Thomist commitments. Their encounters would doubtless have taken different twists and turns had they been, for example, process theologians or Barthians. Dependence of text on *con*text is a standard motif in the study of religion, and the thinkers we have explored make no attempt to mask or "neutralize" their Thomistic moorings. We will be able to appraise their comparative projects at a more profound level, however, as well as develop them further along interesting pathways, if we are sensitive not only to their differing interpretations of Advaita but also to the particular *Thomist* themes and thinkers motivating their engagements.

In the case of Upadhyay, we have seen that he was influenced by the sort of "Manual Thomism" associated with the neo-Scholastic Leonine revival of the late nineteenth century. This Scholastic influence comes through most clearly, as Lipner has shown, in Upadhyay's acceptance of an emphasis on the *discontinuity* between the "natural" and the "supernatural," and between "reason" and "revelation." This vocabulary allows him to position Advaita Vedānta as the *natural* philosophical framework through which the *supernatural* truths that have been graciously revealed in Christianity can be articulated from, and received within, Hindu lifeforms.

While it does nothing to advance the "nature versus grace" debate in Christianity to caricature either side of it or to portray it in mutually excluding binary terms such as "Arminian" versus "Calvinist," there is something prima facie counterintuitive about Upadhyay's position on the conceptual spectrum of possible options between the two extremes. If the spectrum covers those who would want to emphasize that grace is *intrinsic* to nature, and grace is always already encapsulated within the natural domain, on the one hand (the extreme end of this part would collapse the soteriological distinction altogether and claim, in effect, that nature is not in any need of redemption), and those who would want to stress that grace is only *extrinsically* related to the natural order, on the other (the extreme end of this part would be the notion that grace is merely an accidental footnote to the main text that is naturally constituted), we would surely expect someone sympathetic to Advaita to veer toward the "intrinsicalist" position since there are not, *ultimately*, two orders of reality (nature + grace).[120] Although this continuum raises all sorts of complex historical and doctrinal questions that I cannot address here,[121] Upadhyay's seemingly counterintuitive starting point of a discontinuity between "nature" and "grace" perhaps helps to explain why

Lipner is suspicious of the degree of genuine convergences between Thomas and Śaṁkara in Upadhyay's work.

While this particular theme of a putative "pure nature" in contrast to the sheer gratuity of grace was opposed in the generation after Upadhyay by Thomist scholars like E. Gilson (1884–1978), A. C. Pegis (1905–1978), and Henri de Lubac (1896–1991) and criticized by them as a *Neo*-Scholastic misreading of the master,[122] another trend in Thomist scholarship is particularly important when it comes to the figures we have examined. Aquinas was still being read, until well into the twentieth century, against an Aristotelian background that tended to underestimate the influence of (neo-)Platonism in his thinking.[123] This Aristotelian emphasis is clearly evident in Dandoy's essay, not least in the stress he puts on the reality of the material world as the unquestionable starting point of Thomist philosophy. The strong contrast he draws between a bottom-up Scholastic system grounded in the empirical realm, which only then ascends to God via analogical predication, and the top-down monistic Advaita philosophy which is led to deny the full-blooded reality of the material because of its starting point in pure spirit, reflects the broader tenor of nineteenth-century Neo-Scholasticism. Aristotle and Aquinas were being used in (especially English and French) Catholic theology to provide a realist buttress against the perceived threats of philosophical idealism—not least what was seen as the inevitable conclusion of idealism in pantheism and subjectivism.[124] Dandoy was not only approaching Vedānta through a Thomist lens, then, but also he was working during a period dominated by a specifically *Aristotelian-inflected* Thomism.[125] Having written his 1919 essay on Advaita in English (presumably for the sake of the readership of the *Catholic Herald* of India, where it was first published), Dandoy's treatise was later translated into French by Louis-Marcel Gauthier, and the widely accepted contemporary preeminence of Aristotelianism is evident even in the preface, where Gauthier contends that:

> Peripatetic Scholasticism is the key, the only one we have, to unlock the doctrines of Hinduism. Indeed, without its vocabulary, one could not even think of attempting a worthwhile translation [of Hindu doctrines]: ". . . this language (Aristotelian and Scholastic) is, moreover, for this case, the least inadequate of those at our disposal in the West."[126]

It is also telling that there is, in the French version of Dandoy's essay, a short afterword written by Jacques Maritain (1882–1973) in praise of Dandoy's "Catholic exegesis of Vedānta."[127] Maritain read Aquinas as being largely opposed to the Neoplatonism of figures like Pseudo-Denys, and emphasized the ontological *difference* between divine being and finite beings,[128] so it is hardly surprising that he is sympathetic to Dandoy's critique of Advaita.[129]

By the time of De Smet and Grant, in the second half of the twentieth century, however, the landscapes of Thomist scholarship had changed considerably, not least in Belgium. There was a far greater appreciation of the influence of Neoplatonism in Thomas's theology and of the influence of Pseudo-Denys, in particular.[130] This was a rather different (reception of) Aquinas from the one seen through the "Neothomist" lenses operating in the background of the work of Upadhyay or even of Dandoy and Johanns:

> From the perspective of the Neothomists, Neoplatonism appeared as an ally of modernity, the predecessor and support of its idealisms. The positive present interest in Neoplatonism depends on a reversal of this judgement. In the last third of the twentieth century, the dead Neothomism and Neoscholasticism of the nineteenth-century revival, appears, instead of Neoplatonism, as having been thoroughly infected with modern objectifying rationalism.[131]

One of the trends in Thomist scholarship most open to the role of Neoplatonism in Aquinas's thought was "Transcendental Thomism," whose origins can be traced to Louvain and the work of the Belgian Jesuit, Joseph Maréchal, SJ (1878–1944).[132] Both Johanns (who studied at Louvain) and Maréchal became important influences on De Smet's approach to Thomas and—we might reasonably speculate—also on his subsequent approach to Advaita and Śaṁkara.[133] While most early twentieth-century Thomists were agreed in their opposition to the "modern" (from Kant onward) "turn to the subject" because of concerns that this move inevitably led to some form of Idealism, Transcendental Thomists daringly took it as their starting point:

> In other words, the Transcendental Thomist project endeavoured to show that the modern subject is not a self-enclosed autonomous absolute but rather a dynamic openness to the Absolute Self.[134]

This "transcendental turn" meant not only bringing Thomas into creative conversation with Kant and German Idealism, but also digging deeper into Thomas's own idealist influences—not least, the influences of Neoplatonism, via figures like Proclus and Pseudo-Denys.[135]

This development in Thomist scholarship has several intriguing implications for and connections to my own broader argument. First, it is interesting to note that Transcendental Thomism was associated mainly with Jesuit (rather than, say, Dominican) scholars. Beginning with Maréchal, significant Jesuit theologians such as Erich Przywara, SJ (1889–1972), Bernard Lonergan, SJ (1904–1984), Karl Rahner, SJ (1904–1984), and W. Norris Clarke, SJ (1915–2008) all explored the relations between Thomas's thought and modern philosophy, particularly in terms of how consciousness shapes reality.[136] Second, one of the most important (re-)discoveries prompted by this greater openness to the Neoplatonic influences on Aquinas was of the participatory character of his concept of *esse*.[137] C. Fabro (1911–1995) was one of the first to emphasize Thomas's understanding of creaturely existence as a finite "sharing in" the infinite act of divine being,[138] and his work has been picked up and continued by contemporary Thomists like F. O'Rourke, W. Hankey, V. Boland, and R. Te Velde. I argue in Chapters 4 and 5 that the ways in which De Smet and Grant try to harmonize Aquinas and Śaṁkara by reading non-duality with the vocabulary of contingency can be further developed by looking at the focus of these contemporary Thomists on Neoplatonic themes like "participation":

> Fabro showed that at the heart of Aquinas's understanding of the one and the many, especially as that problem gets worked out at the level of the relationship between God and the world, is that the many get their metaphysical value by somehow sharing, in a limited and causally derivative fashion, a perfection that belongs by nature to the One who is its source.[139]

As indicated by Shanley, this metaphysics of participation implies a God who is both the source and the sustainer of Being or, indeed, is Being itself; a God who is, therefore, able to "cause" existence not by pantheistically transforming Godself into finite beings but by "containing" all beings as God's "effects." The "created" order, or what an Advaitin would refer to simply as "the world," has no independent reality of its own, but exists only by participating in its ontologically grounding cause. Again, it is only possible to appreciate fully the extent to which Thomas was working with such a notion of divine causality when the Aristotelian language and the conceptual architecture of formal, material, efficient, and final causation are seen alongside Thomas's indebtedness to Neoplatonic concepts of causation. This is most apparent in Aquinas's commentary on the *Liber de Causis*, which I will discuss in Chapter 4.[140]

Conclusion

A nineteenth-century revival of Thomism that had been explicitly Aristotelian and *anti*-idealist had travelled, by the middle of the twentieth century, a considerable hermeneutical distance in a different direction—toward an understanding of Thomas as influenced also by (Neo-)Platonism and by the idealist metaphysics of divine ideas, of causation as a form of emanation in which the effect preexists in the cause, and of creaturely being as a *less-than-fully-real* participation in divine being. In the next chapters, I want to suggest that these Neoplatonic themes in Aquinas are the ones most likely to offer new insights into the God-world dialectic in the in-between spaces across Thomism and Advaita. For Grant, one of the key challenges that Advaita poses to Christian theology is its call to revive and revitalize the apophatic dimensions of Christian faith and its keen sense of the "relative nonbeing of all created things."[141] If uncovering the resonant parallels, at a depth level, between Śaṁkara and Thomas involves drawing Advaita Vedānta back from its tendencies toward illusionistic monism, it may also be that the resultant invitation to Christian theologians is to be open to an inverse conceptual movement of Scholasticism—that is, to underscore a strain of idealist metaphysics that allows for a distinctive form of Christian nondualism.[142] This will mean remaining alert to the Neoplatonic themes of "emanation" and "participated being," which lie in the background of Aquinas's metaphysics of creation, and the radical parallels *and* differences between these concepts and associated metaphysical tropes in Advaita Vedānta.

The exciting result of this Scholastic-Vedāntic comparative engagement is, according to Grant, the "Copernican revolution," which it could bring about in Christian theological understandings of God—not as a distant entity "out there" to whom many people find it increasingly hard to relate, but as the transcendent and yet immanent Self of our own self—and also of grace, not as somehow "coming in from outside," but as the essence and the power of God as supreme being already present in creation by the very fact of it "being there" at all.[143]

> Obviously, Christian thought-patterns have been challenged on these and other points from other quarters too, but so far as advaita is concerned the challenges all stem from the radically different metaphysical assumption underlying them, namely, that the tendency to "objectify"

the ultimate Mystery and identify it with "names and forms" of any kind whatever is the root of all error . . . For both the Questing Beast and the Tamil saint Sadashiva, it was the root of all spiritual alienation in an apparently dualistic world, as it must be for anyone who has begun to apprehend, however dimly, that "in every "I" which I attempt to utter, his "I" is already glowing.[144]

4 Creation: "Ex Nihilo" or "*Ex Deo*"?

There was neither non-existence (*asat*) nor existence (*sat*) then: there was neither the realm of space nor the sky which is beyond. What stirred? Where? In whose protection? Was there water, bottomlessly deep?

There was neither death nor immortality then. There was no distinguishing sign of night nor of day. That one breathed, windless, by its own impulse. Other than that there was nothing beyond.

Desire came upon that one in the beginning; that was the first seed of mind. Poets seeking in their heart with wisdom found the bond of existence in non-existence.

Who really knows? Who will here proclaim it? Whence was it produced? Whence is this creation? The gods came afterwards, with the creation of this universe. Who then knows whence it has arisen?

Whence this creation has arisen—perhaps it formed itself, or perhaps it did not—the one who looks down on it, in the highest heaven, only he knows—or perhaps he does not know.[1]

In Chapters 1, 2, and 3, I have made a case for exploring the unique nature of the distinction-and-relation between the world and God by bringing Christian and Vedāntic theologies into conversation. With the help of contemporary theologians like Robert Sokolowski, David Burrell, and Kathryn Tanner in Chapter 1, I started to uncover—and recover—glimpses of a Christian "non-dualism" latent in the reflections of Pseudo-Dionysius, Meister Eckhart, and Nicholas of Cusa, to highlight only a few of those who have insisted that the world cannot, ultimately, be other to God. Our main focus, however, was on the metaphysics of creation found in Thomas Aquinas and his attempt to articulate the sui generis relation between creature and Creator through an engagement not only with Greek philosophy and Christian revelation, but also often with medieval Jewish and Islamic voices. Next, in Chapter 2 and Chapter 3, I responded to Burrell's invitation to expand this conversation beyond Abrahamic frontiers by turning to the Calcutta School of Jesuit Indologists and their comparative Scholastic engagements in the first half of the twentieth century. Inspired particularly by Richard De Smet's work on Śaṁkara, Sara Grant later focused on the Hindu tradition of Advaita Vedānta and the possibilities of a "non-dualist" Christianity. Through a careful examination of the concept of relation in Aquinas and Śaṁkara, she argues that both were making fundamentally the same point: that the nonreciprocal causal arrow of dependence running from the world to God means that the world simply could-not-*be*-without God. There are not *really* two separate ontological realities (world + God) but nor is there simply one, in the arithmetic sense in which this sentence is being typed on "one" computer. The least misleading way of describing the relation between the world and God, then, is to say, along the *via negativa*, that they are "not-two" (*advaita*).

In the previous chapter we saw that Aquinas explains this God-world dialectic as a "mixed" relation—the world is really related to God, but God is not really related to the world. We now need to look more closely at the ontological structure of this relation and at how the world comes to "be" at all, for Christian theology claims that the world is created "from nothing" (ex nihilo)—that it is the bursting forth of something ontologically new—while the Vedāntic doctrine of causality known as *satkāryavāda* suggests that the world, as an effect (*kārya*), always already implicitly exists (*sat*) in Brahman, its cause (i.e., that it is never really "created" at all). In this chapter, I will argue that a comparative exploration of Aquinas's understanding of the nature of divine causation ex nihilo and Śaṁkara's causal conception of *satkāryavāda* shows that these prima facie conceptual differences can be resolved, or even *dis*solved, in terms of a more fundamental alignment.

Creation Ex Nihilo versus *Satkāryavāda*

The intriguing echoes between the Ṛg Vedic verses at the beginning of this chapter on the production of the world and the opening lines of the book of Genesis will surely resonate with a Christian theologian.[2] The poetic seeds of a metaphysical doctrine of world production from nothingness and the emphasis on a willed, even "desired," world provide rich soil for comparative theological engagement—and yet, it is precisely in their respective understandings of divine causality that Christianity and Vedāntic Hinduism are often thought to differ in kind, and not merely in degrees of emphasis.[3] As a result of their ostensibly different starting points (creation ex nihilo versus *satkāryavāda*), Christian teaching on creation tends to stress the ontological *distinction* (or even, according to certain Christian theological understandings and artistic expressions, gap or gulf) between the finite temporal world (produced "from nothingness") and the unlimited eternally existent God,[4] while Advaita Vedānta insists that, in the ultimate analysis, the world is ontologically *not-other* than its supreme cause (Brahman). It would be difficult to imagine two worldviews that are prima facie more diametrically opposed.

It is tempting, moreover, to see these contrasting accounts of divine causality as inevitably drawing the Christian theologian toward an emphasis on the transcendent *otherness* of God to the world and the Vedāntin toward the immanent *presence* of Brahman in and to every finite effect. Yet, of course, the Christian also wants to talk of God in more Vedāntic-sounding imagery as the God in whom "we live and move and have our being" (Acts 17:28) and, conversely, the Advaita Vedāntin maintains, as does a Christian, that Brahman is (at least, from a conventional viewpoint) entirely different from the empirical world (*jagad-vilakṣaṇa*).[5] I will argue that a more nuanced understanding of their respective doctrines of causality provides ample philosophical and theological grounds—contrary to first impressions—for a Christian to underline God's immanence and an Advaitin to highlight Brahman's transcendence. If creation ex nihilo is taken seriously, it means precisely that God is present, at all times and in all places to all things, sustaining every contingent effect in being; while *satkāryavāda*, understood properly, insists that every effect exists latently in its cause, but not vice versa—in its inexhaustible ontological abundance, the cause would remain the "cause" even without the production of its effect.

It is more helpful, therefore, to see transcendence and immanence as mutually constituting concepts, rather than to set them against each other as bipolar alternatives. Although the characteristic imageries of transcendence involve the dimension of "height" and those of immanence the dimension of "depth," we should keep in mind that neither dimension applies, strictly speaking, to God who is not localizable as either *here* or *there*. As we saw in Chapter 1, it is precisely *because* God is understood to be transcendent to creatures in a non-contrastive sense in

Christian theology that God can also be said to be intimately present to and in them—in the way that, according to the Chalcedonian definition, divine and human natures coexist in the undivided person of Jesus the Christ without separation or confusion.

It might be objected, however, that introducing the doctrine of incarnation into this discussion is a red herring—that it has unique application and that the ontological non-difference between God the Father and God the Son, who are co-*eternal* and *con*substantial, cannot be extrapolated to explain the simultaneous distinction-and-relation between God and every *created* effect. The crucial difference is that, according to the Nicene creed, Jesus the Christ was "one in being with the Father" (*homoousios*) because he was, in his divine nature, "begotten, *not made*." As a result, the fact that God is incarnate in the human individual Jesus of Nazareth (i.e., they are "one in being") does not entail that God is one in being (*con*substantial) with the world. As J. Lipner argues, a Christian theologian can certainly speak of "God dwelling in the creature," in the sense of "keeping it in existence" or "being present to it," but this does *not* mean, he claims, that God is "constitutive of its [very] being."[6] The most that the doctrine of *creatio ex nihilo* allows for, in other words, is what Lipner calls "de-entitative immanence,"[7] which differs crucially from entitative immanence in the following way:

> We are assured by Aquinas, and most Christian thinkers would make the same point, that the theory of creation allows for no entitative union whatsoever between the divine being and the created order . . . the accent remains [in the doctrine of *creatio ex nihilo*] on God's presence within and to his creature, rather than on his being its very ground of existence, the wellspring of its reality. The overriding emphasis in the Christian teaching on creation is on the impassable gulf between the infinite and the finite.[8]

On this reading, the disagreement at the level of fundamental ontology between Christianity and Vedāntic Hinduism is a significant one: understanding divine causality as *satkāryavāda* as opposed to ex nihilo entails the "*entitative* pervasiveness of Brahman in the whole of the finite order" such that the world is—ultimately speaking—not ontologically other to Brahman.[9] This leads Lipner to suggest that "Vedāntins have a theory of natural divine immanence with respect to the Absolute and the empirical order, while Christians only speak of such intense indwelling as occurring on the supernatural plane," and that, in the final analysis, "the more literally such unitive language is taken, the less compatible does it become with the doctrine of creation ex nihilo."[10]

In this chapter, I want to suggest that Lipner is correct when he says that the "accent" and the "overriding emphasis" of Christian teaching on creation tends to be on the ontological *difference* between ultimate reality (God) and mundane reality (the world). I will argue, however, that if we keep in mind the fundamentally *non*-contrastive nature of this difference, creation ex nihilo and *satkāryavāda* are much more closely aligned than they first appear to be. That is to say, the finite world and the infinite (*non*finite) divine reality should not be contrastively posited as two individuals pulling away at opposite ends of the same piece of rope, such that the former is only an enumerative addition to, or a quantitative extension, of the latter; rather, in both Christian doctrine and Advaita metaphysics, the latter *non*-contrastively encompasses, envelops, and encapsulates the former by sustaining it in its very finitude. Interpreted thus, both worldviews would agree that the world is not produced from some-one-thing and both doctrines also agree, I will contend, that *no*thing comes from no*thing* (ex nihilo nihil fit). As a result, there is a sense in which it is possible to talk of the world as emanating from God in *both* Christianity and Vedānta.

More specifically, in the distinctive ways in which divine causation is understood by Aquinas and Śaṁkara, I will argue that creation ex nihilo can be seen as a form of *satkāryavāda*. This will be clearer when I set the two doctrines in their historical contexts and against the thematic backgrounds of their most obvious philosophical-soteriological alternatives. Both Christians *and* Vedāntins avoid speaking *univocally* of the world and God through worldly vocabularies, albeit from two contrasting perspectives: Christians uphold this epistemic stricture by emphasizing the "ontological difference" between the two and Vedāntins by denying the ultimate reality of anything other than God. I will argue that there is, in Lipner's words, "no entitative union whatsoever between the divine being and the created order"—in *either* tradition's understanding of creation. There is no *union* because we are talking about different orders of being, which, as I argued at length in Chapter 1, cannot be contrasted or united with each other any more than the words on this page can be contrasted or united with the thoughts in my head that are giving rise to them. There is an ontological distinction between my thoughts and these ink marks, such that being one does not exclude simultaneously being the other. If I have first thought of the word

"Advaita," and then inscribed the word "Advaita" on a piece of paper, the inscription is metaphysically dependent on ideation in a *non*-contrastive, and thus *non*competitive, manner.

I suggest that stressing the ontological "gap" in Christian theology and denying the full-blooded ontological reality of the world in Advaita Vedānta are two parallel strategies motivated by the same conviction: that God and the world should not be contrasted as if they were two enumerable entities existing alongside or opposed to each other. The reason why the Christian response and the Advaita response to this conviction can seem so divergent is because of their distinctive patterns of emphases: the former maintains that the relatively *real* world is sustained in its relative (that is, contingent) existence by God and the latter holds that the *relatively* real world continues to be (empirically) real through its rootedness in Brahman. In neither case should the notion that the divine reality "constitutes" the finite world be explicated in the materialistic sense in which clayey stuff constitutes the pot—we should rather speak of the divine reality as transcendentally, that is, non-contrastively, constituting the existence of the world. Therefore, the non-contrastive nature of this "impassable gulf between the infinite and the finite" does not, *pace* Lipner, mean that (the Christian) God cannot be entitatively immanent to the world. Rather, it is precisely because the gulf is "impassable," where the term "impassable" should be understood in a non-contrastive and not in a spatial sense, that God can be the "very ground of its existence, the wellspring of its reality," and without this "ground," again understood non-contrastively and not with spatial metaphors, the world would simply not "be" at all.[11] This is because, as we have seen in previous chapters, the distinction-and-relation between the world and God is one in which the effect is really related to its cause (since its very being is, as Sara Grant has shown, an *esse-ad-creatorem*) but the cause is only related conceptually—and not metaphysically—to its effect. Separated from God, the world indeed has no reality in itself.

Satkāryavāda versus *Asatkāryavāda* in Indian Philosophy

The thought-schools of Vaiśeṣika and Sāṁkhya are often presented as exemplary types of two different—even, opposed—theories of causality in Indian philosophy: namely, of *asatkāryavāda* (Vaiśeṣika) and *satkāryavāda* (Sāṁkhya).[12] *Asatkāryavāda* is the doctrine that an effect does not preexist in its material cause but is, rather, brought into existence from nonexistence in the process of causation.[13] *Satkāryavāda*, on the other hand, is the theory that any effect or product (*kārya*) is already ontologically present in its material cause and, therefore, that nothing really—that is, substantivally—new emerges in the process of causation. As Dasgupta puts it, "[t]he causal operation (*kārakavyāpāra*) only renders that manifest (*āvirbhūta*) which was formerly in an unmanifested condition (*tirohita*)."[14]

While *asatkāryavāda* and *satkāryavāda* might seem to exhaust the logically possible ways of conceiving the relation between effect and cause (either the effect preexists in the cause or it does not), W. Halbfass questions whether the opposition between the two doctrines (at least insofar as they are understood by Vaiśeṣika and Sāṁkhya philosophers) is as obvious and unambiguous as it seems at first blush:

> in spite of much dialectical interaction and various tacit accommodations, what characterizes the debate [between Vaiśeṣika and Sāṁkhya] most is a certain refusal to address each other's basic premises concerning the nature of being and the different meanings in which the words *sat* and *asat* are used. The transition from "nonbeing" to "being" that the Vaiśeṣika accepts is not identical with the one that the Sāṁkhya rejects. With the appropriate semantic adjustment and clarification, the Vaiśeṣika theory itself could easily be called *satkāryavāda*. The debate is as much about the meaning and usage of words, as it is about the nature of reality and causality.[15]

The point Halbfass is making is that Vaiśeṣika accepts—as much as Sāṁkhya does—that some*thing* cannot arise out of utter nothingness, because while the Vaiśeṣika philosopher avoids the language of potentiality and latency, he, too, is committed to understanding the world in terms of the combinations, aggregations, and separations of eternally existing atoms;[16] the debate seems to be more about a *stipulative* conception of how high a bar on an ontological scale the effect must reach in order to be considered as genuinely "new" and different from its cause. Both philosophical systems agree that "being" (specific and differentiated) emerges neither from *asat* understood substantivally as a second principle of "Non-Being" in dualistic opposition to Being, nor from *asat* understood as the sheer non-dialectical absence of Being. That is, the *asatkāryavāda* that Vaiśeṣika defends is not the doctrine that first there is utter nothingness and then there is some*thing*: rather, there are new emergents because of antecedently existing atoms. Therefore, the Parmenidean principle of *ex nihilo nihil fit* does not seem to be under challenge in either case (Vaiśeṣika or Sāṁkhya), and Śaṁkara himself takes both Sāṁkhya and Vaiśeṣika views on causality to be different versions of *satkāryavāda*.[17]

The philosophical reasoning behind *satkāryavāda* can be found in Īśvarakṛṣṇa's *Sāṁkhyakārikā*:[18]

> *asadakaraṇād upādānagrahanāt sarvasambhavābhāvāt/*
> *śaktasya śakyakaraṇāt kāraṇabhāvāc ca satkāryam//*

The first reason given in the verse for *satkāryavāda* and the basic premise of Sāṁkhya causality is that it is impossible to produce some-one-*thing* out of *not*-any-thing-whatsoever (*nihil*) or, to put it another way, no-*thing* can arise out of utter nothingness. As a consequence, the verse affirms that any effect requires a material cause.[19] Moreover, any given cause can only produce what corresponds to its particular potential (i.e., an acorn can only give rise to an oak, not to a house) and thus the effect and the cause are said to share the same fundamental nature. Śaṁkara accepts the *satkāryavāda* doctrine of causality and addresses each of these reasons for supporting it, though, as we will see, he disagrees with the specific ways in which the doctrine is interpreted by both Vaiśeṣika and Sāṁkhya philosophers.

Production Ex *Materia* versus Creation Ex Nihilo (or *Satkāryavāda* versus *Asatkāryavāda*?) in Christian Thought

The intellectual history of the doctrine of *creatio ex nihilo* in Western Christian thought can be seen to mirror debates on the nature of originative causality in Indian philosophy in interesting and important ways.[20] Like the (supposed) conceptual opposition between *asatkāryavāda* and *satkāryavāda*, the Christian doctrine of creation *from nothing* can also be understood in contrast with philosophical systems, which explain the world as the product of some sort of *preexistent* cause.[21] Some scholars put this point more strongly: that creation ex nihilo was developed as an ontological doctrine *precisely* as an antithesis to the idea of world formation from eternal matter.[22] Whether in the shape of primordial material elements in the pre-Socratics, intelligible Ideas in Plato, or prime matter in Aristotle, a marked preference for some analog of *satkāryavāda* had been established in Greek philosophy long before Christian theologians began to contemplate the kind of causality involved in creation.[23] Some early Christian Fathers, shaped by Platonic cosmogonies, also regarded creation primarily as the ordering of unformed matter[24] and accepted, along with Greek thinkers at least as far back as Parmenides (and, unknowingly, with their Sāṁkhya and Vaiśeṣika cousins), that being does not arise from nonbeing (ex nihilo nihil fit).[25]

Influential Christian thinkers like Theophilus of Antioch (d.183–185 CE), Irenaeus (130–202 CE), and Origen (184–253 CE), however, gradually began to develop a doctrine of creation ex nihilo in opposition to these widely accepted notions of the production of the world *ex materia*. Indeed, Christian theology and later (i.e., "neo") Platonism came close to each other in late antiquity precisely on this point—namely the denial of preexisting matter. Both Christian and pagan (Neoplatonist) thinkers criticized the sort of cosmogony found in Plato's *Timaeus* (i.e., that the demiurge or creator god works with already existent materials) because they saw such productivity as placing limitations on the divine power.[26] Motivated by a recognition of the sheer contingency of existence (i.e., the fact that the world cannot provide the sufficient reason for its own existence) and of the unlimited power of the sovereign God, key figures in the early and medieval Church like Augustine, Boethius, and Anselm followed this lead and established creation ex nihilo as the authoritative Christian understanding of originative causality. According to a standard reading of the doctrine,

> creation is a thrusting into being, so to speak, of a *reality* not existing qua being hitherto . . . of being that had not pre-existed or remained hidden qua being before the creative act (except in the loose and related senses of being objectively possible to God and existing in him as seminal ideas). Thus, creation, in this understanding, is not an emanation or transformation of pre-existing reality, but, by the power of God, the emergence of something real from the void.[27]

At first sight, this seems to place Christian metaphysics squarely on the *asatkāryavāda* side of the Indian debate (as an even "purer" example of *asatkāryavāda*, strictly speaking, than any of the Indian systems), and Greek and Vedāntic metaphysics on the *satkāryavāda* side. *Asatkāryavāda*, to recall, is the doctrine that effects do not preexist in their material cause but are, rather, brought into existence from nonexistence in and through the process of causation. To be more precise, according to the Vaiśeṣika doctrine of causality known as *ārambhavāda*,

> when the *upādāna kāraṇa* [material cause] gives rise to an effect, such as cloth from woven threads, or a jar from prepared clay, not only the jar qua jar, but also the jar qua being is a totally new product. Hence, the effect is neither a manifestation nor a transformation of its material cause: it is defined as the "counterpositive of its own prior nonexistence" (*prāgabhāvapratiyogin*).[28]

Before we too quickly assume, however, that the Christian doctrine of creation ex nihilo is the paradigmatic example of a metaphysics of causality in which the effect is *not* ontologically existent in its cause (*asatkāryavāda/ārambhavāda*) and that, therefore, creation ex nihilo must be diametrically opposed to the Vedāntic understanding of causality as *satkāryavāda*, we would do well to heed the example of Halbfass's careful delineation of the opposition between Vaiśeṣika and Sāṁkhya. In that case, we saw that disjunctive binaries tend misleadingly to divert attention away from the subtler conceptual convergences and disagreements in seemingly opposed systems by forcing their basic premises into preconceived schemas. The problems occur when we stop at the schemas and forget the Aristotelian principle (used also by Thomas) that *eadem est scientia oppositorum*—affirmations and their corresponding negations only make sense against some kind of shared background. It is, I contend, a shared conceptual background that brings Śaṁkara's *advaitic* interpretation of *satkāryavāda* very close to Thomas's understanding of the divine causality involved in creation. I will argue that Halbfass's analysis of the Vaiśeṣika theory of causality can be applied, mutatis mutandis, to the Christian conception of creation ex nihilo—namely, that it, too, "[w]ith the appropriate semantic adjustment and clarification . . . could easily be called *satkāryavāda*. The debate [in this case, between creation ex nihilo and Vedāntic *satkāryavāda*] is as much about the meaning and usage of words, as it is about the nature of reality and causality."[29]

The Relation of the One to Its Many in Advaita Vedānta—Śaṁkara's Understanding of *Satkāryavāda*

To understand better the Vedāntic conception of originative causality, we must take into account not only the philosophical background of debates between Vaiśeṣika and Sāṁkhya, but also the pertinent Vedic and *Upaniṣadic* texts.[30] As Uttara Mīmāṃsā, Vedānta is, after all, a philosophical-theological school that sets out its positions primarily through means of exegesis on scripture. We can clearly see this emphasis in the section of Śaṁkara's commentary on the *Brahma-Sūtra* which is specifically dedicated to originative causality.[31] He notes, first of all, the seeming ambiguity of scripture when it comes to the question of the production of the world—with some *Upaniṣads* lending support to the *asatkāryavāda* doctrine by suggesting in certain passages that the world came from nonexistence (e.g., *Taittirīya* II.vii and *Chāndogya* III.xix.1), while in other passages pointing toward *satkāryavāda* by asserting that the world emerged from the already existent (e.g., *Chāndogya* VI.ii.1–2).

Śaṁkara explains this seeming disagreement by arguing that any talk of nonexistence prior to the production of the world is not to be understood as referring to an utter void or *sheer nothingness* (because there never was a time that *Brahman* was not, and Brahman did not come into being), but as referring to the undifferentiated absence of *manifest* "names and forms" (i.e., the absence in the empirical realm of seemingly distinct and particularized pots and jars).[32] He is arguing, in other words, that the scriptures are referring to nothingness understood as the contrastive negation of some-one-*thing*, or what we could call a "dialectical" absence (henceforth, nothingness$_{\text{dial}}$). This is quite different from nothingness understood non-contrastively as the sheer and absolute negation of being altogether (henceforth, nothingness$_{\text{non-dial}}$). Such non-dialectical absence (i.e., the denial of being *tout court*, which, unlike nothingness$_{\text{dial}}$, is not a conceptualizable denial-relative-to-a-particular-*x*) cannot even be conceptualized. Indeed, Śaṁkara maintains that "the theory of non-existence, fancied by the people of dull intellect, is raised and repudiated with a view to strengthening the idea of Existence"[33] because even commonsense observation shows us that particular effects only arise when there is a corresponding power in the cause. If there were not this ontological relation between effect and cause, and any particular effect could emerge from utter nonexistence (i.e., when it had not existed in some sense prior to its manifestation), there would be no reason why curds could not arise from clay and pots could not come out of milk—since the absence of the relevant potential in milk and clay to produce those particular effects would have no bearing on them.[34] Rather, "as a result of this possession of potency by the state preceding origination, the theory of the non-existence of the effect before creation [*asatkāryavāda* or nothingness$_{\text{non-dial}}$] will fall through, and the theory of the pre-existence of the effect [*satkāryavāda*] will stand confirmed."

To summarize, Śaṁkara insists that there is no contradiction in the scriptures, but that "the universe is said to be non-existent before being evolved through name and form [i.e., before its temporal manifestation, in the sense that I "did not exist" before my birth] . . . as a concession to common sense."[35] He rejects, however, the particular understandings of *satkāryavāda* that he finds in Vaiśeṣika and Sāṁkhya philosophy. His objection is that they both, in different ways, presuppose something *other than* Brahman to be the ultimate cause of the world's existence—a beginningless agglomeration of atoms that rearrange themselves, in Vaiśeṣika, and an insentient underlying prime matter (*pradhāna*) in Sāṁkhya.[36] For Vedānta, the only cause in which the effect/world (*kārya*) is ultimately and always existent (*sat*) is Brahman.

Śaṁkara is quite clear, then, that causality only makes sense if an effect *is* ontologically preexistent in its cause prior to its manifestation (*satkāryavāda*), and disagrees with *asatkāryavāda* if this is taken to mean that effects are produced from sheer nothingness (nothingness$_{\text{non-dial}}$). By analogy, he would have defended the viewpoint that the entire universe cannot have been produced ex nihilo (if this is taken to mean that it was produced from a total absence of Being or nothingness$_{\text{non-dial}}$, because there never was a time when Brahman was not), but that it must have been produced *ex deo*, since the potency existed, as it were, in Brahman. This is not a cosmological point about the temporal beginnings of the universe, but a fundamental ontological statement about the ongoing dependence of the universe (the product) on its cause (Brahman), just as a gold necklace only exists through all the three times insofar as it exists substratively "in" gold:

> Because it can be understood that even as today, the effect (universe) has existence only *in identity with* its material cause (Existence-Brahman), so it had its existence in that very way even before creation. For even now, this creation does not exist independently of the Self that is its material source . . . But the existence of the product as the cause before creation is in an indistinguishable form.[37]

The crucial phrase "in identity with" here is a rendering of *kāraṇātmanā*—that is, grammatically speaking, *kāraṇa* (cause) with *ātman* in the instrumental case. So, literally: with the (material) cause as its inner self or inner essence. Parsed carefully in this way, I will argue that Thomas, too, could say that the world has existence only in identity with God.

The Relation of the One to Its Many in Christian Theology—Aquinas's Understanding of *Creatio Ex Nihilo*

Śaṁkara disagreed with both Sāṁkhya and Vaiśeṣika views on causality because of their positing of some kind of a second entity alongside of or instead of Brahman to explain the production of the world. On this particular point, the Christian doctrine of creation ex nihilo is in complete agreement—there is no preexistent entity other than God out of which the world is produced (whether atoms, water, ideas, or matter, to mention a few of the candidates ruled out by creation ex nihilo). Indeed, it was precisely in opposition to this sort of interpretation of *satkāryavāda* analogues in Greek philosophy that ex nihilo was formulated (i.e., to insist that the creation of the world was "not-from-some-one-thing"). This point is made by Augustine and Anselm,[38] and is abundantly clear in Aquinas, as the following passages show:

> Those who posit an eternal world would say that the world is made by God from nothing, not because it was made after nothing (which is how we understand the term "creation"), but because it was not made from something.[39]
>
> If someone holds that something besides God could have always existed, in the sense that there could be something always existing and yet not made by God, then we differ with him: such an abominable error is contrary not only to the faith but also to the teachings of the philosophers, who confess and prove that everything that in any way exists cannot exist unless it be caused by him who supremely and most truly has existence.[40]

In other words, the doctrine of creation ex nihilo, as understood by Aquinas (and all orthodox Christian theologians), is couched in terms more of a denial than an affirmation. It does not pretend to explain precisely *how* the world came into being but merely rules out certain doctrinal errors—in particular, that of thinking that God produced the world from some-one-thing.[41] The danger of forgetting this apophatic nature of the doctrine is that "nothingness" can easily become an extremely rarefied kind of some*thing*, an essentialized substratum "out of which" God then makes, fashions, or crafts the world—which is precisely the kind of dualistic thinking between God and not-God in the creative process that the doctrine was originally formulated to reject.[42] A. Maryniarczyk is correct in saying that

> the theory of *creatio ex nihilo* does not mean that being was called into existence "out of non-being," but that the Creator is the cause of everything that is—form, matter, properties, and substance—and that nothing exists apart from Him that did not come from Him. The universe was and is a work of creation (*creatio continua*).[43]

On this point, then, Aquinas and Śaṁkara are in agreement: there is no-*thing* "out of which" the world is produced. We could call this standpoint the rejection of *satkāryavāda*^{a} (i.e., the kind of *satkāryavāda* associated, in different ways, with Sāṁkhya and Vaiśeṣika philosophy in Indian contexts, and with pre-Socratic as well as Platonic and Aristotelian philosophy in Western contexts). The disagreements between Aquinas and Śaṁkara—if there are any—must, then, revolve around two questions: first, does Aquinas *affirm* what Śaṁkara *denies* when it comes to the possibility of something arising from sheer nothingness or nothingness$_{\text{non-dial}}$ (what we might call "pure" *asatkāryavāda*)? Second, and conversely, does Aquinas *deny* what Śaṁkara *affirms* when it comes to Brahman/God as the sole originative cause of the world (i.e., that any created effect always already exists "in" God—let us call this *satkāryavāda*^{b})?

As we have seen, Śaṁkara rejects "pure" *asatkāryavāda* as metaphysically impossible since effects only arise when there is a corresponding potency.[44] As such, the world could no more emerge ex nihilo (out of nothingness$_{\text{non-dial}}$) than curds could be produced from clay or pots from milk. The world "exists," even if only latently and not manifestly, according to Śaṁkara, in the potency of Brahman. At first sight, this position does seem to be a rejection of what creation ex nihilo affirms—that creation, as Lipner puts it, "is a thrusting into being, so to speak, of a *reality* not existing qua being hitherto . . . of being that had not pre-existed or remained hidden qua being before the creative act."[45] In his discussion of the question of whether God could cause something that has always existed, Aquinas seems to confirm Lipner's point:

> notice that before an angel is made, we may say, in a certain manner of speaking, that the angel cannot be made, since no passive potentiality precedes its being, for an angel is not made from pre-existing matter [*quia non praeexistit ad eius esse aliqua potentia passiva, cum non sit*

> *factus ex materia praeiacente*]. Nevertheless, God was able to make the angel, and he was able to cause the angel to be made, for God made it, and it was made.[46]

Read carefully, however, it is clear that what Aquinas is rejecting in this passage is *satkāryavāda*[a]—he is rejecting the position that created effects (whether angels or otherwise) are made from preexisting matter and that, prior to their creation by God they possess some kind of "passive potentiality." In other words, "being made" or "being caused" should not be understood as the preexistence of a passive potentiality (as if the essence of a creature could be separated from its existence) "out of which" things are produced by God.[47] Rather, Aquinas is affirming, along with Śaṁkara, that, *notwithstanding* the absence of any*thing* to "work with," God is somehow able to make the angel. Again, this is why when reading Lipner's characterization of *creatio ex nihilo* as "the emergence of something real from the void,"[48] we must be careful not to imagine "the void" as a subtle abyss of passive potentiality existing as nothingness$_{\text{dial}}$ with respect to or alongside God. The "void" here—and more generally "nothingness"—signals not an ontic space over and above God, or in addition to God, but merely a logical space that has to be invoked by human categorical understanding to make contrastive sense of the *nihil* in the doctrine of creation ex nihilo.[49]

Equally crucially, Aquinas cannot be affirming the "pure" *asatkāryavāda* of created effects arising from nothingness$_{\text{non-dial}}$ either, for, if he were to allow for that, none of his Five Ways of demonstrating the existence of God could get off the ground. It is not quite as clear-cut, then, as S. Oliver's seemingly commonsense contention makes it sound, that creation ex nihilo "clearly contradicts the classical philosophical maxim first articulated by Parmenides . . . *ex nihilo, nihil fit*."[50] Admittedly, Aquinas does suggest that this "common opinion" of ancient philosophers (viz. *ex nihilo nihil fit*) "has no place in the first emanation from the universal principle of things,"[51] but, nonetheless, in his third Way, Aquinas makes his rejection of "pure" *asatkāryavāda* abundantly clear:

> if everything is possible not to be, then at one time there could have been nothing in existence [*nihil fuit in rebus*]. Now if this were true, even now there would be nothing in existence, because that which does not exist only begins to exist by something already existing [*quia quod non est, non incipit esse nisi per aliquid quod est*]. Therefore, if at one time nothing was in existence, it would have been impossible for anything to have

begun to exist; and thus, even now nothing would be in existence—which is absurd [*si igitur nihil fuit ens, impossibile fuit quod aliquid inciperet esse, et sic modo nihil esset, quod patet esse falsum*].[52]

Aquinas's solution to this problem, of course, is that there never was a time when there was sheer *nothingness* understood as complete absence of being (nothingness$_{\text{non-dial}}$). The existence of the contingent order now (or at any point) can only be explained by the sustaining presence of a necessarily existent cause—and that, as Aquinas pithily concludes, is what all people call "God." On closer inspection, then, we can see that Aquinas and Śaṁkara are in agreement on these points: originative causality cannot be explained either by *satkāryavāda*^{a} or by the "pure" *asatkāryavāda* of nothingness$_{\text{non-dial}}$. The *nihil* in the Christian doctrine of creation is more mysterious than it first appears: it must not be understood as a dialectically structured "nothingness" or nothingness$_{\text{dial}}$, which precedes some-one-thing (the sort of "passive potentiality" we have seen Aquinas reject), let alone as a kind of physical/spatial nothingness, but it is also difficult to render it as sheer absence of being or nothingness$_{\text{non-dial}}$ as well.[53] The *nihil* seems to dissolve into a merely logical or grammatical constellation of Christian teachings, the essence of which is that the world is nonexistent without and but for God even though God does not become ontologically diffused into or dispersed across the world. Having rejected both *satkāryavāda*^{a} and "pure" *asatkāryavāda*, Śaṁkara's own solution is *satkāryavāda*^{b}—that Brahman/God is the sole originative cause of the world and any created effect always already exists "in" God, in the sense that it is ontologically rooted in God as the hyper-being. If there is any disagreement on originative causality between Śaṁkara and Aquinas, it must be here.

What Kind of Cause Is Brahman?

Śaṁkara notes that if Brahman is that from which (*yataḥ*) the world is born, in the sense that Brahman is the cause with the power to produce the effect (the universe), Brahman could be understood either as the *efficient* cause (along the lines of a potter or a goldsmith) or as the *material* cause (as clay and gold are to pots and necklaces) or as both.[54] He agrees that Brahman certainly is the ultimate efficient cause of the universe, since there could be no other. This insistence is not surprising, as all Vedāntic schools take the existence of Brahman as timeless, indivisible Being as their starting point, and see Brahman as the one cause of the world's origin.[55] As E. Lott puts it: "Brahman 'in the beginning was only one, one without a second,' and from this one Being all finite beings have derived."[56]

Śaṁkara wants to maintain, however, that Brahman is "that from which the world derives" also in the sense of being its material cause, and "entitatively immanent" in it. At first sight, this claim seems more problematic, as Śaṁkara's opponent recognizes, because "this universe, which is a product, is seen to be composite, insentient, and impure; so, its material cause, too, must be of the same nature, since the cause and effect are seen to be similar. But Brahman is known to be devoid of such a nature."[57] In other words, as we saw in Īśvarakṛṣṇa's *Sāṁkhyakārikā*, the effect shares the same fundamental nature as the cause. Brahman, it would seem, cannot be the material cause of the world because of the dissimilarity in fundamental nature between Brahman and the world.[58]

An entire section of Śaṁkara's commentary (BSBh II.i on *avirodha*/noncontradiction) deals with this and other similar objections to the idea of Brahman being a material cause, suggesting that he recognizes this as a doctrine that is open to considerable philosophical and theological misunderstanding. We can draw out several key lines of argument from his defense. First, he maintains that holding Brahman as the material cause of the universe is the only valid inference from the sorts of *Upaniṣadic* passages that affirm Brahman as all that existed prior to the production of the world.[59] In other words, since there was no*thing* else (viz., no other "material") besides Brahman prior to the world (and, as already established through *Upaniṣadic* exegeses, effects cannot arise out of sheer nothingness), Brahman cannot have depended on anything else that is not-Brahman in order to produce the world. Just as milk has the potential to turn into curds or a spider can spin its own threads without help from anything else, so "Brahman . . . is possessed of the fullest power and It has not to depend on anything else for imparting an excellence."[60] Second, he argues that Brahman must be the sole material cause in order to make sense of scriptural passages that say by knowing this one (Brahman), a person will know all (e.g., Ch.Up.VI.i.2–6, Br.Up. IV.v.6). Such an argument only works if Brahman is, in some sense, the substrative material cause of every finite thing that exists and not merely the efficient cause, in the same way it is by knowing clay that one knows, as it were, everything that is made of clay, and not simply by knowing the individual potter.

Perhaps most importantly, however, we must remember that the "material" cause, whether in Greek (*hyle*) or in Sanskrit (*upādāna kāraṇa* or, sometimes, *prakṛti*) philosophical contexts, simply means the substrate from which the effect derives its existence or, in more Aristotelian idiom, that which becomes a particular thing by receiving form. While that substrate may well be physical matter in many of the most common examples that spring to mind (e.g., the bronze or stone out of which a statue is made), there is no particular reason—for Aristotle or for Śaṁkara—why the material cause has to be "material" in the sense of physical "stuff."[61] Confusion arises when we begin with the assumption that the "material world" is essentially physical and then balk at the idea of Brahman being a "material cause" as physical. Śaṁkara's starting point, in contrast, is Brahman as *sat* (Being) and *cit* (Consciousness). As the only possible substrate out of which the world can have been derived (since it can neither have been derived from another nor from sheer nothingness), positing Brahman as the "material" cause in fact tells us something interesting about the essential nature of the world:

> Hearing from the Vedas that creation has Consciousness as its material cause, we can understand on the strength of this, that the whole universe is conscious, for the characteristics of the material are seen to inhere in the product. The non-perception of consciousness [e.g., in wood or lumps of earth] is caused by some peculiarity of the transformation [i.e., consciousness is expressed in some particular forms and not others].[62]

We might still reasonably object, however, that Śaṁkara has not shown how the world (which is "composite, insentient, and impure") can be *of the same nature* as Brahman, and yet, this must be the case, if Brahman is "One-without-a-second (which is putatively outside of or beyond Brahman)." The Vedāntic commitment to *satkāryavāda* and to a single, indivisible source of all being (Brahman) means that Brahman must be both the efficient (*nimitta kāraṇa*) cause *and* the material (though not "physical") cause (*upādāna kāraṇa*) of the phenomenal world in the same way that the "one clod of clay" is the material cause of "all that is made of clay." To make this puzzle of how two entities that are qualitatively different can yet be of one ontological nature (which is what *satkāryavāda* entails) even more difficult, Vedāntins take the simplicity and the immutability of Brahman to be axiomatic.[63] This is why Śaṁkara cannot accept the Sāṁkhya interpretation of the *satkārya* idea—that the effect is a real transformation (*pariṇāma*) of the cause or that the world is a real transformation of Brahman. As he explains, if Brahman has changed into the world *wholesale*, Brahman would no longer be self-subsistent; and if *part* of Brahman has changed into the world, Brahman will no longer be simple.[64]

Śaṁkara seems to be left with an irreconcilable combination of three theological and philosophical premises: (i) that prior to the world's existence there was only Brahman; (ii) that effects are ontologically preexistent in their causes because *no*thing can come from no*thing* (i.e., that the world emerges from Brahman and is ontologically indistinct from Brahman); and (iii) that Brahman does not undergo any fundamental change. The distinctively *advaitic* (dis)solution of this seemingly inconsistent triad is to deny that there are "really" two different entities at all: Brahman + world. This is not an empirical statement about the way things look or seem because, prima facie, the properties of objects in the universe are certainly not identical with the scriptural characterizations of Brahman (infinite, unchanging, eternal, etc.). Indeed, Śaṁkara does not deny that there is an *empirical* difference (observed in common experience) between effects and causes, but he maintains that there cannot be any real *ontological* diversity at a fundamental depth level because Being is One-without-a-second. Just as we can distinguish between waves and bubbles, while recognizing that, in an ontological sense, "they are [merely] modifications of the sea and non-different from it, which is but water,"[65] we can distinguish between the world and Brahman while recognizing that they are ultimately not-two in the sea of being, Brahman.

This (dis)solves the problem of how the effect (world) can share the nature of its cause (Brahman) because there are not *really* two "different" ontological realities that need to be harmonized or correlated. Similarly, Brahman "has not changed *into* another thing, the world, since what we call as 'world' is not an ontological entity in its own right; it is not something other than the material cause, Brahman itself."[66] As the immutable and infinite plenitude of Being—One-without-a-second—there can be no ontologically distinct and separate "second" thing (i.e., the world) into which Brahman could become transformed.[67] In this sense, to ask whether the *Upaniṣads* are talking about the products or about their cause involves, from a transcendental vantage point, a false distinction. We can thus understand more clearly what Śaṁkara means by saying that the effect (universe) has existence only *in identity with* its material cause.[68] The world has Brahman as its "inner self" or "essence" (*kāraṇātmanā*) because it is—and can only be, given the philosophical and theological premises taken as axiomatic—some sort of "manifestation" of the transcendental cause (*kārya*) in which it always already exists (*sat*), namely, Brahman.

It is hard to deny, though, that this dissolution of the conundrum of how the many can be related to the One has some peculiar-sounding and highly counterintuitive ramifications. It means that the "modifications" or "transformations" of which Brahman is the Self,[69] are not *really* modifications or transformations of Brahman at all from the transcendental perspective; it is only from the unenlightened perspectives of ignorance (*avidyā*) that Brahman is mistakenly regarded as having undergone modifications or transformations into the world. In a conceptual move strikingly similar to Aquinas, Śaṁkara insists that the ontological causal arrow only points in one direction, for "though cause and effect are non-different, the effect has the nature of that cause and not vice-versa," in the manner in which a necklace does not transfer its individual peculiarities to gold.[70] These individual peculiarities—or, more generally, the "modifications" and "transformations" that we think of as particularized empirical effects—originate in speech and "exist" only in name at the conventional (*vyāvahārika*) level, *sub specie temporis*, and not from the transcendental (*pāramārthika*) standpoint, sub specie aeternitatis. Just as we might call a particular object a "pot" even though it is *really* just clay, so everything without exception is *really* Brahman in the sense that no modification can exist separately from Brahman (for that would be to exist separately from Being and, therefore, not to exist at all). So, in spite of what seem to be genuinely different particularized objects,

> in reality, this difference does not exist, since a non-difference between those cause and effect is recognised. The effect is the universe, diversified as space etc. and the cause is the supreme Brahman. In reality it is known that the effect [*kārya*] has non-difference [*ananyatvaṃ*] from, i.e. non-existence in isolation from [*vyatirekeṇa-abhāvaḥ*], that cause [*kāraṇa*].[71]

Hence, the momentous conclusion of the *Chāndogya Upaniṣad*: "All this has That as its essence; That is the Reality; That is the Self; That thou art."[72]

What Kind of Cause Is God?[73]

We have already seen that the primary meaning of the doctrine of creation "ex nihilo" was precisely the denial of ontological dualisms—*non ex materia sed ex nihilo*—and the corresponding affirmation of the noncontrastive transcendence of God over every sort of dependence and limitation.[74] This sets Christian teaching on originative causality apart from the mainstream Greek philosophical traditions that tended to understand creation as a process dependent on some sort of preexistent reality alongside and extraneous to God (at least up until the Middle Platonist period, in any case).[75] Divine causality in Christian theology is more radical because it answers the question of why there is any-one-*thing* at all. God is not merely the efficient cause of the world because "according to Aquinas, God is not simply a being among other beings, albeit of the most perfect kind. He is Being Itself (*ipsum esse per se subsistens*), and as such He comprises in himself the fullness of being."[76] This is why De Smet insists that when created effects are produced, "their supreme cause is neither decreased nor increased" since nothing can be added to God who is, as Anselm describes God, "that than which a greater cannot be thought." Oliver, too, repeatedly insists that creation should not be understood as the change from there being one thing (God) to there being two things (God + world).[77]

This theme is potentially problematic for a Christian theologian, though, because if the world (as effect) emerges neither from sheer nothingness or nothingness$_{\text{non-dial}}$ (as we see in Thomas's third Way) nor from any preexistent some-one-thing, it seems that the world must emerge *ex deo*—that is, from God, the only possible cause, the One-without-a-second, and that the world is, therefore, "of one being" with God.[78] Aquinas seems to reject this conclusion when, for example, he castigates David of Dinant for teaching the "absurd thesis" that God is prime matter.[79] His objection is that God cannot enter into composition with anything, either as a formal or as a material principle since this compresence would impinge on God's simplicity and immutability. There is, however, no direct disagreement with Śaṁkara on these points. As we have seen, a material cause (*upādāna kāraṇa*) can, and does, mean a kind of eternal stuff that undergoes change in *some* Indian and Western philosophical systems (e.g., Sāṁkhya or Vaiśeṣika; Greek Atomism or Manichaeism) but that cause, which provides the substantive ground of created effects, need not be thought of as some spatiotemporal entity. For Śaṁkara, Brahman *is* the *upādāna*, but not in a "material" sense. De Smet is surely correct when he says that "if we were to ask [Aquinas] whether the Godhead is the world-*upādāna* in the sense used by Śaṅkara in the same topic, i.e., the innermost Cause that provides the whole substantial reality of the creature, he would fully answer yes." The creature as created, he writes, "is not the essence of God but its essence is from God" (*non est ex essentia Dei, sed est ex Deo essentia*: S.Th. I,41,3,2).[80] As long as we are careful, therefore, not to assume that a material cause has to be some kind of physical "stuff"—and neither Śaṁkara nor Aquinas do intend it this way when talking about divine causality—there seems to be no reason why we cannot speak of God as the "material cause" of the world: that is, the "innermost Cause that provides the whole substantial reality of the creature."[81]

In fact, the Graeco-Latin philosophical traditions of which Aquinas was an inheritor, have their own epigrammatic version of *satkāryavāda*. The principle that an effect always bears a certain resemblance to its cause can be found also in Plato and Aristotle, as well as in Neoplatonist figures like Plotinus and Proclus, and was taken as axiomatic by just about every major Scholastic thinker including Aquinas.[82] E. Gilson has pointed out that few formulations occur more often in Aquinas's writings than *omne agens agit sibi simile* (causes can only produce effects that are similar to themselves).[83] This does not mean that there is necessarily a physical likeness between effect and cause, but that the power to produce the effect must be present within the cause—which Aquinas takes to mean the same as saying that the effect, in an ontological sense, is pre-contained in or always already exists in its cause (i.e., *satkāryavāda*):

> As every agent causes something similar to itself, the effect of the agent must necessarily in some way be in the agent.[84]
>
> The effects proceed from the efficient cause insofar as they pre-exist in it, as every agent causes something similar to itself.[85]
>
> The effect pre-exists virtually in the efficient cause.[86]

These passages seem to suggest, then, that Aquinas's understanding of causality is a Christian variation on *satkāryavāda*. It might be objected, however, that God is not a cause like any other and that divine originative causality is sui generis—such that the principle *omne agens agit sibi simile* cannot be applied to the God-world relation. This does not seem to be applicable to Aquinas, though. Indeed, his whole justification for *theo-logia* rests on the principle that created effects (viz. the world) resemble their supreme cause (God); we would simply not be justified in speaking about God at all if there were no such *analogia entis*.[87] While I would, therefore, agree with Lipner that "the fact that we may be able to speak intelligibly of God [does not] in any way logically predetermine[s] the intensity of his ontological relationship with us,"[88] I would contend that Aquinas thinks that "the intensity of God's ontological relationship with us" *does* logically predetermine the ways in which we can intelligibly speak of God. In other words, it is because God is—in some sense (which I will seek to clarify in the following section)—"entitatively immanent" in all created effects that we can say anything at all about God.[89] To repeat, this style of immanence does not obliterate the ontological distinction between creatures and Creator, but, in fact, relies on it and reinforces it—for it is precisely the *non*-contrastive nature of the distinction that allows God, as cause, to be both transcendent to *and* immanent to the world. Far from being an exception to the rule, the God-world relation is *the* most important example of the principle *omne agens agit sibi simile* because God is *the* primary cause and, as such, produces effects that analogically resemble God.[90] It is only a short logical step from here (if any kind of step at all) to affirm that all created effects (viz. the world) must be pre-contained in their supreme cause (God) or, to put it in the slightly more daring terms not unknown to some medieval Christian mystics, that the world exists "in" God—which is precisely Śaṁkara's (and, I have argued here, also Aquinas's) position: in a word, *satkāryavāda*[b].[91] Effects cannot emerge out of sheer nothingness or nothingness$_{\text{non-dial}}$, and *creatio ex nihilo* insists that the world does not come from some-one-thing either: it can, therefore, only come from God.

In attempting to show that the respective understandings of originative causality in Vedānta (*satkāryavāda*) and in Thomism (*creatio ex nihilo*) are much closer than they might first appear, I am only elucidating what theologians of the Calcutta School had already argued. Johanns and De Smet, for example, both affirmed that the reality of the world is contained in God:[92]

> The world, as it is in itself cannot exist . . . It has reality, but in God, it has *cit* and *sat*, but in God. *It is but not in its own way of being*—as finite and material but in God's own way of being—as infinite and spiritual, without any opposition or limitation.[93]

Where Johanns sought to synthesize the *advaitic* position with the Christian doctrine of *creatio ex nihilo*, however, by emphasizing the dependent contingency of the world while resisting what he saw as the problems of univocity associated with *satkāryavāda*, I am arguing more strongly that no such active "synthesis" is even necessary, since *creatio ex nihilo* simply *is* a Christian form of the proper understanding of *satkāryavāda*.[94] This is even clearer in De Smet, who maintains that

> we can very well uphold that effects pre-exist in their cause without thereby implying that they abide there actually and causation simply manifests instead of causing them. For, it is enough to hold that they are in the power of their cause *bhavisyena rūpena*, viz. "in the state of future realities." When they are produced, their supreme cause is neither decreased nor increased, neither transformed, nor perfected, but they now exist in the present instead of being mere futures.[95]

De Smet wants to resist the idea that created effects (viz. the world) are somehow latent in God, simply awaiting actualization, precisely because of the understanding of *creatio ex nihilo*—the world is not produced from any-one-thing, whether preexisting matter, form, or essence, but originates in its entirety from God. If effects had their own *independent* (pre-)existence, they would be ontologically independent of God, who would merely, in demiurgic fashion, "activate" them from "outside" them. As we have seen, however, this is precisely the sort of metaphysical dualism that *creatio ex nihilo* was formulated to reject. At the same time, as an effect, the world can only emerge from a cause with the power to produce it—thus, De Smet can say that:

> Virtually, however, or, to use Śaṅkara's terminology, as still undifferentiated, it [the world] pre-exists in the power of its Cause, just as it [the world] is eternally known by it [the Cause] independently of its production . . . This is an important application of the theory which the Indians call *satkāryavāda*, namely, of the virtual pre-existence of an effect in the being of its cause.[96]

It seems, then, that *creatio ex nihilo* can be understood as a form of *satkāryavāda* (more precisely, what I have been calling *satkāryavāda*^{b}), which is synonymous with *creatio ex deo*. While the "surface grammar" of the statements "God creates the world ex nihilo" and "Brahman is the *upādāna-kāraṇa* of the world" seem starkly different, a meticulous analysis of their "depth grammar" indicates that the first statement is to be parsed as "God produces the world from (a logical and not onto-logical) nothingness$_{\text{non-dial}}$," which means that God does not produce the world out of some-one-thing, which is nothingness$_{\text{dial}}$ with respect to God—and this, in turn, amounts to the Christian correlate of the Vedāntic claim that the world does not emerge out of some-one-thing other than Brahman. I would argue, therefore, that we *can* speak of genuine entitative divine immanence in Thomas's understanding of creation in the sense that the world does not have its "own being" separately or contrastively from God.[97] In this manner, we can foreground a Christian doctrine that belongs to the foundations of Christian faith but which rarely receives sufficient attention in systematic theology—namely, the omnipresence of the God who is *in* everything.

Nevertheless, a Christian theologian could still insist that the Advaitin goes further than Thomas would, for the following reason: while Śaṁkara agrees that there *is* a distinction between the world and God from a conventional perspective, he denies that this distinction is an ontologically real one. For the Advaitin, there are not *really* two orders of being: God + world (or wave + water). In other words, there is not, *really*, an "ontological distinction" between creature and Creator, for the paradigmatic features of that distinction on the side of the world (i.e., its finitude, transience, mutability, etc.) are only *relatively* real at an empirical level. That is to say that the world, viewed as contingent effect, is indeed finite, transient. and mutable, but Brahman, its causal substrate, is of a different—and more ontologically fundamental—order of being. It is because these "two" orders of being are radically incommensurable and do not exist in a relation of mutual competition that the Advaitin concludes that they are not really "two" at all. Therefore, from the ultimate perspective, there are no "orders" of being: there is Brahman alone, being itself. In what follows, I want to show that this denial of two distinct "orders" amounts to the same concept (intriguingly and ironically) as the Christian emphasis on the "ontological distinction": *because* this Christian distinction, too, is *non*-contrastive, there are not *really* "two" mutually independent orders of being (God + world) in Christian understandings either.

Creation as Emanation: Aquinas and Neoplatonism

As we saw in Chapter 1, Aquinas's formulation of the doctrine of creation was a thoroughly interreligious exercise, influenced by Greek, Jewish, and Islamic philosophical thinking.[98] A key metaphysical question within these medieval Abrahamic contexts was how to conceive of the relation of God to the universe if the universe was eternal, as it had been held to be by the majority of Greek thinkers, including Plato and Aristotle. Islamic thinkers like Al Farabi (875–930) and Avicenna (980–1037) who accepted this picture of the eternal world but refused to see the world as somehow existing independently "alongside" God explained creation in terms of an eternal overflowing or "emanation" out of God—an ontological metaphor influenced by the work of Neoplatonists like Plotinus (204/5–270) and Proclus (412–485).[99] Others, like Al Ghazali (1058–1111)[100] and Maimonides (1135–1204),[101] through whom Aquinas learned of these debates, argued that an eternal world was the antithesis of a created world and rejected the concept of emanation as contrary to their belief in divine freedom. The problem was that creation by emanation sounded too much like a necessary "unfolding" or "bubbling over" of God into the world and also, in Neoplatonic schemes, tended to involve various hypostatic intermediaries in the creative process. The debate became framed disjunctively as one between *necessary* emanation and *free* creation, and, indeed, Burrell recognizes that this conceptual opposition has shaped much of his comparative work.[102] The reason why these debates are interesting for our dialectical situation is because thinking of creation as emanation *ex deo* seems to be a natural corollary of the sort of interpretation of *creatio ex nihilo* for which I have been arguing—namely, that it is a form of *satkāryavāda*[b] in which the effect (world) exists "in" and is empirically distinct from, but metaphysically not-other-than, its cause (God).

While Aquinas (and Śaṁkara) deny that God is a material substance; that creation is effected via intermediaries; that God is changed or transformed in creating;[103] or that creation is necessary and constrained rather than free and sovereign, Aquinas sees "creation" and "emanation" as complementary ideas rather than as bipolar alternatives, for, "having removed any hint of necessity or mediation in creating, Aquinas turns to Plotinus' metaphor, now set free from the accompanying model of logical deduction, and offers a lapidary formula for creation: 'the emanation of the whole of being from the universal cause of being [God].'"[104] It is worth quoting the relevant section of Aquinas's exposition of creation in full:

> As said above (I.44.2), we must consider not only the emanation of a particular being from a particular agent, but also the emanation of all being from the universal cause [*emanationem totius entis a causa universali*], which is God; and this emanation we designate by the name of creation [*et hanc quidem emanationem designamus nomine creationis*]. Now what proceeds by particular emanation, is not presupposed to that emanation; as when a man is generated, he was not before, but man is made from

> "not-man," and white from "not-white." Hence if the emanation of the whole universal being from the first principle be considered, it is impossible that any being should be presupposed before this emanation [*Unde, si consideretur emanatio totius entis universalis a primo principio, impossibile est quod aliquod ens praesupponatur huic emanationi*]. For nothing is the same as no being [*Idem autem est nihil quod nullum ens*]. Therefore, as the generation of a man is from the "not-being" which is "not-man," so creation, which is the emanation of all being, is from the "not-being" which is "nothing" [*ita creatio, quae est emanatio totius esse, est ex non ente quod est nihil*].[105]

Here, we see Aquinas clearly affirming *satkāryavāda*[b]—that particular effects emanate from particular agents and that the world (viz. "all being") emanates from God, the "universal cause." He is also careful to explain that this emanation does not mean that the world existed as distinct from God "in" God prior to its production, any more than a particular man exists prior to his generation, for this would contradict his belief in creation ex nihilo (i.e., that the whole of being emanates from God, not from anything else, including something merely potential). Nevertheless, this is not an affirmation of creation from sheer nothingness either, for the power to produce the effect must exist *in* the cause. That is why man is made from "not-man," white from "not-white," and, more generally, being from "not-being" (i.e., man cannot be made from "not-tree," for example). In other words, "prior" to creation, there simply was no being (no-*thing*) at all other than God, who, alone, had the power to produce being. This is made even clearer by Aquinas in a passage in his *De Potentia*:

> now all created causes have one common effect which is *being*, although each one has its peculiar effect whereby they are differentiated: thus heat makes a thing *to be* hot, and a builder gives *being* to a house. Accordingly, they have this in common that they cause *being*, but they differ in that fire causes fire, and a builder causes a house. There must therefore be some cause higher than all other by virtue of which they all cause being and whose proper cause is *being*: and this cause is God [*Oportet ergo esse aliquam causam superiorem omnibus cuius virtute omnia causent esse, et eius esse sit proprius effectus. Et haec causa est Deus*]. Now the proper effect of any cause proceeds therefrom in likeness to its nature. Therefore, *being* must be the essence or nature of God [*Proprius autem effectus cuiuslibet causae procedit ab ipsa secundum similitudinem suae*

> *naturae. Oportet ergo quod hoc quod est esse, sit substantia vel natura Dei*]. For this reason, it is stated in *De Causis* (prop. ix) that none but a divine intelligence gives being, and that *being* is the first of all effects, and that nothing was created before it.[106]

Again, to emphasize, this is only teasing out the entailments of certain convictions that both Śaṁkara and Aquinas hold as axiomatic: that the world cannot have emerged ex nihilo if this means from sheer nothingness, and that it did not emerge *ex materia* either—rather, the world emanates from God, "for comprehending all in itself, [God] contains existence itself as an infinite and indeterminate sea of substance."[107] Moreover, there is no reason to conclude that creating places any kind of constraint on divine freedom because it is a free act of love entirely consistent with God's nature.[108] It is no coincidence that Aquinas's treatment of creation in the first part of his ST follows immediately upon his extended discussion of God as Trinity (Q.27–43) because it is in seeing creation as a reflection of the inner life of God that creation can be seen both as an unmediated extension of God's nature and as entirely free.[109] Aquinas summarizes much of what I have been arguing in the following passage from Q.45 on creation:

> To create is, properly speaking, to cause or produce the being of things. And as every agent produces its like [*omne agens agit sibi simile*], the principle of action can be considered from the effect of the action; for it must be fire that generates fire. And therefore, to create belongs to God according to His being, that is, His essence, which is common to the three Persons.[110]

It is instructive here to return to the Nicene distinction between "making" and "begetting." The difference between these two manners of production is that one can *make* something unlike (in fundamental nature) oneself (as, for example, a builder makes a house), whereas one can only *beget* something of the same kind (as a human begets a human). God the Son is "eternally begotten" of (rather than created or made by) God the Father, which is why the creed affirms that Jesus the Christ (the incarnate Son) is "consubstantial" with the Father. The Christian doctrine of creation ex nihilo and the Vedāntic doctrine of *satkāryavāda* seem opposed if we interpret the former as an example of "making" and the latter as an example of "begetting," and, from there, draw the inference that what God "makes" is not of the same nature as God—that is, the world is not "of one being" (*homoousios*) with God (or that God is not "entitatively immanent" in it).[111] Indeed, Aquinas emphasizes this very point when commenting on St. Paul's Letter to the Romans, in which Paul says that "everything there is comes from him and is caused by him and exists for him":[112]

> It should be noted that another Latin word for "from" is *de*, which seems to suggest the same relationships; however, *de* always designates a consubstantial cause. For we say that the knife is from [*de*] the iron, but not from [*de*] the maker. Therefore, because the Son proceeds from the Father as consubstantial with Him, we say that the Son is from [*de*] the Father. But creatures do not proceed from God as consubstantial with Him; hence, they are not said to be from [*de*] Him but from [*ex*] Him [*Creaturae vero non procedunt a Deo tamquam ei consubstantiales; unde non dicuntur esse de ipso, sed solum ex ipso*].[113]

However, given Aquinas's insistence on the principle that *omne agens agit sibi simile* (which applies preeminently to God as the non-contrastive cause of the world) and his explicit use of the language of emanation, I would suggest, somewhat arguing with Aquinas against him, that we can also talk, in some sense, of God "begetting" being and, therefore, of God's creating as a kind of "begetting" in which the effect (the world) analogically shares the nature of the cause (God), but not vice versa. Śaṁkara denies the full-blooded ontological reality of the world in order to dissolve the seeming paradox of correlating the ostensibly distinct natures of Brahman and the world, and Aquinas adopts a surprisingly similar strategy. The reason we cannot speak univocally of creatures and Creator (i.e., talk of them as being "con-substantial") is not, I would argue, because they possess two different natures, but because:

> every effect which is not an adequate result of the power of the efficient cause, receives the *similitude of the agent not in its full degree, but in a measure that falls short*, so that what is divided and multiplied in the effects resides in the agent simply, and in the same manner; as for example the sun by exercise of its one power produces manifold and various forms in all inferior things. In the same way, as said in the preceding article, all perfections existing in creatures divided and multiplied, preexist in God unitedly.[114]

There *is*, in other words, an "ontological distinction" between creatures and Creator (they are not straightforwardly "con-substantial" as

God the Son *is* consubstantial with God the Father), but it is not a distinction between two *different* ontological orders separate from or in competition with each other. At the same time, I am not suggesting that this conception implies that God and creatures are positioned on differently graded rungs of the *same* ontological ladder either. The distinction remains non-contrastive and asymmetrical. This is why I think that we can speak of God "begetting" the world *in a sense*, but I would not want to push this language too far lest it sound like the world is ontologically *continuous* with God. We must remember that even in Advaita, it is not really a case of ontological *continuity* between the world and Brahman because there are not ultimately two different and metaphysically independent realities to be continuous with each other on a shared ontic backdrop. Indeed, Śaṁkara gets to the heart of the matter when he talks of the "unreality" of the world, for the key to the distinction between the world and God is the world's ontological nothingness apart from God. It is this radical and nonreciprocal dependence that explains both the ontological "distance" between the world and God, and also why the world is intelligible only if God *is* entitatively immanent in it. Where Śaṁkara describes this divine presence in terms of the non-difference of the effect from its cause, Aquinas speaks of the effect "receiving the similitude of the agent not in its full degree, but in a measure that falls short"—a concept known as *participation*, which Aquinas borrows from his Neoplatonic sources, as Burrell recognizes:

> From pseudo-Dionysius he adopts the notion of causal participation, where creatures are said to participate not in the cause itself but in its "similitude" (since "creation is not a sort of divine expansion"), and "the similitude of the divine essence is multiplied and distinguished into many and diverse effects, each of them bearing a likeness in a distinct and partial way."[115]

This concept will be the focus of my discussion in the following chapter, but it is important to notice at this stage how deeply indebted Aquinas's metaphysics of divine originative causality is to the philosophical-theological thought-worlds of Neoplatonism. This is evident not only in his use of the language and the ontology of emanation and participation, but also in his striking use of the Neoplatonic *Liber de Causis* to explain what it means to say that God is the "cause of being."[116] As Burrell has noted, the strategy that this enigmatic text offered Aquinas was "a description of that emanation in which the One first created *being* [*esse* = "to-be"], and through this *being* everything else that is."[117] So, in his commentary on Proposition 4 ("The first of created things is being and there is nothing else created before it"), Aquinas affirms that created being is one since it is produced by God, but comes to be multiple because of the presence in it of intelligible forms.[118] This is clearly not a straightforward case of "making" something of a different nature, since the reason why "being" is the first created effect is because God is "to-be" and has the power to produce this effect: "For God himself is goodness itself and "to be" [*esse*] itself, encompassing virtually in himself the perfections of all beings."[119] It is, however, not a straightforward case of "begetting" either, since God "is" in a different way to which all effects "are," as Aquinas explains by citing Pseudo-Dionysius: "For God is not somehow existent, but he prepossesses the whole of being in himself in an absolute and uncircumscribed way."[120] In other words, God is entitatively immanent in the world in the non-contrastive sense that Being is what all effects have in common, but there is no ontological continuity or univocity as such because each being (*ens*) only "has" in a finite, limited, and particularized way what God unqualifiedly "is" (*esse*): "So, it is necessary that *the cause* be *in* the effect *in the mode* belonging to the effect and that the effect be in the cause *in the mode belonging to the cause*."[121] The nature of divine transcendence allows God to be fully immanent in the world without being straightforwardly identical to or ontically exhausted by it.[122] As Dionysius puts it, "It is not that He is this and not that, but that He is all, as the cause of all."[123] As I have argued throughout, the concepts of identity and distinction between creature and Creator are mutually implicating and mutually implicated.

Conclusion

The echoes of the *Liber de Causis* in some of Aquinas's best-known metaphysical tropes (e.g., that God is the First Cause, giving being [*esse*] to others by way of creation; that Being [*esse*] is the first created thing and the most proper effect of God; and that God is innermostly present in all things as their Cause, preserving each thing in being) are undeniable.[124] Although we should not exaggerate the specific role of this text in his formulation of these concepts (since many of these ideas were part of a common and developing intellectual heritage from antique pagan philosophy into medieval Christian theology), it is striking that Aquinas took the time toward the end of his life to write a detailed commentary on this Plotinian and Proclan-inspired Arabic work.[125] Perhaps what motivated him was the metaphysical structure it offered for explaining how God could, in a sense, be *in* all things without being pantheistically reduced to them.[126] For the first cause is not "Being" shared out among creatures, but "above being inasmuch as it is itself infinite "to be" [*esse*]."[127] Language cannot adequately describe this Cause, which is beyond any genus, but I have argued in this chapter that the unique manner of divine originative causality that Christians call "creation" is much closer conceptually to the Vedāntic idea of *satkāryavāda* than first appearances might suggest. I think that Christian theologians can speak of "entitative" divine immanence in the world without entailing straightforward consubstantiality, but I will only be able to defend this claim further through an examination in the next chapter of the metaphysics of divine ideas and participation in Aquinas.

It is interesting to note that Burrell attributes his own inquiry into the importance for Aquinas of the *Liber de Causis* to four distinct sources: Sokolowski's work on "the distinction"; Bernard McGinn's questioning of the juxtaposition of "emanation" and "creation"; his own reading of Eriugena and Eckhart and their use of Neoplatonic themes; and, finally, Sara Grant's work on Śaṁkara and non-duality (which, he says, began to dispel his fears of pantheism).[128] The common thread is that the distinction-and-relation between the world and God is a non-contrastive or *advaitic* one in which the "two" (world and God) are "not *other*, yet not the *same* either."[129] As I indicated in Chapter 1, the macrocosmic question: "How is God related to the created world?" can be answered by borrowing some language from fifth-century Christian attempts to answer the microcosmic question of how human and divine natures are related in the one person of Christ: the world and God are distinguished-and-related "without confusion, without change"—thus steering away from an undiluted pantheism,[130] and "without separation, without division"—thus moving away from a deistic dualism.[131] In the case of creation ex nihilo, as in the case of Chalcedon, then, we cannot pronounce clearly on what creation is, but only stutter about what creation is not.[132]

5 How Real Is the World?

BEING AND NOTHINGNESS IN ŚAṀKARA AND THOMAS

Despite differences of interpretation among Advaitins regarding the ontological status of the world, non-duality always refers to the unity of all being in the One. The world in all its multiplicity is never "outside" or external to its infinite simple Source nor can the two be added up as if they were entities in a series. The world exists by participation in the supremely Real, so that it may be said that while the two—the world and its Source—are distinct, they are not realities set apart.[1]

Introduction

In the previous chapter, I argued that Aquinas's understanding of the divine originative causality that Christians call creation ex nihilo is much closer conceptually to Vedāntic *satkāryavāda* than first appears to be the case. I also suggested that Christian theologians can speak of "entitative" divine immanence *in* the world without entailing straightforward con*substantiality* between the world and God. This is because what we call "world" and what we call "God" are distinguished-and-related *non*-contrastively such that all things are, in a manner of speaking, *not-other* than God but no-thing is *identical* with God either: the "two" (world "and" God) are neither separate nor the same.

For the Christian theologian, the ontological "difference" between the world and God consists in the fact that God could and would be God even without the world, whereas the world only exists at all *in relation to* its Creator.[2] In other words, God is ontologically self-standing, while the world exists because it is ontologically dependent on God. Hence, the Christian insists, there *is* an ontological difference between the two. The Advaitin also affirms that Brahman is infinite fullness of Being and, as such, that "the world" adds nothing to Brahman, but pushes this logic of infinity to its conceptual and linguistic limits by concluding that the world is, therefore, "unreal" in itself. Precisely *because* the world is entirely ontologically dependent on Brahman, it makes no sense to talk—from an ultimate perspective—of an ontological difference because there are not *really* "two" separate realities (God + ~~world~~) at all.[3] There would be genuine disagreement here only if the "ontological difference" of Christian theology entailed a dualism between two ontologically separate and self-standing realities (God + world), but, as we have seen repeatedly, this would be to misunderstand what it means to be God and what it means to be world. The fact that the world only exists in (dependence on) God means—to the Christian—that "God" and "world" cannot be ontologically identical (since God does not exist in dependence on the world) and simultaneously means—to the Advaitin—that they cannot be ontologically separate either. The language of non-duality allows us to see that both of these positions can be held coherently together without entailing any contradiction or disagreement at the level of fundamental ontology as opposed to the levels of, say, ritual worship or devotional practice. This is another case where *eadem est scientia oppositorum*.

In spite of the case I have made so far in this book for conceptual alignment between Christianity and Vedāntic Hinduism (as refracted through the specific understandings of creation / world production in Aquinas and Śaṁkara) it would, however, be misleading to give the impression that there are no areas of difference. In this final chapter, I want to suggest that there are limits to how far the case for convergence can be pushed, by examining what each tradition means by saying that the world—as effect—exists "in" God, its supreme cause (what I am calling *satkāryavāda*[b]). First, I will argue that Aquinas and Śaṁkara both have recourse to ostensibly similar metaphysical strategies to explain how the world is pre-contained in, "unfolds" out of, and continues to exist "in" God. They do this via the concepts of *nāmarūpa* (in Śaṁkara) and of divine Ideas (in Thomas). Second, I will explore the implications of these doctrines for the ontological status of the world and contend that Aquinas would agree that the world is metaphysically "unreal" in the carefully qualified senses in which that term is used by Śaṁkara. As Richard King puts it, even for a Christian, "on the last analysis God must be the sole ultimate reality, or at least be more real than the thing which he creates."[4] Indeed, King claims (and I would agree) that "any theistic belief system which accepts the absolute nature of God (i.e. divine omnipotence, omniscience, etc.), will inevitably shade into a form of pan-en-theism (all-in-divine-ism) when taken to its logical conclusion."[5]

True as that may be, Aquinas pulls back from the brink of dissolving the reality of the world straightforwardly into the reality of God because he does not want to let go of the real value of every individual creature precisely in its distinct particularity. While the Advaitic sensibility encourages the seeker to pierce through the "name and form" of the pot to see that all is ultimately clay, Aquinas wants to safeguard belief in a God who has counted every hair on our head and calls each sheep by name.[6] This concern for particularity is brought out in Aquinas's doctrine of participated being—a doctrine that would be difficult to assimilate, I think, into *advaitic* universes.

How Does the World Exist "in" Brahman? The Concept of *Nāmarūpa*

As we have seen, the Vedāntic conception of *satkāryavāda* entails that nothing ontologically new emerges in the production of the world (because the "clod of clay" / Brahman and "all that is made of clay" / the world are metaphysically *a-dvaita*). Śaṁkara argues that any apparent modifications of Brahman (viz. the objects and the events of the finite world) are not *ontologically* distinct entities but merely "name and form" (*nāmarūpa*), superimposed (*adhyāsa*) upon undifferentiated Being (e.g., calling the clay a "pot") and taken to be real through ignorance (*avidyā*).[7]

According to some scholars, however, there is a gradual hermeneutical shift discernible in the Advaitic tradition from seeing ignorance (*avidyā*) as an epistemological error to speaking of it (or cognate terms like *māyā*) as if it were an enigmatic some-*thing* out of which the world is produced.[8] We can detect the subtle quasi-substantializing of "*avidyā*" in the following verse from Sadānanda's fifteenth-century *Vedāntasāra*: "Consciousness associated with ignorance (*avidyā*), possessed of these two powers [viz. the power to conceal reality and to project illusion], when considered from its own standpoint is the efficient cause, and when considered from the standpoint of its *upādhi* or limitation is *the material cause* (of the universe)."[9] Here, the root cause (*avidyā*) of the appearance of a separate phenomenal world starts to look not so much like misconception due to ignorance (i.e., taking the world to have its own independent existence as a result of failing to distinguish between the eternal and the noneternal), but like a quasi-substantial entity out of which the world evolves. This principle increasingly came to be referred to as "*māyā*" (rather than *avidyā* or *nāmarūpa*),[10] which is why Advaita has for centuries been known as "*māyāvāda*"—especially by its critics.[11] While "*māyā*" had been used from Gauḍapāda on within the Advaita tradition to gesture to (if not explain) the enigmatic (non-)relation between Brahman and the world, Hacker claims that "only with [Śaṁkara's] disciples is the Advaita system a *māyāvāda* in the sense that it reflects on the nature of *māyā* and develops a theory of it. With them, indeed, *māyā* is sometimes much more the matter of concern than Brahman or liberation."[12] Rambachan goes so far as to call this focus on *māyā* a "post-Śaṅkarite myth"[13] and Pandey, similarly, regrets the "harm done by thinkers of the post-Śaṅkara era."[14]

The "harm done" by later disciples in the tradition must arguably be due to the disproportionate attention given to the precise nature and status of *māyā* (and its cognates) in their writings, which risks giving the impression that the Advaita tradition is primarily "about" ignorance and illusion, rather than about Brahman and liberation. As for the quasi-substantializing of ignorance, however, the seeds of this conceptual move can be traced back to Śaṁkara himself—except that he initiated it with the concept of *nāmarūpa*.[15] Although this term might also be thought to have a predominantly epistemological status (i.e., we superimpose "names" and "forms" onto undifferentiated reality when we call the clay a "pot"), Alston notes that Śaṁkara "much more commonly uses the term [*nāmarūpa*] in the singular in the same [cosmological] way as it is used in the older texts [viz. the Brāhmaṇas], where it implies a kind of unitary entity that unfolds into the many names and forms of the pluralistic universe."[16] When commenting upon *Bṛhadāraṇyaka* 1.4.7 ("this universe was then undifferentiated"), for example, Śaṁkara explains that the world "diversified through names and forms, was in the beginning in a state of latency [*bījāvasthā*], devoid of differentiation" prior to its manifestation.[17] Indeed, Śaṁkara sometimes explicitly refers to *nāmarūpa* as the "seed of the world," as in the following passage from the *Upadeśasāhasrī*:

> Brahman . . . is, by virtue of Its inscrutable power, the cause of the manifestation of unmanifested name and form which abide in the Self through Its very presence, but are different from It, which are the seed of the universe [*nāmarūpayor jagadbījabhūtayoḥ*], are describable nei-

ther as identical with It nor different from It, and are cognized by It alone.[18]

This seems precariously close to positing a kind of eternal prime matter that was somehow already present and "unmanifest" in Brahman, and which was then "unfolded" into the empirical world—a position that would have Śaṁkara teetering on the edge of an ontological dualism, which, as I argued at length in the previous chapter, Śaṁkara rejects.[19]

Hacker, however, sees no contradiction in Śaṁkara's use of the *nāmarūpa* concept, and, indeed, thinks that it fits perfectly with his understanding of *satkāryavāda*, because everything already exists in potential and nothing can come from nothing. Thus, Hacker explains that:

> For him [Śaṁkara] material cause and product are identical, and the object to be *effected*, already latent in the subject, is at the same time also the object to be *affected*. With his term *nāmarūpa* Ś[aṁkara] brought about the consummate expression of this theory. Material cause and product, which are identical, are even designated by the same word. That which is formed out of *(avyākṛte) nāmarūpe* at the same time develops into *(vyākṛte) nāmarūpe.*[20]

This is no doubt true, *but* (and it is a significant "but") this conceptual device still leaves Śaṁkara on the horns of a dilemma: on the one hand, *nāmarūpa* cannot be a material cause ontologically *independent* of Brahman because this independence would violate his non-dual interpretation of the *Upaniṣadic* texts; at the same time, however, empirical *nāmarūpa* (e.g., the "names and forms" of particularized pots, trees, people, and so on) cannot be straightforwardly *identical* to Brahman either because Brahman is eternal and immutable. Somehow, the "relation" must be a *tertium quid* in which *nāmarūpa* is *a-dvaita* with Brahman, even though Brahman is not really related to *nāmarūpa*.[21] As we have already seen in the discussion of *satkāryavāda*, Śaṁkara is only too aware of this difficulty, and seeks to dissolve it by taking perhaps the only route possible—namely, to claim that such a dilemma only exists from within the *vyāvahārika* (empirical or conventional) standpoint, conditioned by a false view of reality. In other words, there is no *real* transformation of Brahman, so all appearance of change is only perceived; *nāmarūpa*, whether in the "unmanifest" or the "manifest" state, are themselves the product of *avidyā*.[22] To be clear, although it is true *from a certain standpoint* to say that the particular pot exists in a state of latency in the clay before its manifestation and is then "unfolded" into the world as "this pot," there is, *ultimately*, no such ontological reality as "pot" separately identifiable from the clay—and never has been. This point, however, simply returns us to our question of the ontological status of the pot/world (or, which is the same point, of *nāmarūpa*): although the pot might not be *as* "real" as the clay, it is clearly not absolutely "unreal" in the sense of "nonexistent" either—so *how real* is it? Śaṁkara enigmatically describes the ontological status of *nāmarūpa* as *anirvacanīya*—indeterminable or inexpressible (as either identical to Brahman or as something other than Brahman):[23]

> It is *nāmarūpa* that constitutes the limiting adjunct of the Supreme Self, and in becoming manifest, *nāmarūpa* cannot be categorically stated as either a real thing (*tattva*), or as something else, analogous to [the relation between] foam and water.[24]

The analogy here is used to suggest that names and forms (viz. the pot or the world) can be empirically distinguished from their underlying reality (viz. the clay or Brahman) just as foam can be empirically distinguished from water, but that they are no more "categorically real" or "something else" than Brahman than the foam is really other than the water. Although the term *anirvacanīya* occurs in Śaṁkara's writings, it is chiefly later Advaitins who use it to express the ontological *indeterminability* of the world as either real or unreal (like the ontological status of the foam):

> Thus, *anirvacanīya* within the Advaita must be seen as directly related to name and form and in fact constitutes the definition of name and form as the explanatory principle of the origin of the world contained within the *avidyā* structure. The world then as *anirvacanīya* cannot be defined as existent or non-existent, as either one with Brahman or different from Brahman.[25]

The concept of an ontological category that cannot be described as either "being" or "nonbeing" (*sadasat*) can be traced further back, of course. As we saw in the previous chapter, the Ṛg Veda enigmatically describes the state prior to the origin of the world as "neither being nor nonbeing"[26] because "one cannot say that before its origin the world did *not* exist [because then, according to Vedāntic metaphysics, it never could exist] . . . however, one also cannot say that at that time there was *something*; for being has not yet arisen."[27] The paradox that we must always bear in mind, of course, is that, for Advaita, nothing ontologically distinct from Brahman ever *does* emerge, which means that the liminal status of the world "before" its appearance applies as much to its status now when it does phenomenally exist. As Hacker rightly says: "The world is also to be characterized as 'indeterminable' in relation to that which truly exists in itself, to *sat* or the self . . . Since in reality there is only one, indivisible Being, everything that exists, exists only insofar as it is endowed with the being of the One."[28] Before exploring this notion of the (un-)reality of the world any further, I want to look first at a possible parallel to the doctrine of *nāmarūpa* in Aquinas. In his use and development of the Platonic doctrine of Ideas, Aquinas seems to be saying something similar to Śaṁkara: that the world exists "in" God and "unfolds" into the manifest realm.[29]

Nāmarūpa in Thomas Aquinas? The Doctrine of Divine Ideas[30]

Aquinas's conviction that creation is the paradigmatic example of the dictum *omne agens agit sibi simile* means that it is true for Aquinas as well as for Śaṁkara that the world exists "in" God prior to its manifestation (in the sense that God has the power to produce it)—when it is in an unfolded "seed-state," as Śaṁkara would put it—just as it exists in God now (when the world is "manifest").[31] Śaṁkara articulates this "precontainment" of diverse effects in a single undivided cause via the concept of *nāmarūpa* and Aquinas via the concept of divine Ideas. We will see that Aquinas and Śaṁkara end up with strikingly similar understandings of *nāmarūpa* and divine Ideas because, somewhat intriguingly, the doctrines traveled in opposite directions on their historical hermeneutical journeys of "mediating" unity with multiplicity. The quasi-*ontologizing* of the *nāmarūpa* concept (expressed in terms of *avidyā* or *māyā*) in the Advaita tradition after Śaṁkara results in a notion similar to Plato's doctrine of Ideas in its ontological "thickness," whereas the gradual *de*-ontologizing of the Ideas in the Christian tradition means that we arrive, by the time of Aquinas, at a far more ontologically fragile concept, closer to Śaṁkara's understanding of *nāmarūpa*.[32]

The theory of a finite sensible world that is somehow dependent on an eternal intelligible realm of unchanging Forms or Ideas (*eidos*) is, of course, associated preeminently with Plato (ca. 428–ca. 348 BCE).[33] In the *Timaeus*, it is the Forms or Ideas to which the divine craftsman (*demiurge*) looks in order to shape the sensible world out of matter.[34] Like an artist who beholds an image in the mind and then fashions it after that intellectual archetype, the whole world reflects the intelligible Forms contemplated by the demiurge. What is more, these Ideas are themselves described by Plato as divine because they are "unconditioned, timeless realities" in which particular instances share.[35] It is also crucial to note that these Ideas are "causes or givers of being, in some sense, to the things of this world"[36] and that the distinction between them and their particular instantiations is a *non-contrastive* (and non-reciprocal) *meta*physical one, such that there is no opposition or separation between a Form and a particular.[37] As E. Perl puts it,

> Plato's understanding of reality as form, then, is not at all a matter of setting up intelligible forms in opposition to sensible things, as if forms *rather than* sensible things are what is real. On the contrary, forms are the very guarantee of sensible things . . . in virtue of which they are what they are and so are anything at all.[38]

By the time of Middle Platonism (ca. first century BCE–second century CE), Roman philosophers such as Cicero (106–43 BCE) and Seneca (4 BCE–65 CE), and the Hellenistic Jewish philosopher Philo of Alexandria (ca. 13 BCE–47 CE) had come to understand the Ideas as "intradeical"—that is, as thoughts *in* the mind (*logos*) of God.[39] The divine mind (*Logos*), which contained the intelligible Ideas was in an intermediate position between the transcendent Godhead and the sensible many.[40] This then led to the next stage in the development of the doctrine, which was the collapsing in toto of the divine Ideas into the divine mind.[41] (Neo-)Platonist thinkers like Plotinus (204–270 CE) insisted not only that the Ideas did not exist independently of the divine mind (as Plato seems to have held, in some sense at least),[42] but that they were, in fact, the essence of mind (*nous*) itself.[43] *Nous* does not think thoughts that are separate from itself (since it is eternally actual and does not stand to gain anything from outside), and is identical with its thoughts[44]—a doctrine influenced by Aristotle's notion of thought thinking itself.[45] Boland argues that this Plotinian synthesis of Platonism and Aristotelianism crystallized a crucial difference between two ways of understanding the divine Ideas: "the demiurgic notion that the Ideas are *in* the divine mind as God's thoughts and the Plotinian notion that the Ideas in the divine mind must *be* the divine mind."[46] Both of these hermeneutical strands can be found in St. Augustine (354–430 CE), whose understanding of the Ideas as divine exemplars (*rationes aeternae*) of created things would be directly influential on Aquinas.[47]

The problem for Christian thinkers was that, although the Ideas were no longer ontologically independent of the divine creator, they were nonetheless *real* and, therefore, really diverse (since they corresponded to the diverse objects of the sensible world into which they emerge). Neoplatonists like Plotinus and Proclus (412–485 CE) tackled the problem of how there can be multiplicity in the Absolute by making *nous* a second hypostasis below the supreme and strictly nondual unity of the One, which is beyond being. The Ideas were somehow latent (unmanifest or "un-unfolded") without multiplicity in the One (since all reality is pre-contained in the One), and only unfolded or manifested in *nous*. However, although a mediating Logos or *nous* provided one way, philosophically, of relating multiplicity to an indivisible unity, it became a problematic solution for Christian theologians who associated the Logos with Christ and yet wanted to avoid subordinating the Son to the Father.[48] As Boland puts it:

> The question of the multiplicity which this [i.e., identifying the Ideas with the divine mind] seems to introduce to the divine substance must be faced sooner or later. Plotinus' solution of subordinated hypostases is not available and Christians must face directly the question of a multiplicity of Ideas in the supreme principle.[49]

As we will see, this is a problem directly addressed by Aquinas. To help him solve it, the Christian authority he most frequently turns to, in addition to Augustine, is Pseudo-Dionysius and, specifically, the following passage:

> The exemplars of everything preexist as a transcendent unity within It [God]. It [God] brings forth being as a tide of being. We give the name of "exemplar" to those principles which preexist as a unity in God and which produce the essences of things. Theology calls them predefining, divine and good acts of will which determine and create things and in accordance with which the Transcendent One predefined and brought into being everything that is.[50]

For Dionysius, these exemplars are not merely paradigms but are, in some sense, aspects or attributes of the creator in which God wills creatures to share.[51] Given the simplicity of God, however, these exemplars cannot involve real multiplicity, but exist, as Dionysius puts it, "as a transcendent unity." The introduction of the language of "will" at this point alerts us to what Boland sees as "the fundamental difference between pagan and Christian neoplatonism—"[52] (i.e., the difference between voluntary creation in Christianity and some sort of necessitarian unfolding of the Ideas in pagan Neoplatonism). As I argued in the previous chapter, however, setting up creation in disjunctive opposition to emanation can be misleading—not least because it encourages an unhelpful bifurcation between the divine will (associated with creation ex nihilo) and the divine nature (associated with emanation). I will return to the ramifications of such a "will versus nature" paradigm in the conclusion to this chapter.

Given what I argued in Chapter 4 about Aquinas's reading of the *omne agens agit sibi simile* doctrine as entailing the pre-containment of an effect in its cause, it is perhaps unsurprising that he uses the metaphysics of divine Ideas to explain how the finite creaturely realm emerges.[53] Specifically, the divine Ideas provide a way of articulating how all being is pre-contained in God and how God knows all things.[54] Like the later Platonic tradition, Aquinas denies that the Ideas are realities in themselves, independent of God (as we have seen, he rejects any possibility of a creation *ex materia*),[55] but unlike Neoplatonist thinkers such as Plotinus and Proclus, he did not see the divine mind as some sort of lower hypostasis subordinate to God, but simply as Godself.[56] Aquinas was also an inheritor—and, indeed, synthesizer—of the two hermeneutical traditions we have seen within the intellectual history of the doctrine. On the one hand, he speaks of the Ideas existing *in* the mind of God: "In the divine mind, there are exemplar forms of all creatures, which are called Ideas, as there are forms of artefacts in the mind of an artisan."[57] On the other hand, these Ideas cannot be a "second something" existing as part of, limiting, or extraneous to, God, but must, in some sense, simply be *not-other than God*. As Doolan puts it: "Unlike the human artisan . . . whose Ideas are originally derived in some way from the external world, God's Ideas are not derived from anywhere other than himself. The divine Ideas, therefore, must somehow be present in his very essence."[58]

If, however, the Ideas are "in" God (but not as separate realities), such that they are—we might say—*a-dvaita* with God, the vexed question of how a multiplicity of Ideas can be reconciled with the simplicity of God again rears its head. As I have noted, the strategy of subordinating mind to God is not one that sits easily with orthodox Trinitarian Christianity, so Aquinas borrows the distinction we saw earlier in Dionysius to solve this problem. While the intelligible exemplars preexist in God in a singular way (since God's essence is simple), God knows this essence as imitable by different things in different ways. In other words, "The things that he [God] knows . . . do not exist in his intellect according to the same mode of distinction they have in themselves: in themselves, things exist separately in an essential way but not so in the divine intellect, just as things also exist materially in themselves but immaterially in the divine intellect."[59] This is a microcosmic example of what I have been emphasizing throughout this study: speaking about God is a "sui generis discourse" because God cannot be compared and contrasted with anything else.[60] So, while it is true that *omne agens agit sibi simile*, Boland is also right to point out that "if an agent is in no genus its effect cannot be like it either specifically or generically but only *secundum aliqualem analogiam*."[61] The divine Ideas are not simply "unfolded" pantheistically into the world because no created effect can "be" in the same unqualified manner that the infinite, unlimited plenitude of divine Being "is."[62] By the same logic, as we have seen, God cannot be *really* related to anything:

> The divine essence as known is the Idea of all things while the plurality of Ideas arises from the imperfect imitations of that essence which creatures are. Although the relation of God to the creature is not "real" in God, it is "notional" for us and so can be in God's mind too.[63]

There is, thus, no *real* diversity or multiplicity in the divine intellect because the Ideas simply are the divine Being *insofar as it can be imitated by finite creatures*.[64] Much more could be said about Thomas's understanding of the divine Ideas and the role they play in his theology, but I will bring this part of our discussion to a close with a passage in which he summarizes much of what I have been trying to elucidate:

> Inasmuch as He knows His own essence perfectly, He knows it according to every mode in which it can be known. Now it can be known not only as it is in itself, but as it can be participated in by creatures according to some degree of likeness [*similitudo*]. But every creature has its own proper species, according to which it participates in some degree in likeness to the divine essence. So far, therefore, as God knows His essence as capable of such imitation by any creature, He knows it as the particular type and Idea of that creature; and in like manner as regards other

creatures. So it is clear that God understands many particular types of things and these are many Ideas.[65]

I will return presently to what exactly Aquinas means by creatures "participating in some degree in likeness to the divine essence," but before that, I need to summarize where I have reached so far.

SUMMARY: NĀMARŪPA AND DIVINE IDEAS

In terms of parallels, it seems clear that Śaṁkara and Thomas have recourse to the metaphysics of *nāmarūpa* and divine Ideas for similar reasons—that is, to explain how the world preexists in and emerges out of the Absolute, and (which is to say the same thing in different words) to explain how multiplicity can come from unity. The diverse "names and forms" or Ideas that somehow "become" the sensible world are always already "precontained" in Brahman/God, the unlimited fullness of Being and reality. In Advaita, these names and forms are "unfolded" into finite material reality while remaining radically not-other-than Brahman; in Christian Platonism, particular created realities "participate" in their exemplar Forms that (at least for later pagan and Christian Platonists) are not-other-than the mind of God itself. Neither the Advaitin nor the Christian theologian wants to suggest that there is any real change or multiplicity in Brahman/God, so they avoid this implication by downplaying (albeit in different ways) the ultimate reality of the names and forms / Ideas. This is achieved by associating *nāmarūpa* with *avidyā* in Advaita (i.e., we only perceive and talk of names and forms anyway because of a spiritually naïve dualistic ignorance) and by distinguishing in Christian theology between the different ways or modes in which God (as simple unity) and creatures (as finite and particular) exist.[66]

There also seem to be significant differences in the two doctrines, however. While *nāmarūpa* in Advaita is essentially ephemeral and only provisionally real or true *sub specie temporis*, the divine Ideas, at least in Plato, are what are "really real" and the very guarantor of the reality of sensible objects.[67] In the later developments of this Platonic doctrine which put the multiple Ideas in the indivisible Mind of God, it would also be hard to straightforwardly equate these Ideas with (quasi-real) *nāmarūpa* in Advaitic understandings since there cannot be any second thing besides Brahman. It is tempting to conclude that the crux of the difference is that *nāmarūpa* was only ever intended to be a logical device, with a merely linguistic-conceptual reality, whereas the Platonic doctrine (at least as traditionally understood) is a metaphysical (and not purely epistemological) one in which the Ideas do enjoy some kind of ontological integrity. Nonetheless, as we have seen in Christian Platonists like Aquinas, these Ideas cannot be ontologically other to God either; like *nāmarūpa*, the Ideas must be—in some sense—*advaita* with God.

There are, however, potentially troubling implications for a Christian theologian pressing this line of argument: we seem to be teetering on the ontological abyss of suggesting that the world, which is virtually precontained in the divine nature, has very little (if any) ontological integrity of its own and that what a Christian thinks of as the created order is merely some sort of (necessary) unfolding of God. Indeed, the twin specters of pantheism and determinism were seen to pose enough of a threat historically that the doctrine of divine Ideas all but disappeared in Christian thought after Aquinas.[68] I sought to show in the previous chapter that the second part of this conclusion (necessary emanation) need not follow (and, in fact, only does so if we work with a particular anthropomorphic notion of freedom as God sequentially choosing between alternatives) and that finite creatures can be intimately and radically related to God without being some kind of Spinozistic modes that are metaphysically necessitated. The question of the relative *reality* of the finite realm, however, is yet to be fully addressed. In the following section, therefore, I will examine more closely the question of the (un)reality of the (created) world vis-à-vis Brahman/God in Advaitic and Thomist understandings.

The (Un)Reality of the World in Advaita Vedānta

> This plurality [viz. the empirical world] does not exist as identical to the Self [Ātman-Brahman], nor even does it somehow exist of its own accord. Those who know reality know that nothing exists different [from the Self] or as identical [to the Self].[69]

We are familiar by now with the distinction indicated here by Gauḍapāda: for the one who is liberated and "knows reality," non-difference from Brahman means that there is, metaphysically speaking, no empirical world to inquire about, and, hence, no "problem" in need of a solution.[70] Until we have come to see reality in such a way, informed by a proper metaphysical understanding of what *is*, however, the perceived reality of the phenomenal realm seems to cry out for an explanation. The fact that Advaitins have to navigate deftly between the Scylla of ontological dualism and the Charybdis of pure illusionism leads them, as we have seen, to explain the "difference" between Brahman and world as one only in "name and form," not in essential nature (as, for example, a "round clay pot" makes the essential nature of the clay itself neither "round" nor "pot-like")—a position that leaves the ontological status of the pot (i.e., "world") hovering mysteriously somewhere between being unequivocally real and utterly unreal. In the following section, I will address this seeming paradox (that the world exists, but that Brahman does not change into the world) by looking at precisely how Advaita distinguishes "real" from "unreal," and what "measure" of reality (if any) the tradition is willing to grant to the world. Much will depend, as we will see, on the "point of view" one adopts.

CRITERIA OF "REAL-ITY" IN ADVAITA

If Brahman alone is Real (*satya*), this is the same as saying that something is "Real" only if it, and insofar as it, corresponds to the divine *sat* (Being/Existence) that is Brahman.[71] In other words, in classical Advaita, "unqualified Reality" (*sat*) is infinite, simple, and unchanging—which is why the transient empirical world logically comes to be seen as not possessing the ontological plenitude of *sat*.[72] This leads Gauḍapāda, Śaṁkara, and Advaitins generally to the conclusion that origination, dissolution, and, indeed, change of any kind are, therefore, only *empirically perceived* and not a feature of fundamental reality.[73] This is why a further criterion of "reality" in Advaita is *causal independence*, since the unchanging is, by definition, uncaused. In his commentary on the verse from the *Bhagavadgītā* to which I referred earlier (2.16), Śaṁkara summarizes thus:

> There is no *bhāva*—no being, no existence—of the unreal (*asat*) such as heat and cold as well as their causes. Heat, cold, etc. and the causes thereof, which are (no doubt) perceived through the organs of perception, are not absolutely real (*vastu-sat*); for they are effects or changes (*vikāra*), and every change is temporary . . . Thus every effect is unreal because it is not perceived as distinct from its cause. Every effect, such as a pot, is unreal, also because it is not perceived before its production and after its destruction.[74]

Another way Advaitins tend to express this equivalence is to emphasize the difference between something that is "real" and therefore cannot be sublated (*abādha*)—because, as unchanging, no future experience of the "real thing" could falsify a previous experience of it—and things that are subject to change and are, therefore, sublatable by later experience.[75] In other words, my experience of a clay pot could be sublated by a later experience of seeing it in pieces after it has fallen off a table (in which case, I would no longer say there is a "pot"), but my experience of "clay" would remain the same whether it was still on the potter's wheel, baked in an oven, or shattered into small parts—it is always a cognition of clay.[76] This is why (according to Advaita), Āruṇi tells Śvetaketu that "all that is made of clay" is really "only clay" because the clay is never *really* transformed (*pariṇāma*) in its essence (i.e., its intrinsic nature, or *svabhāva*, does not change), but only in "appearance" (*vivarta*).[77] The apparent transformation only "arises from speech" (i.e., the clay is only a "pot" for the period of time we name it as such). When we perceive a "clay pot," then, Śaṁkara says that this cognition involves a "twofold consciousness"—" the consciousness of the real (*sat*) and the consciousness of the unreal (*asat*)"[78] and he goes on to explain that:

> the distinction of reality and unreality depends on our consciousness. Now, in all our experience, twofold consciousness arises with reference to one and the same substratum (*samānādhikaraṅa*) as "a cloth existent," "a pot existent" . . . Of the two, the consciousness of pot, etc., is temporary as was already pointed out, but not the consciousness of existence. Thus, the object corresponding to our consciousness of pot, etc., is unreal, because the consciousness is temporary; but what corresponds to our consciousness of existence is not unreal, because the consciousness is unfailing.[79]

In the same way that the pot is causally dependent on the clay (and, therefore, is "less" real), we can say that the clay is causally dependent on Existence or Being and is, in turn, "less" real than "*that*," which is Brahman. More importantly, what Śaṁkara is indicating through these analogies is that the empirical world *as such* (not just cloths and pots) is causally dependent on its hyper-ground and that the "distinction" between the empirical world (unreality) and the hyper-ground of being (Brahman) "*depends on our consciousness*"; they are not two ontologically separate or separable realities, any more than "existence" and "pot" are when we perceive an "(existent) pot." In the same way, "of the two," the consciousness of the empirical world is temporary, but not the consciousness of unqualified existence.[80] It is clear, then, that according to Advaitic (interrelated) criteria of "reality"—namely: (i) permanence/immutability, (ii) causal independence, and (iii) unsublatability, the objects corresponding to our experiences of the world (viz. the world) are metaphysically unreal, but "what corresponds to our consciousness of existence is not unreal."

The difficulty then, is how to speak of the reality-unreality of "two" things (clay and pot / world and Brahman) that are not substantially distinct (i.e., the pot just *is* the clay, and yet we still want to be able to speak of our experience of a "pot"). It seems either we know (and can speak of) the world but not Brahman, or we know (and can speak of) Brahman but not the world, and yet there "is-not-two."[81] The way out of this paradox taken by Śaṁkara is to be clear about the perspective from which we are looking. It is to this crucial aspect of Advaita that I will now turn.

DIFFERENT "LEVELS" OF REALITY

There are at least two "levels" or standpoints of reality recognized in Advaita:[82] an "absolute" (*pāramārthika sat*) level, from which all is experienced as *a-dvaita*;[83] and an empirical or "relative" level (*vyāvahārika sat*) from which change and duality are experienced. Within this second, *vyāvahārika* level, later Advaitins made a further distinction between that which is utterly non-real (*vikalpa*), like the son of a barren woman, and that which is illusorily real (*prātibhāsika*), like a mirage or a rope snake—the difference being that even an illusion has to have a substratum external to the cognizing subject in order to be experienced at all.[84] Thus, as Hacker explains, while the phenomenal world is *asatya* in relation to Brahman, it is *satya* in relation to an illusion within mundane experience (e.g., a rope snake) and even more so compared to utter non-reality (e.g., a square circle): in other words, much depends on one's frame of reference. Śaṁkara makes this point explicit in his commentary on aphorism 2.1.14 of the *Brahma-sūtra*:

> Assuming, for the sake of argument, an *empirical* difference between the experiencer and the things experienced, the refutation (under the previous aphorism) was advanced by holding that "the distinction can well

> exist *as observed in common experience*." But *in reality*, this difference does not exist, since a non-difference between the cause and effect is recognized. The effect is the universe . . . and the cause is the supreme Brahman. *In reality* it is known that the effect has non-difference from, i.e. non-existence in isolation from, that cause.[85]

Even Śaṁkara, then, admits that the phenomenal world of change and duality exists from an empirical point of view, but the mistake, cognitive as well as spiritual, that is recognized from the transcendental perspective, is to see it as existing separately from its source.[86] Indeed, if the empirical world is *a-dvaita* with Reality, even talking of the "unreality of the empirical world" as if it were something *different* from Brahman/Reality is somewhat paradoxical.

We must, then, bear two things in mind when reading Advaitic texts: while, in the final analysis, the world is not-other-than Brahman, the fact that we usually do not perceive it this way means that two different perspectives on R/reality emerge, and we must be alert to the perspective from which any given statement is made if we are not to misunderstand it.[87] As Hacker rightly says, "Only for the wise or enlightened is the world unreal; for the unenlightened person who lives in the world, its reality remains unshaken. The concept of unreality is therefore relative, depending on the standpoint of the knower."[88] The "difference" is not in Brahman, but in our "consciousness" or vantage point.[89]

DEGREES OF REAL-ITY IN DIFFERENT ADVAITINS

Early Advaitins[90] like Gauḍapāda and Śaṁkara were careful to distinguish different "levels" in our understanding of reality (chiefly, the transcendental and the empirical) as a concession to the seeker who is still stuck within a worldly perspective, but they did not really develop a theory of "gradations" of reality—from more real to less real—precisely because their whole point was the nonduality of Reality. The question of just what this means for the ontological status of the world, however, would not go away, and Advaitins from Sureśvara (ca. 900 CE) onward found themselves driven by intra-Vedāntic polemic and apologetics to spell out their position with increasing subtlety.[91] When one puts the tradition under a conceptual microscope, it is therefore possible to detect slightly different emphases, such that the question of whether the world can be considered "real" becomes more properly a question of *how* real it is in the treatment of different Advaitins. This is why Barua argues that

> Advaitins . . . can be placed on a *conceptual* spectrum ranging from the affirmation that the world has some "measure" of phenomenal reality (what we shall call the Weak Advaita of, for instance, the fourteenth century Advaitin Prakāśātman) to the denial that the world possesses any "degree" of phenomenal substantiality whatsoever (what we shall call the Strong Advaita of, for instance, the seventeenth century Advaitin Prakāśānanda).[92]

This spectrum is often depicted in secondary literature as a more general post-Śaṁkara division of the Advaita tradition into two loosely defined sub-schools, named after their typical way of characterizing the reality of the empirical self (i.e., in "distinction" from the *ātman*, which is pure consciousness).[93] Thinkers like Padmapāda (ca. 900 CE) and his commentator, Prakāśātman (ca. 1300 CE), who would later be viewed as representatives of the so-called *Vivaraṇa* school, focus resolutely on the *oneness* of Brahman, and therefore describe the finite self/empirical world merely as a kind of "reflection" (*pratibimbavāda*). As a consequence, they seem to resolutely downplay the reality of the empirical world as far as they can go, which is why Barua refers to this as "Strong Advaita." In contrast, the *Bhāmatī* school, represented by figures like Vācaspati Miśra (ca. 900 CE)[94] describe individual selves as being like jars that "contain" or "limit" the space (analogized with *ātman-brahman*) that is "in" them and all around them (*avacchedavāda*).[95] Although the purpose of this analogy is clearly to highlight the illusory nature of any real distinction between the space "inside" the jars and the space "outside" them (i.e., between finite selves and the Self), the image seems to imply more of a willingness to attribute some degree of reality, albeit only gossamer-like, to the empirical world, which is why Barua calls this "Weak Advaita." Finally, some later Advaitins analyze the phenomenal world in terms of constructions by perception, thus going even further down the spectrum of "Strong Advaita" than the "reflectionists" had. In the most straightforwardly "idealist" of any of the post-Śaṁkara thinkers, Prakāśānanda (ca. 1600 CE), "the world-appearance has no reality whatsoever, all talk of causation or production is substantively ungrounded, and Brahman is the sole reality."[96]

It is interesting to note how far we *seem* to have come since Śaṁkara to arrive at Prakāśānanda.[97] Although the basic problem remains the same (i.e., that of reconciling the *Upaniṣadic* teaching of One changeless Brahman with the evidence of the senses, which imply a manifold and changing phenomenal world), it could be argued that the tradition tied itself up in dialectical knots in the intervening 800 or so years—ironically, by taking too seriously the very empirical "ignorance" that is ultimately to be sublated.[98] Śaṁkara's own enigmatic refusal to enter into these sorts of "Scholastic" discussions should alert us to the risks of becoming entangled in what are—from an Advaitic soteriological perspective—little more than distracting pseudo-problems.[99]

The (Un)Reality of the World in Christian Theology

We have seen that in Advaita the immutability and the metaphysical independence of Brahman are held up as the measuring stick of Reality. As such, only that which is independent of, and unlimited by, anything else; which is indivisible and unchanging; one and eternal, is "really real."[100] This is what De Smet means when he says that Śaṁkara "is a radical valuationist who measures everything to the absolute Value, the Brahman, and declares its inequality to it rather than the degree of its participation in it."[101] Compared to Brahman—the "really Real"—the world is relatively unreal (*asat*), albeit not utterly nonexistent or a mere figment of our imaginations.[102] Again, to be clear, this is because Brahman is the ontologically stable ground on which the world depends. De Smet sums up Śaṁkara's position as follows:

> He said this: that man and the world cannot be truly comprehended apart from, and independently of, God, for they depend entirely upon him as upon their total cause; that since they are totally his effects, they are nothing by themselves, yet by him they are in their own imperfect way what he is in his own most perfect way; and that, therefore, they are neither sheer non-being nor being in the highest sense of the term (*sad-asad-vilakṣaṇa*).[103]

No Christian theologian is likely to object to the Advaitic characterization of ultimate Reality as one, simple, eternal, unchanging, etc., but they might be more reluctant to use the language of *unreality* when it comes to the world. In this section I want to examine the possible reasons for such reluctance and to ask how far a Christian theologian, if pushed, could agree with the Advaitin that the world is metaphysically "unreal."

If "unreal" is used in contrast to the supreme reality of God, it would be hard to see how a Christian who defends "perfect being theology" could disagree that the world is unreal. It is, after all, lacking in the intrinsic divine characteristics that would make it unequivocally real: seen from an empirical perspective, the world is changing, transient, temporal, and complex.[104] Its radical relation of dependence on God, established and maintained by creation, means that creatures apart from God are, in Upadhyay's favorite phrase, *tenebrae, falsitas et nihil.*[105] Johanns, likewise, agrees that the world does not have its "own" being or independent reality,[106] and that, therefore, "[w]hen there is question of what the world is by itself, in itself, and for itself, the answer must always be that it is nothing, thorough unreality."[107] De Smet points out that authorities whose orthodox credentials can hardly be doubted, such as Augustine, Anselm, Bonaventure, and Aquinas also used this sort of language—but in moderation, "for it can mislead the untrained mind."[108] In fact, the history of doctrine suggests that talk of the "unreality" of the world in Christian contexts can be heady stuff even for minds that *are* highly theologically trained. The twenty-sixth article of Meister Eckhart's teaching, which was found, after careful examination by the Magisterium "to contain the error or stain of heresy as much from the tenor of [its] words as from the sequence of [its] thoughts"[109] runs as follows:

> All creatures are one pure nothing. I do not say that they are a little something or anything, but that they are pure nothing.[110]

Eckhart was unrepentant in his defense, moreover, citing John 1.3 in support ("All things were made through him, and without him was made nothing"), and even argued that "to say that the world is not nothing in itself and from itself, but is some slight bit of existence is open blasphemy. If that were so, God would not be the First Cause of all things and the creature would not be created by God in possessing existence from him."[111] As Eckhart states so clearly, the conclusion that the world is ontologically unreal in itself—a pure *nihil*—is simply the logical (and, one might think, uncontroversial) entailment of a standard Christian understanding of creation: the world would *not-be* if it were not related at every moment to its grounding reality-giving cause. Yet, as Burrell points out, "most varieties of "Christian philosophy," and most notably "Thomism," succeeded in avoiding this implication [i.e., the world is nothing *in itself*] for centuries, spooked as they were by the specter of 'pantheism' or 'monism.'"[112] I will now turn to examine these concerns and Aquinas's ways of mitigating them.

PROBLEMS WITH THE LANGUAGE OF UNREALITY IN CHRISTIAN THEOLOGY

I hope I have made it clear enough by now that it is not necessary to interpret non-dualism (even with references to the world as "nothing" or as unreal) as illusionistic monism (indeed, that it would be incorrect to interpret Śaṁkara—let alone Thomas—in this way). I have argued, rather, that, in both Christian and Vedāntic contexts, it is true to say that "there is no such *ontologically-separate-from-God* thing as world" (i.e., world and God are *a-dvaita*) and that it is appropriate for a Christian theologian to describe the God-world dialectic as a form of pan-*en*-theism ("all-in-God-ism").[113] I do not think, therefore, that having a keen sense of the *relative* unreality of the world need raise pantheistic or monistic fears for Christian theologians.

However, the language of unreality does raise a different challenge. If Brahman is unlimited *(ananta)* plenitude of Being (*sat*) and the spiritual-experiential "goal" of the Advaitin is to become aware of the relative *unreality* of the physical world of name and form (i.e., to become aware that all "this" is, ultimately, Brahman),[114] we might wonder what purpose and value the dependent world has at all. This question could equally be posed to the Platonist, whose aim is similar—to ascend out of the cave to see things as they really are, that is, to see the intelligible Forms or Ideas of things (in and through those things).[115] It might be pointed out, in response, that it is only ignorance (*avidyā*) that causes us mistakenly to treat the physical world as if it were a subsistent reality that is nothing more than "what meets the eye" and that the language of liberation/salvation (whether in pagan Greek, Indic, or Christian contexts) is often couched in spatial metaphors that should not be taken literally. The "really real" does not, in other words, exist "somewhere else" but is right in front of our eyes, if we can only see it as such. This is the point King makes:

> The Non-difference model also allows Advaita Vedānta to avoid the criticism that it is world-denying; the world in fact is Brahman! On this model one can conceive of liberation as the transfiguration of the world through the Brahman-realisation . . . The classic Advaita Vedānta view

> is that Brahman is the sole reality. The created world is empirically real (being practically efficacious), but is not ultimately real; or perhaps one might say that the world is real insofar as it is really Brahman.[116]

Even if not "world-denying," though, the language of "liberation" and "transfiguration" surely suggests that there is a deeper reality than the purely physical. Although this might be trivially true for anyone who would describe themselves in any way as "religious," Christianity has to tread a thin line between a materialistic reductionism and a Gnostic spiritualism (not least because of its emphasis on incarnation and sacramentality). At the risk of oversimplification, I could argue that this is why Christian philosophical theology has sought to hold together Aristotelian and Platonic instincts (matter and form; particular and universal; temporal and eternal; finite and infinite, etc.) in a creative tension—and there are few better examples of this "hylomorphic" structure of Christian doctrine than the work of Thomas Aquinas.

One particular danger is that the more the Platonizing strands in Christian theology are accentuated—as I have tentatively been doing in this book—the more they risk downplaying the ultimate value and the distinctive particularity of the embodied creature. This same risk is posed, mutatis mutandis, by pressing the argument for convergence between Thomism and Advaita. Even Grant admits that, in spite of the broad agreement she argues for between Śaṁkara and Aquinas on the question of the distinctive relation between the world and God, there remains a difference of emphasis that is reflective of their respective traditions:

> it is undeniably true that while reading Śaṅkara the "searcher into majesty" is so "overwhelmed with glory," as the Imitation of Christ puts it, that his own finite selfhood fades into insignificance—so much so that even today it remains an open question whether or not Śaṅkara personally believed in the ultimate survival of the individual as such. Most commentators would probably say he did not. In Thomas, on the other hand, what holds the attention is the flowing-out (*emanatio*) and return of creatures from and to God their Source and End, in all their rich diversity.[117]

In other words, even if an Advaitin is willing to accept the *relative* reality of the world, its status as real has much less incarnational significance than it does for many Christian theologians. Grant is perhaps correct that this is more a difference in emphasis than it is a substantive metaphysical disagreement (for the world is *empirically* real for Advaita), but it is a noteworthy difference nonetheless. I would, therefore, agree with McGinn that "the issue of the reality of matter and history . . . [is] a far more serious problem for Christian Platonism [and Christian Advaita] than that of supposed pantheism."[118]

This problem is exacerbated by the doctrine of divine Ideas if this doctrine is taken to mean that the effect in the cause (i.e., the Idea in God) is *more real* than the material manifestation or unfolding of the Idea. For Plato, the intelligible Forms certainly are "more real" than sensible particulars[119] and a full-blooded Christian Platonist (or Christian Advaitin) would surely be drawn to similar conclusions: that the (eternal, immutable) intelligible Ideas in God are more robustly real than their (temporal and changing) embodied instantiations. This seems to be the case for Eckhart, and perhaps accounts for the suspicion aroused by his insistence on the nothingness of the creature, for he follows the dialectical logic of the creature-Creator relation to its inevitable (Platonic) end:

> In so far as God's existence is existence in the fullest and absolute sense of the word, in comparison with which the existence of creatures is best seen as nonexistence, that mode of existence which creatures have in God is more real, by far, than their existence in themselves as finite entities.[120]

This does not mean that particular creatures or the world at large do not exist at all, but that their "virtual" (and undivided) existence in God is what is *most* real. This is why Eckhart can speak of "the fundamental *identity* of God and creature when the creature is viewed in terms of its ground."[121] Hayes summarizes Eckhart's position as follows:

> What "I" am in the deepest sense is identical with what "I" am in my virtual existence in God. There is a precreational oneness of the creature with God which constitutes the truest reality of the creature.[122]

This is perhaps as clear a statement of Christian Advaita as there can be—but is it still recognizably *Christian*? What is the telic value of history and eschatology if my beginning is also my end—if I always already "was" and "am" what I will "become"?[123] Is salvation simply a case—as it is for the Advaitin—of "accomplishing the accomplished"[124] and of realizing our presently established ontological (and not eschatological) at-*one*-ment with God? Is this uncovering of what we essentially are what it means to say that Christ has redeemed the world? Hayes' concern is that while Christian Platonists (and, we could add, Christian Advaitins) can be exonerated from the charge of pantheism, "it is not clear: 1) what sort of world they best account for, and 2) what difference the existence of the world makes in the final analysis."[125] He is right, I think, that the key questions raised by the coming together of Christian theology and (Neo-) Platonism (and Advaita Vedānta) are, as McGinn also indicates, those associated more generally with philosophical *idealism*, rather than those associated with pantheism.[126]

I raise these questions in a deliberately speculative and open-ended manner for I cannot pursue them fully here.[127] What I can do, however, is to show whether they are applicable to Thomas—for our main focus, after all, has been on the degree to which Aquinas's metaphysics of creation can be considered non-dualistic. I will return, then, in the final part of this chapter, to Aquinas's understanding of divine Ideas and ask whether, as in Eckhart, they are "more real" than their sensible instantiations (i.e., the material world).

AQUINAS ON THE REALITY OF FINITE CREATURES: DIVINE IDEAS AND PARTICIPATION[128]

Doolan points out that Thomas never really asks himself the question: "Are the Ideas or sensible objects 'more' real?"[129] but his awareness of the nature of the distinction is clear when he says that "Plato held that the separate Man was the true man (*verus homo*), whereas a material man is man by participation."[130] It is important here to remember what we earlier saw Aquinas saying—things exist in God in a different way from which they exist in themselves: "Hence, something that is in God exists in him according to an uncreated *esse* (*per esse increatum*). By contrast, the thing exists in itself according to created *esse* (*per esse creatum*), in which there exists less truth of being than exists in uncreated being."[131] This sounds like Thomas is saying (like Eckhart) that creatures *do* exist "more truly" in God (*per esse increatum*) than they do in themselves (*per esse creatum*). In *De Veritate*, he makes the same point by way of a further distinction, explaining that "as regards logical truth [*veritas praedicationis*], something exists more truly in its essence than where it exists by a likeness [*verius est aliquid ubi est per essentiam quam ubi est per similitudinem*]. As regards ontological truth [*veritate rei*], however, it exists more truly through the likeness that is its cause."[132] Since the divine essence is the likeness [*similitudo*] of every created thing (because created perfections exist first and foremost in God and only analogically in creatures), Thomas is saying that the world exists, in an ontological sense, more truly in God, its cause. Indeed, in God, things are not-other than the divine essence.[133] This, quite clearly, is an iteration of *satkāryavāda*. Aquinas admits that a particular creature exists more in itself as regards "logical truth" (*veritas praedicationis*) because a particular material horse is more properly *called* "a horse" than is the Idea of it. Nevertheless, its logical truth is dependent on its ontological truth (*veritas rei*), because, while in the case of human knowledge it is the particular object that makes our knowledge of it true, in the case of God's knowledge, it is the other way around: the object enjoys any truth and reality it has *because* God knows it (as we saw previously, a divine Idea is God's knowledge of God's essence as imitable in diverse analogical ways).[134] As such, Thomas's final position on our question is a complex one:

> Thomas's replies to the objections in *De veritate* q. 4, a. 6 appear to suggest, in a certain respect, an affinity between himself and Plato regarding what constitutes the really real. Nevertheless, as is frequently the case for Thomas, his stance in fact entails both *sic et non*. Although he offers a qualified Platonic *sic* in reply to these objections, the replies that he provides in response to the *sed contra* arguments from the same article offer an Aristotelian *non*.[135]

This Aristotelian *non* is particularly clear in Q.18 of the ST where Aquinas admits that if what it meant to be a creature consisted entirely in that creature's intelligible *form*, then the creature would certainly exist more truly in God than in itself.[136] However, although it is true that *esse increatum* (God) exists more than *esse creatum* (creatures)—which is, according to the leitmotif I have developed throughout this book, with its emphasis on the non-reciprocal relation of dependence, uncontroversially true—what it means to be *this* particular creature is *not* just a question of form. Thus, Thomas nuances his earlier comments, as Doolan explains, by noting that

> as regards *this esse* (*esse hoc*)—such as a man or a horse—natural things have *esse* more truly in their own nature than in the divine mind. For, as he explains, it belongs to the truth of what man is to have *esse* in a material way (*esse materiale*), a mode of being that man does not have in the divine mind. Similarly, he observes, a house has a more noble mode of being in the mind of the artisan than it does in matter, and yet, Thomas

> insists, the house in matter is more truly said to be a house than the one that exists in the artisan's mind because the latter is only a house in potency whereas the former is a house in act.[137]

In other words, it is not straightforwardly true to say, for Aquinas, that I exist more in God's Idea of me than I do in myself because God gives me (as a material being) my own existence (*actus essendi*). By emphasizing existence as well as essence, Aquinas's point is that I only *really* exist "as me" in this embodied hylomorphic state, imperfect as it may be. This is also why Thomas insists that God has Ideas of individually existing creatures. In other words, God has an Idea of Peter that is separate and distinct from the Idea of Paul—not merely a universal Idea of "Man."[138] It is here, Boland claims, that "Saint Thomas 'shows his hand' as a thinker who prefers an Aristotelian to a Platonist ontology."[139] His emphasis on particularity is also motivated by what his faith demands—namely,

> that God's bestowal of *esse* means he is responsible for everything there is in things, that God's knowledge therefore extends to the very least traces of existing things, that divine providence includes within its concern the last and least details of the created world, "drops of rain and grains of sand."[140]

Rather than "preferring" an Aristotelian ontology to a Platonist one, however, I would suggest that Thomas skillfully manages to hold the two together. Indeed, it is his skillful reworking of the (Neo-)Platonic metaphor of "participation" that allows him to preserve the integrity of each individual existing thing.[141]

As we saw in Chapter 1, a "being" (*ens*), in Aquinas's understanding, is not an essence to which existence (*esse*) is subsequently "added" but something that is intrinsically defined in-relation-to *esse*. In other words, without existence (*esse*), there simply is "no-thing." This is why it would be wrong to picture the divine Ideas as "essences" that are lingering in an ontic limbo from which they may or may not be later summoned into full-blooded existence. They exist in God in the mode appropriate to the divine nature and in themselves in the mode appropriate to finite creatures. Any degree of existence and reality the creature enjoys is limited by its essence (by what it means to be "that creature") whereas existence in God (who is *ipsum esse subsistens*) is entirely unlimited.[142] Thus, to return to our language of unreality, Thomas is clear that—relative to God—the creature is "almost nothing at all" (*quasi nihil*).[143] While this sounds similar to the language of unreality in Advaita, the doctrine of participation introduces a subtle difference between Thomas and Śaṁkara. Both would agree that the finite order is inherently dependent on God for its very being, and could, in that sense, be described as *advaita* with God, but Thomas's emphasis on creaturely being as a divinely willed, and divinely sustained, participation in God's being seems to accord the finite realm its own integrity, not just provisionally (*vyāvahārika*) but also in an ultimate sense (*pāramārthika*).

Participation (*methexis*) by its very nature suggests a *partial* sharing.[144] A creature may be dependent on God, but could never be said simply to *be* God. As Aquinas puts it: "The effects of God do not imitate Him perfectly, but only as far as they are able; and the imitation is here defective, precisely because what is simple and one, can only be represented by diverse things."[145] This has, as Te Velde notes, both positive and negative connotations for finitude—the creature bears some likeness to God through participation, but the creature is not God since its existence is "borrowed" rather than coterminous with its very essence.[146] If, as I have argued throughout this book, De Smet and Grant are correct to insist that Advaita is not the same as ontological illusionism, there might appear to be no disagreement here between participation in Thomas and "identity" in Śaṁkara. After all, we have seen that "identity" even in Advaita means, when parsed carefully, not that "I = God" but that "I cannot exist without God." This seems to be the very heart of Aquinas's understanding of participated being. Nevertheless, it is hard to imagine Śaṁkara talking about the proverbial pot as a "limited sharing" in the reality of the clay because this would be to give too much ontological weight to the pot—just as it would be hard to imagine Aquinas talking about an individual creature merely as a "name and form." For the former, the preferred locution is "the *clay* that somehow appears as a pot," whereas the latter, especially in writings on the incarnational, soteriological, and ecclesiological dimensions of the faith, would speak of "the *pot* that truly participates in the clay." Again, for the former, the pot cannot be ultimately real because it is "dependently real," but for the latter, it is precisely because the pot is "dependently real" that its ultimate reality-in-God is transcendentally secured, preserved, and redeemed by God. For Aquinas in these Aristotelian moments, "creatures form a substantial reality with a proper consistency and as existing in themselves they have their own specific truth *which cannot be simply reduced to the higher truth in their origin*,"[147] whereas spiritual progress in Advaita surely means precisely the opposite (i.e., seeing that the truth and reality of the finite realm is indeed reducible to the higher truth of Brahman). Perhaps the only way we could decisively settle the question of whether there is a substantive *ontological* (as opposed to a linguistic or epistemic) difference between Advaita and Thomism would be to see things from God's own perspective: whether this is Brahman or the Triune God. Of course, this is not an impossible goal, whether for the *jīvanmukta* or for the blessed saints in Christian heaven, and both ends simply mean recognizing who "I" am in my deepest nature—but here I can only meet this question with humble silence.

Conclusion: Much Ado about Nothingness?

In Chapter 4, I examined Thomas's understanding of the Christian doctrine of creation ex nihilo and Śaṁkara's explanation of world production by *satkāryavāda*, and concluded that, in spite of prima facie linguistic differences, there was no fundamental conceptual disagreement between them. In this chapter, I have probed further into what exactly it means to talk about the world (pre-)existing in Brahman/God and have argued for parallels as well as differences.

In terms of parallels, both Śaṁkara and Thomas have recourse to strikingly similar metaphysical strategies to explain how a world of diverse and particular objects can be pre-contained in and emerge out of an Absolute principle that is one and undivided. Śaṁkara does this via the concept of *nāmarūpa* and Thomas via the Platonic notion of divine Ideas. Similar questions arise in each case of how there can be real multiplicity in God and of how *nāmarūpa*/Ideas are related to God/Brahman and to the world—and it is here that certain differences (at least in emphasis) become apparent.

Although some scholars have argued for a gradual quasi-substantializing of *nāmarūpa* in the hermeneutical developments of the Advaita tradition, Śaṁkara described the ontological status of these "names and forms" as *anirvacanīya* (indeterminable as either real or unreal). They cannot be substantivally real because this would introduce real multiplicity and division into Brahman, but they are not totally unreal either since they account for the empirically perceived world of diversity and change. In short, *nāmarūpa* are neither identical with Brahman nor ontologically separate—the relation is an *advaitic* one.[148]

In a similar way, Aquinas understands the divine Ideas as exemplars of the material world. The Ideas "exist" in God and, insofar as they are not-other than the divine essence, can be said simply to *be* God. There is, however, no real multiplicity in the divine nature because the Ideas exist in God in the mode appropriate to God (*per esse increatum*) and in creatures in the mode appropriate to creatures (*per esse creatum*). God's knowledge, moreover, is not merely speculative but productive, because God's knowledge of the Ideas does not depend on the Ideas, but vice versa: any truth and reality enjoyed by the Ideas is owed precisely to the fact that God knows them. In this sense, it would be a mistake to picture God thinking the Ideas and "then" bringing them into being in a kind of two-stage creative process. God grants existence to a thing by the very act of thinking it.

In the light of their understandings of *nāmarūpa* and divine Ideas, I also argued that Thomas could largely agree with Śaṁkara that the world is unreal in itself. Ontological commitment, founded on scripture, to a single enduring Reality (*ātman-brahman*) whose nature as unchanging, uncaused, and unsublatable becomes the standard against which "Real" is measured makes it difficult for Advaita to accord any substantial reality to the empirically perceived world of manifold change. We can speak somewhat meaningfully of this phenomenal realm, nevertheless, owing to the concession within the tradition to conceptual standpoints (the *pāramārthika* and the *vyāvahārika*). This allows us to talk about the world as at least "empirically" real (i.e., within its own conceptual domain), and different Advaitins emphasize this "provisional" reality more or less than others. Few take the ultimate unreality / falsity (*mithyā*) of the world to mean that it is entirely fictitious or a bundle of mental projections. On the other hand, it cannot be denied that from the transcendental perspective of Brahman (which is the soteriological goal/foundation of Advaita), all change and duality is said to be absent/sublated. This brings us back again to the more general philosophical principle in Vedāntic metaphysics of *satkāryavāda* and its implication that an effect is ontologically subordinate to its cause because it cannot exist independently of it (i.e., an effect does not have its "own nature" in the way a cause does).

There is not much here that a Christian theologian—if pushed—could disagree with. Just as for Śaṁkara the effect is non-different (*an-anyat*) from the cause,[149] so too, for Aquinas, "The creature is no part of the essence of God but its essence is from God" (*non est ex essentia Dei sed est ex Deo essentia*).[150] Both the Thomist Christian and the Advaitin could surely agree, therefore, that the relation between the world and God is well encapsulated by the Vedāntic notion of *tādātmya*—the creature has its "self" in God. As I have been arguing throughout this study, "[t]he language of theism emphasizes the distinction between God and the world . . . however, it is not possible to speak of 'distinction' without 'identity.' For him [Aquinas], 'distinction' is not a descriptive term by which God is somehow located *there*, over and against the world *here*, as if God occupies a certain region of reality. Distinction (God is not the world) goes together with identity (God is the world in some sense)."[151]

Nevertheless, it is hard to deny that there is a greater emphasis in Christian theology than there is in traditional Advaitic exegetical streams on the relative *reality* of the created order.[152] Aquinas develops the doctrine of divine Ideas in ways that would be difficult to directly transpose onto Advaitic understandings of *nāmarūpa*, for example, due to his concept of ontological participation, which is not really found in Śaṁkara. This allows Aquinas not only to affirm that there are individual divine Ideas of each creature but also that the creature, in a sense, exists more—*as a creature*—in itself than it does in God. It would be hard to imagine Śaṁkara talking about individual things or persons in this uncompromising way since it is precisely their empirically differentiating characteristics of "name and form," which must be sublated on the spiritual path. In other words, although, for Thomas, God knows Peter as distinct from Paul, and this irreducible particularity encapsulated in the divine milieu is soteriologically significant, the truth from an Advaitic point of view is that such empirical distinctions do not exist from a transcendental perspective, where there are no fine-grained haecceities and all *is* Brahman.

It is, perhaps, Aquinas's use of the language of *participation* rather than "identity" (as in Eckhart) that marks the thin line between acceptable Christian God-talk and suspicion-arousing heresy.[153] Whereas Aquinas veers back from the brink and describes the creature as "*almost* nothing" (*quasi nihil*—cf. fn.143), Eckhart bites the ontological bullet and provocatively calls the world a "pure nothing."[154] Indeed, the more we focus on metaphysical doctrines such as divine Ideas and *satkāryavāda*, the more the emphasis falls on the divine nature (as opposed to divine *fiat*) and the closer we get to seeing the world as a production *ex deo*, intimately and radically ontologically related to its creator. As Burrell reminds us, "'Nonduality' is the paradoxical term invented to articulate this constituting relation whereby each thing's *to-be* (*esse*) is a *to-be-towards* (*esse-ad*)."[155] The risk this entails of blurring the distinction between the world and God seems to have been worrying enough for certain figures in the Christian tradition that the whole notion of Ideas virtually (though not completely) disappeared after Aquinas, to be replaced with a strong emphasis on the divine will as the explanation for why there is a world at all.[156] This voluntarist downplaying of the Ideas (as in figures like Duns Scotus and William of Ockham) comes at a cost, however. It can lead to a theologically suspect opposition between God's nature and God's will and—most perniciously—to a spiritually stultifying caricature of God as an entity separate from the world rather than as the sustaining ground of our very being.[157]

Conclusion

> Realization . . . does not involve an abandonment of the world in any pessimistic or destructive sense, but rather is the discovery that the deepest Reality within oneself is the deepest Reality at the heart of all being.[1]

Sara Grant's motivation for her academic and spiritual engagement with Advaita Vedānta was primarily twofold: on the one hand, to return to the original Sanskrit sources in order to reevaluate what had become a widely accepted interpretation of Śaṁkara as an acosmic monist, and, on the other, to explore "the implications of the Hindu experience of non-duality for Christian theological reflection."[2]

As we have seen, Grant argues that much confusion about Śaṁkara's real meaning boils down to linguistic issues and, in particular, to his resort to the language of unreality and illusoriness to express the ontological dependence of the physical world on Ātman-Brahman and the sui generis (in)distinction-and-(non)relation between them.[3] If correcting this misreading of the Advaita tradition was one of Grant's primary motivations, the other driving force was "her conviction that a right understanding of non-duality could serve as an important corrective to much widespread popular Christian misconception about God and creation."[4]

As I indicated in the introduction to this book, David Burrell has long been suggesting that Grant's work on non-duality in Śaṁkara and Aquinas can offer precisely this sort of corrective by articulating the "not-otherness" of creature and Creator, which we have also seen in different formulations in Christian voices ranging from Pseudo-Dionysius, Meister Eckhart, and Nicholas of Cusa, to Robert Sokolowski, Kathryn Tanner, and Denys Turner. Like Burrell, Grant focuses on the particular expression of this non-duality which she finds in Aquinas's metaphysics of creation and the sui generis (in)distinction-and-(non)relation between creature and Creator which this articulation undergirds. Her hope, in so doing, is to show that "non-dualists are not confined to the East, though perhaps they are less common in the West,"[5] and that her arguments

> might find an echo in the heart of at least a few other crypto non-dualists and so help them to recognize their own identity and come to terms with it, and also, especially if they were from a Christian background, help them to recognize and relate to the ultimate non-dualism of Christian revelation.[6]

One of my key arguments has been that this modality of non-dualism, in which God is the "hyper-ground" of the world, shapes the thought systems of both Advaita and Thomism in their respective understandings of production of the world from God. While their surface grammars are stylized with distinctive scripturally shaped vocabularies—one speaks of projection from *Brahman* and the other of creation out of *nihil*—I have argued that a deeper analysis reveals that these understandings of how the many are related to their One are not as conceptually far apart as they first appear. In particular, I have suggested that the Christian doctrine of God's creation ex nihilo should be parsed as creation "not-from-some-one-thing extraneous to" God, and since this expression is merely a string of words with no ontic referent, it becomes, in logical space, indistinguishable from the noncontrastive expression "creation from God."

This sort of language of creation *ex deo* and the (quasi) nothingness of the creature has historically raised the spectres of pantheism and monism in both Christian theology and Advaita. I have contended, however, that "pantheism" is a conceptual bogeyman that has for too long haunted debates between Advaita and Thomism and should now be carefully exorcised from these spaces. Depending on what that rather slippery term connotes, vast tracts of both Hindu and Christian worldviews can be, with some definitional rewiring, re-presented as, at least, pan-*en*-theistic.

The more vital, and conceptually fine-grained, question relates to the status of the particularity of things in these systems of hyper-grounding the world "in" God. One difference between the two systems is that the finite creature in Thomism seems more robustly real than in Advaita. Christian theologians, in other words, do not tend to speak as unequivocally as Advaitins do of the surpassing of the particularity itself of the "I" as the final end of its eschatological perfection, due to their belief, drawn from scripture and Church teaching, that even after earthly death, God will sustain, preserve, and redeem the "I" precisely in its quiddity as that very "I."[7] Even here, though, I would not want to insist too strongly on this point as a clear demarcation of the two traditions. We have seen that Christian theologians, too, are aware of the vocabularies of worldly nothingness and unreality and of the fragility of the created order that is "swept away by God like a dream—like grass which flourishes in the morning and in the evening fades and withers."[8]

Therefore, rather than setting up Christian teaching on creaturely particularity in (dualistic) opposition to an emphasis in Advaita on Brahman being all-in-all (for the New Testament, too, can speak in these registers of the God-rootedness of all),[9] this is another case where it is more helpful to see these modes of discourse as non-contrastive and, indeed, functionally complementary ways of talking about God and the world.[10] Kathryn Tanner points out that there are two ways of looking at the non-dualistic rules for speaking of this God-world dialectic, which I have taken as my leitmotif throughout this study:

> The rule for talk of the creature as directly dependent in its entirety upon God can be used either to highlight what the creature has in dependence upon God or to underscore the very relation of dependence by which the creature has it. The first use promotes theological discussion of the creature in itself, its own value and dignity . . . [t]he second use fosters discourse that subordinates the creature to God. Created reality becomes a transparent reference to the God upon whom it depends.[11]

Although it may be *generally* true that Christian theologians tend to focus on the "creaturely" dimension of this dependence relation (i.e., the creature has an ontic integrity upheld by God), and that Advaitins tend to focus on the dependence itself (i.e., the creature is nothing without God), these two vantage points are not mutually exclusive. Indeed, part of the argument of this book is that an engagement with Advaita need not push Christianity toward a rejection of this world as an illusory realm but can help to revivify and reinforce a sense of the world as iconic and theocentric—to see the world, in other words, as a sacrament of the divine who is omnipresent at the heart of every created being.

As Grant is keenly aware, however, scholastic argumentation and philosophical reasoning can be (and are) employed in Advaitic circles as a pedagogic tool toward the catalysis of the intuitive realization of ultimate non-duality, but can only take us so far to the frontiers of the reasoning mind. Likewise, academic disquisitions such as this one may help to shed some light on what is at stake, but can—at best—serve as modest pointers toward deeper truths:

> This teaching (*advaita*) can be understood only by those who have renounced all longing for external things, who seek for no other refuge . . . and as regards the understanding of the true, it cannot be acquired unless it is sought after and prayed for; hence [Śaṁkara] says, "This understanding itself one must seek to understand."[12]

This is surely why Śaṁkara and Thomas both submitted their own teaching to the teaching of their respective scriptures and also explains the single-minded purity of heart required of the inquiring disciple, who must be prepared "to take nothing for the journey"[13] in order to discover that even without anything, they are yet "lacking nothing."[14]

Where Have We Got To?

I said at the very beginning of this book that I saw it as an exercise in comparative theology, but the fact that there is a burgeoning literature on the nature, methods, and aims of this discipline[15] more than twenty-five years after Francis Clooney set the template for it in his *Theology after Vedānta*,[16] perhaps suggests that I ought to say a little more about how I understand it.

Insofar as I am shaped by my own Roman Catholic faith and have been inspired by the work of Thomist scholars like Sara Grant and David Burrell, my work could reasonably be described as confessional. This is true not only in a descriptive, but also in a normative sense, in that I have taken certain contours of the Christian theological tradition as my discursive parameters and worked within, and through, them. This might mean that my book will primarily be of interest to others who identify with these milieus and broadly accept a shared and inherited set of Christian criteria for discerning what is true, good, and valuable. The great benefit of comparative engagement with other religious traditions is that it can mitigate the risks of such confessionally rooted theology becoming simply an intellectual echo chamber—for the goal of the comparative exercise is not merely the disinterested advance of scholarship (though this will likely be a concomitant good) but also the spiritual transformation it can catalyze in its practitioners, audiences, and students.

Clearly, this assumes an existential commitment to a "home tradition" as well as an openness to the presence of truth in the beliefs, texts, and practices of other traditions—here, specifically, in the teachings of Advaita Vedānta. Although there might be some degree of arbitrariness in this choice of conversation partner (motivated, in my case, by my reading of Sara Grant), I hope it has been clear throughout that this is not about the rapacious appropriation or instrumentalization of the other for the sake of cherry-picking only what is convenient or comfortable to "take home." Rather, I have been inspired by the epistemic humility shown by Grant in her engagement with Śaṁkara's Vedānta (and, indeed, by Aquinas and the intellectual regard in which he held pagan Greek, Jewish, and Muslim voices) to listen carefully to what Advaitic thinkers are saying—in their own contexts shaped by their scriptural constraints. I have focused on a "slow reading" of particular texts and tried to hear how indigenous commentators have understood these texts from within Vedāntic milieus.[17]

The purpose of this kind of comparative engagement is, as I have already affirmed, the potential it holds for transformative theological learning—*fides quarens intellectum*. Admittedly, the learning is somewhat asymmetrical, in that the primary orientation of my work has been toward greater self-understanding of my home tradition. However, by building on Grant's meticulous exposition of Śaṁkara, I like to think that there may be something of interest here for the Vedāntic nondualist as well. This would be less likely if I had focused only on questions of obvious interest to a Christian, but by exploring certain key issues central to both traditions (i.e., the nature of the relation between the temporally dispersed many and the eternally established One), and by bringing the particular language and concepts of both into active conversation with each other (e.g., *creatio ex nihilo* and *satkāryavāda*, divine Ideas and *nāmarūpa*), we move toward a fusion of horizons in which our understanding of neither comparand is left quite the same as it was before.

Specifically, it is by reading Śaṁkara and being confronted with his stark insistence on the *not-two-ness* of the world and Brahman that we understand how Aquinas was trying to express a highly resonant nondual intuition through his emphasis on the sui generis nature of the relation between creature and Creator. Clearly, other Christian thinkers have explicated this motif via other means—such as Burrell's emphasis on Thomas's engagement with non-Christian philosophers and theologians or the work of scholars like Wayne Hankey and Rudi Te Velde on Aquinas's neoplatonic influences—but bringing Aquinas into direct conversation with Advaita Vedānta offers Christians a new way of expressing the world-God relation in the language of non-dualism. To say more about the contribution this "Advaitic Thomism" can make, it is helpful to turn to Catherine Cornille's recent work, *Meaning and Method in Comparative Theology*, in which she delineates some of the different types of learning to which comparative theology can lead its practitioners.[18]

To a large extent, the goal of what Cornille calls "rectification"[19] has already been accomplished for me by Sara Grant and Richard De Smet (and continued by contemporary scholars like B. Malkovsky, H. Nicholson, and A. Rambachan). Their aim is to restore a proper understanding of Śaṁkara's Advaita and to correct earlier Orientalist misrepresentations of it simply as world denying.[20] The key to this retrieval, as we have seen, is to be attentive to the perspective from which a given statement is made: for everyday purposes, it makes sense to talk of a real world that is changing and finite, and a really limited ego-self that exists within it. According to Advaita Vedānta, though, this idiom is merely a convenient fiction (as long as it is understood as such—for if taken as expressive of deep reality, it becomes extremely inconvenient from a soteriological perspective, to say the least) or a façon de parler. The truth is that "you are not the inadequate self you consider yourself to be—you are the self that is free from all limitations . . . the complete, full being lacking nothing, limitlessness itself."[21]

Notwithstanding everything I have argued for in this book, I would contend that this language of the limitlessness of my true self remains shocking for a Christian accustomed to an emphasis on creaturely finitude and original sin. Shocking is good, though, as it reminds us that comparative theology need not hide timidly under a Saidian shadow, as if this exercise of comparative theology were inevitably a form of metaphorical colonialism, but can bravely set out to rediscover through the other, through this defamiliarization of the self, what other religious traditions are saying (just as Aquinas was doing centuries ago) in order to rearticulate what we believe about our own faith. As Cornille rightly says,

> The comparative theologian thus approaches the other religion not from a position of power, but from a position of vulnerability, and with an openness to recognizing the superiority of the other religion in certain areas of religious thought or practice.[22]

This has been my experience in more ways than one. The practice of comparative theology makes one intellectually vulnerable in that it requires one to tread lightly in unfamiliar terrain and to acquire new skills in order to enter into densely stratified conversations with complex layers of linguistic, historical, and theological nuance. It also makes one professionally and publicly vulnerable because theologians working within the confessional "mainstream" can react with ambivalence, suspicion, and occasionally downright rejection—wondering why one would need to seek truth "outside" the already richly woven homespun tapestries of the Christian (or Hindu) traditions. One can appease some of these concerns by highlighting the possibilities that comparative engagement affords of what Cornille calls "intensification" and "recovery."[23] With respect to the former, Grant's theological journey was motivated by what she intuitively recognized as similarities between Thomas and Śaṁkara, and her conceptual exercise led to the amplification of Thomas's emphasis on creaturely dependence. I have developed this intensification of the non-dual implications of Christian teaching on creation by engaging with David Burrell's work and other figures who stress the "non-contrastive" nature of the distinction between the world and God. With respect to the latter, I hope this book will contribute to the rediscovery of figures (like De Smet and Grant) who have been neglected in mainstream Christian theology, and to the recovery of teachings (particularly on God as the divine reality in whom we "live and move and have our being"),[24] which are often underemphasized. A singular focus on the doctrine of redemption—centered around the divine attributes of omnipotence and omniscience—has often been associated with configurations of Christianity in which Christ becomes the deus ex machina who saves the day at the last moment. In contrast, the hermeneutic retrieval of some Advaita-shaped strands of Christianity can modulate or even recalibrate this doctrine with the divine attribute of omnipresence, which rarely receives sustained discussion in Christian doctrinal milieus.

However, this can make comparative theology sound as if it simply helps us to retrieve what was already known. I would argue, more strongly, that the learning goes further than this, and that it can actually lead to fresh insights that would not have been gained otherwise. If my arguments have been convincing, we have learned through the encounter with Advaita that the traditional Christian doctrine of creation ex nihilo can (and should) be seen as a form of *satkāryavāda* or creation ex deo, and that it is the Christian emphasis on the value of embodied particularity that underlines the relative reality of the created order and the individual within it.

Where Are We Going?

David Tracy predicted as long ago as the late 1980s that Christian systematic theology would one day unavoidably have to be comparative.[25] If that means that all Christian theologians should be engaging with the texts and practices of other religious traditions, I am not sure that I agree. For reasons of temperament, interest, and ability, I do not think such a vision is realistic or necessary. If, however, this means something closer to what Michelle Voss Roberts advocates as comparative theology's constructive goal (i.e., to make interreligious learning a *constituent part of Christian self-understanding*), then I wholeheartedly concur.[26] In other words, it is not that every scholar in a Christian theology faculty should be busy learning Sanskrit and reading Śaṁkara, but that every scholar should recognize the efforts of the pioneering one who *is* doing this as an integral part of the systematic jigsaw—as integral as those who bring other disciplinary lights (historical, textual, philological, sociological, etc.) to bear on Christian self-understanding. In short,

> Comparative theology is constructive theology in that it seeks to contribute to or advance the understanding of faith and truth. Sharing this same goal with other classical areas of theology . . . what distinguishes comparative theology is the material it brings to theological reflection.[27]

As we have seen, comparative theology can lead to different types of learning, such as rectification, intensification, and recovery, all of which are in evidence throughout this book. Looking forward, though, I think the real question for my own work and others like it is whether an engagement with Advaita Vedānta contributes toward, or is seen as, a *reaffirmation* of the truth and value of Christian teaching or whether, more provocatively, it triggers, or is seen as demanding, a radical *reinterpretation* of certain aspects of the tradition. Cornille expresses this well when she says that

> It is probably not insignificant that the process of learning through reinterpretation in Christian comparative theology so often involves the Hindu and Buddhist traditions of nondualism. These traditions do have some resonances with certain traditions of mystical [and, I have argued,

> scholastic] thought in Christianity, and they also address some of the modern or postmodern challenges of classical metaphysics. The question as to whether or to what extent this type of learning through comparative theology takes a firm hold in the tradition remains to be seen. They [traditions of nondualism] do seem to have some appeal to Christians in search of a less hierarchical and dualistic understanding of faith and tradition.

This move away from a dualistic understanding of the world and God was what appealed to Sara Grant and it is the appeal that can be seen in contemporary Christian figures like Thomas Keating, OCSO (1923–2018), Laurence Freeman, OSB, and Richard Rohr, OFM. By drawing on nondualist themes and imageries, they seek to reinvigorate a sense of the divine within the mundane. As I suggested in my introduction to this book, a non-dualistic (or advaitic) Christianity has profound ethical, as well as spiritual, promise. It is not difficult to imagine how a sacramental vision of the world as not-other than God could provide theological grounds for bolstering human solidarity, for cultivating greater reverence toward nature, and for a reformulation of the traditional "problem" of evil and suffering, which too often imagines God as a cosmic figure who somewhat capriciously intervenes in the world as if the two existed alongside one another. The risk of an exclusive emphasis on the non-dual, however, is that differences and particularities are eroded—seen from a lofty perspective where all *is* God, we could easily become indifferent to distinctions of ethnicity, class, and gender; to the loss of biodiversity; and to the suffering of *this* particular individual. This is where the traditional Christian emphasis on the importance of embodied "name and form"—which I discussed in the final chapter—can help to ensure that an advaitic Christianity would still be recognizably Christian.

Here, though, is where things get difficult. It would be all too easy to sit comfortably with an exotic-sounding, and yet ultimately anodyne Christian nondualism that offers saccharine platitudes about the deep unity of reality. No Christian could object to Advaita if all it amounts to saying is that the world is radically dependent on God. It is far more daring than this, for, as one of India's best-known twentieth-century Advaitins puts it, "The object of knowledge . . . of Vedānta is oneself," and "The vision of Vedānta is that one is the complete, full being, lacking nothing—that one's nature is limitlessness itself."[28] I have alluded to these issues in Chapter 4—by arguing that creation ex nihilo should be understood as creation ex deo—and in Chapter 5—by arguing that a Christian, too, should view the world as less than fully real—but I think the next step for Christian Advaita should be anthropological. It would mean bringing the questions of this book down to the far less comfortable level of myself and asking who "I" am, in my deepest nature. It would mean asking penetrating and existentially involving questions about what exactly Jesus meant when he said that it is only by losing our life that we will find it.[29] Would a non-dual reading of this invitation *reaffirm* our finitude and limitedness without God or would it force a radical *reinterpretation* of our true identity and encourage us to let go of the small self that is defined by our individual particularities? Should traditional Christian teaching on the metaphysical reality and the value of finite embodiment temper an advaitic propulsion to see beyond "name and form" or should Advaita instead push the Christian off the ontological precipice and dare us to lose our little self in the abyss of God? We might balk at the erosion of individuality implied by St. Paul's affirmation that "it is no longer I that live, but Christ lives in me,"[30] but this expanded sense of self can be liberating (as well as frightening). These questions have profound theological, ecclesiological, spiritual, and ethical ramifications: they would affect how we understand the doctrines of incarnation and atonement; they would influence how we pray; and they would speak directly to contemporary issues of personal identity and related issues of mental health. Would an advaitic Christianity risk doing a disservice to those whose identities are already socioculturally and historically marginalized by encouraging them to dissociate further from their sense of self or would it help to free individuals from the debilitating labels of race and gender, and the anxiety caused by a frenetic world that forces us to compete to be and do ever more? This is where comparative theology makes us not just intellectually and professionally vulnerable, but—with far more existential depth—renders us personally and spiritually vulnerable, too.

The question I am still wrestling with—as theologian and Christian—is whether I could ever say, along with Śaṁkara in his denominational vernacular, *Śivo'haṁ* ("I am Śiva").[31] A Christian can accept Jesus—uniquely—saying that he and the Father are one,[32] but what if Paul, too, had said it in these terms (for is that not the logical entailment of what he did say about Christ living in him)? What if a Roman Catholic priest said, "I am Christ" or, indeed, "You are Christ"? We make such statements more palatable by finessing them with "images," "likenesses," and "participations"—and maybe rightly so, but in that case, this is as far as an advaitic Christianity can go. What, though, if this is a refusal to bite the advaitic bullet? How liberating—or not—on a practical level would it be to affirm that "I am not the mind, the intellect, the ego or the memory, I am not the ears, the skin, the nose or the eyes"?[33] More daringly, could a Christian affirm (with some scripturally shaped linguistic rewiring) that:

> I am untouched by the senses, my form is formlessness, I exist everywhere, pervading all senses, I am neither attached, neither free nor captive, I am the form of consciousness and bliss . . .[34]

Could an advaitic Christian affirm—at the proverbial end of the day—that "I am He"? *Śivo'haṁ, Śivo'haṁ.*

ACKNOWLEDGMENTS

This book is the final fruit of an idyllic three years of full-time doctoral research in Cambridge (2016–2019). I am enormously grateful to the UK Arts and Humanities Research Council for awarding me the funding that made this possible, as well as to the Spalding Trust and the Teape Trust, which generously provided me with extra funding along the way. The Teape Trust also enabled me to spend a month in India, where I benefitted from time spent at the Ajatananada and Swami Dayananda Ashrams in Rishikesh. Sitting at the feet of Swami Atmananda Udasin and Swami Tattvavidananda Saraswati reminded me—if I needed reminding—that this journey into Christian Advaita was never merely an intellectual exercise.

Clare College provided a friendly and welcoming environment within which to live and work, and the Faculty of Divinity was a helpful and stimulating academic home. I am grateful, in particular, to Clemens Gresser and Matthew Patmore in the Divinity Library, who were never too busy to help and who always responded generously to my occasional recommendations for new books.

I have benefitted from a host of outstanding teachers who have all inspired and nurtured my love of learning in different ways. At St Bede's College in Manchester, my interest in languages was kindled by Phil Maree and Terry Barnes, and my ongoing apprenticeship in theology and philosophy began at the hands of Tony McCabe and Matthew Taylor. As an undergraduate, I was particularly influenced by the teaching of Chris Insole. I was first seriously introduced to the possibilities of comparative theology and, in particular, to the fascinating area of engagements between Hinduism and Christianity by Michael Barnes and Martin Ganeri, and I thank them for their ongoing support and friendship. I am grateful to Eivind Kahrs and Vincenzo Vergiani for sharing their expertise and patiently opening my eyes to Sanskrit.

As a secondary school teacher of theology and philosophy, I have been fortunate to work alongside colleagues whose passion for the subject has been infectious. I have learned much from friends in the Religious Studies Departments at Stonyhurst College and St Benedict's, Ealing, as well as from the wisdom transmitted over the ages by the two great Christian traditions to which these schools belong. Teaching at Hills Road Sixth Form College in Cambridge provided an ideal counterbalance to the solitary nature of doctoral research, and I greatly enjoy life in the Divinity Department at Eton. I have been challenged and enriched, personally and academically, by students at all of these schools, and am particularly grateful to my last A-level group at St Benedict's who were extraordinarily kind and encouraging to me when I left them to begin the PhD out of which this book is born.

Over the course of writing, I have benefitted from feedback and critique from a number of esteemed academic colleagues who have given generously of their time and advice. My sincere thanks go to: Mario Aguilar, David Burrell, Francis Clooney, Christian Hengstermann, Julius Lipner, Bernard McGinn, Martin Poulsom, Jacob Sherman, Janet Soskice, John Thatamanil, and Peter Tyler. I am particularly grateful to Brad Malkovsky for his careful reading of various chapters and valuable suggestions. The book as a whole is much the better for the expert input of all of these scholars, though obviously any remaining deficiencies and errors are mine alone.

My time as a doctoral student was enriched by the friends and family who were there throughout. I am especially grateful to Nadya Pohran and Daniel Tolan. My parents, John and Barbara, and my brothers, Barry and Luke, are never anything but completely supportive, and Melissa makes me think, laugh, and work in the way that only she can.

Finally, I have heard it said many times that the most important relationship for a successful doctorate is that between the student and his supervisor. I am doubly lucky in that I had two, and I could not have asked for better. Douglas Hedley has kept an avuncular eye on me ever since I first met him as an undergraduate and he encouraged me to embark on doctoral studies in the first place. I have hugely appreciated his sage advice and owe what little I know about the Platonic tradition to his tutelage. Ankur Barua has kept me on my toes with his encyclopedic knowledge of Indic traditions and his forensic eye for detail—not to mention the emails, reading recommendations, and photocopied articles I regularly receive from him. I find them both inspiring, not only because of their learning, but because of the kind and humble way they go about their work. Their support and friendship are invaluable.

NOTES

Introduction

1. Robert Sokolowski, *The God of Faith and Reason* (Notre Dame, Ind.: University of Notre Dame Press, 1982), 1.
2. As we will see, Thomas Aquinas argues, in somewhat provocative-sounding language, that God is not *really* related to the world at all, but that the world *is* related to God (e.g., ST I.45.3.1).
3. Sara Grant, *Towards an Alternative Theology: Confessions of a Non-Dualist Christian* (Notre Dame, Ind.: University of Notre Dame Press, 2002).
4. Grant (2002), 2.
5. For example, Pseudo-Dionysius and Nicholas of Cusa, whom I discuss in Chapter 1.
6. I am aware that the "triune God" of Christian belief and the "*nirguṇa* Brahman" of Advaita Vedāntic Hinduism are not straightforwardly synonymous. To the extent that both refer, in their particular theological, historical, and sociological contexts, to each tradition's concept of ultimate reality, I use the word "God" in this study for stylistic felicity. Where it is crucial to the argument, I will indicate that I have in mind specifically the Christian understanding of God or the Advaitic understanding of Brahman.
7. For example, John 10:30, "I and the Father are one" or John 15:5, "I am the vine; you are the branches. If you remain in me and I in you, you will bear much fruit; apart from me you can do nothing."
8. Cf. Exodus 3:20–22 and Augustine, *On Christian Doctrine*, 2.40.60.
9. The further question of why and how there might be a relationship between some forms of Greek and Indian philosophical idealisms—specifically, between (Neo-)Platonism and (Advaita) Vedānta—is a long-standing one. My aim here is not to address these questions, but to make a textual case for resonant parallels between Aquinas's more (Neo-)Platonic doctrines and non-dual Vedānta. To follow up the "meta" comparison between Platonism and Vedānta, see J. F. Staal, *Advaita and Neoplatonism: A Critical Study in Comparative Philosophy* (Madras: University of Madras, 1961); R. Baine Harris, ed. *Neoplatonism and Indian Thought* (Albany: State University of New York Press, 1981); Paulos Gregorios, *Neoplatonism and Indian Philosophy* (Albany: State University of New York Press, 2002).

10. Cf. Richard A. Norris, *God and World in Early Christian Theology: A Study of Justin Martyr, Irenaeus, Tertullian and Origen* (New York: Seabury Press, 1965).
11. See, for example, Bede Griffiths, "Transcending Dualism: An Eastern Approach to the Semitic Religions," *Cistercian Studies* XX (1985): 73–87; David Loy, *Nonduality: A Study in Comparative Philosophy*, (New Haven and London: Yale University Press, 1988), 18–21; Cynthia Bourgeault, *The Heart of Centering Prayer: Nondual Christianity in Theory and Practice* (Boulder, Colo.: Shambhala, 2016), 44–45.
12. Loy (1988), 21–25 and 38–95; Bourgeault (2016), 48–50.
13. Loy (1988), 25–36; Bourgeault (2016), 46–48.
14. For example, John J. Thatamanil, "Ecstasy and Nonduality: On Comparing Varieties of Immanence," *Journal of Hindu-Christian Studies* 22 (January 2009): 19–24. "Ecstasy and Nonduality" was the original working title of Thatamanil's monograph *The Immanent Divine: God, Creation and the Human Predicament*, (Minneapolis, Minn.: Augsburg Fortress, 2006).
15. For a good summary of some of these different uses, see Beatrice Bruteau's "Prayer and Identity" (originally 1983), reprinted with an introduction by Cynthia Bourgeault as "Beatrice Bruteau's 'Prayer and Identity': An Introduction with Text and Commentary," *Sewanee Theological Review* 50, no. 3 (Pentecost 2007): 385–407.
16. Grant (2002), 54.
17. Kevin J. Vanhoozer, "A Christian Case for Panentheism? The Case Remains Unproven," *Dialog: A Journal of Theology* 38, no. 4 (Fall 1999): 281–85 (here, 281).
18. Grant (2002), 55–56.
19. For recent critiques of such views, see, for example, David Bentley Hart, *The Experience of God: Being, Consciousness, Bliss* (New Haven, Conn.: Yale University Press, 2014) and Rupert Shortt, *God Is No Thing: Coherent Christianity* (London: C Hurst & Co, 2016).
20. Along with the already mentioned works by Bentley Hart and Shortt, other relatively recent examples in this vein include: Philip Clayton, *The Problem of God in Modern Thought* (Grand Rapids, Mich.: Eerdmans Publishing Company, 2000) and Catherine Keller, *On the Mystery: Discerning Divinity in Process* (Minneapolis, Minn.: Fortress Press, 2008).
21. Philip Clayton, "The Case for Christian Panentheism," *Dialog: A Journal of Theology* 37, no. 3 (Summer 1998): 201–8 and Kevin J. Vanhoozer et al., "A Christian Case for Panentheism? The Case Remains Unproven," *Dialog: A Journal of Theology* 38, no. 4 (Fall 1999): 281–93.
22. Clayton, "The Panentheistic Turn in Christian Theology," *Dialog* 38 (Fall 1999), 289–293 (here, 290, original emphasis).
23. Clayton (1998), 202–4.
24. Aquinas, ST I.8, esp. art. 1, ad. 2, quoted in John W. Cooper, *Panentheism: The Other God of the Philosophers* (Westmont, Ill.: InterVarsity Press, 2007), 330.
25. Other than Aquinas's own works, and articles and monographs mentioned in the body of the book (especially those by Burrell and Sokolowski), I have relied on the following for my understanding of Aquinas's doctrine of creation: Norman Kretzmann, *The Metaphysics of Creation: Aquinas's Natural Theology in Summa Contra Gentiles II* (Oxford: Oxford University Press, 2002); W. Norris Clarke, *The One*

and the Many: A Contemporary Thomistic Metaphysics (Notre Dame, Ind.: University of Notre Dame Press, 2001); John F. Wippel, *The Metaphysical Thought of Thomas Aquinas: From Finite Being to Uncreated Being* (Washington, D.C.: Catholic University of America Press, 2000). For an overview of the literature on Thomas's (Neo-) Platonism, see Chapter 3 of this book.

26. Other than the works on Christian nondualism mentioned previously by Bourgeault, Bruteau, Griffiths, and Thatamanil, see, for example, Vladimir Lossky, *Théologie négative et connaissance de Dieu chez Maître Eckhart* (Paris: Vrin, 1973) and James Charlton, *Non-Dualism in Eckhart, Julian of Norwich and Traherne*, Reprint edition (London: Bloomsbury Academic, 2014).
27. As this book is not *about* Hindu-Christian encounters (in a historical or sociological sense), I do not offer a detailed overview of this broad terrain. For this, see, for example, Harold G. Coward, *Hindu-Christian Dialogue: Perspectives and Encounters*, (Maryknoll, N.Y.: Orbis Books, 1989); J. J. Clarke, *Oriental Enlightenment: The Encounter between Asian and Western Thought* (London: Routledge, 1997); Robin Boyd, *An Introduction to Indian Christian Theology*, Revised (New Delhi: ISPCK, 2000).
28. K. P. Aleaz, *Christian Thought Through Advaita Vedanta*, Reprint of 1996 edition (Delhi: ISPCK, 2008); Bradley Malkovsky, "Advaita Vedanta and Christian Faith," *Journal of Ecumenical Studies* 36, no. 3–4 (Summer–Fall 1999): 397–422 and Malkovsky, ed., *New Perspectives on Advaita Vedānta: Essays in Commemoration of Professor Richard De Smet, S.J.* (Leiden: Brill, 2000).
29. Rudolf Otto, *Mysticism East and West: A Comparative Analysis of the Nature of Mysticism* (London: Macmillan and Co., 1932); Wayne Robert Teasdale, *Toward a Christian Vedanta: The Encounter of Hinduism and Christianity According to Bede Griffiths* (Bangalore: Asian Trading Corp, 1987); Sean Doyle, *Synthesizing the Vedanta: The Theology of Pierre Johanns S.J.*, (Peter Lang, 2006).
30. Examples of this latter genre would be Raimundo Panikkar, *The Unknown Christ of Hinduism*, Revised and enlarged (London: Darton, Longman and Todd, 1981) and Francis X. Clooney, *Hindu God, Christian God: How Reason Helps Break down the Boundaries between Religions* (New York: Oxford University Press, 2001).
31. Thatamanil (2006).
32. Michael von Brück, *The Unity of Reality: God, God-Experience, and Meditation in the Hindu-Christian Dialogue* (Mahwah, N.J.: Paulist Press, 1986). This was originally published in German as *Einheit der Wirklichkeit.*
33. Martin Ganeri, *Indian Thought and Western Theism: The Vedānta of Rāmānuja* (New York: Routledge, 2015).
34. Francis X. Clooney, *Theology after Vedānta: An Experiment in Comparative Theology* (Albany: State University of New York Press, 1993).
35. Un moine d'Occident, *Doctrine de la Non-Dualité (Advaita-Vāda) et Christianisme: Jalons pour un accord doctrinal entre l'Église et le Vedānta* (Paris: Dervy-Livres, 1982, reprinted 2019).
36. I am also sympathetic to the view that comparative theology needs to be more attentive to female voices (like Grant). This important concern is highlighted in the work of Michelle Voss Roberts—see, for example, her intriguing theological comparison

of Mechtild of Magdeburg and Lalleśwarī of Kashmir in *Dualities: A Theology of Difference* (Louisville, Ky.: Westminster John Knox Press, 2010).

37. Francis X. Clooney, *Comparative Theology: Deep Learning across Religious Borders* (Chichester: Wiley-Blackwell, 2010). For a recent overview of the field of "comparative theology," see S. Mark Heim, "Comparative Theology at Twenty-Five: The End of the Beginning," *Modern Theology* 35 (1): 163–80.
38. Cf. John Paul II's Encyclical Letter *Fides et Ratio* (1998).
39. I am not suggesting that Aquinas's Neoplatonic influences are the only—or even the primary—explanation for the fruitful possibilities of theological comparisons between Thomas and Śaṁkara, or Vedānta more broadly. My contention is merely that this particular connection can alert us to some significant parallels and differences. There are plenty of other reasons why these two figures constitute thought-provoking comparative partners—not least due to their wider "scholastic" contexts (i.e., both were scriptural exegetes; both build on tradition and aim for a certain completeness and systematicity in their writings, etc.). For more on these connections, see F. X. Clooney, "Scholasticisms in Encounter: Working through a Hindu Example" in Jose Ignacio Cabezon, *Scholasticism: Cross-Cultural and Comparative Perspectives* (Albany: State University of New York Press, 1998), 177–95.

1. The Distinctive Relation between Creature and Creator in Christian Theology: Non-dualism from David Burrell, CSC, to Sara Grant, RSCJ

1. Thomas Aquinas, *Summa Contra Gentiles* (hereafter, SCG) II.18.2 ("*Non enim est creatio mutatio, sed ipsa dependentia esse creati ad principium a quo statuitur. Et sic est de genere relationis*"). See also *Summa Theologica* (hereafter, ST) I.45.3. ad.3.
2. A slightly amended version of this chapter appeared as "From David Burrell CSC to Sara Grant RSCJ: The Distinctive Relation between Creature and Creator in Christian Theology," *Scottish Journal of Theology* 74, no. 2: 123–34.
3. Plotinus, *Ennead* V.5.9.19. All citations from the *Enneads* will be from the edition by A. H. Armstrong, Loeb Classical Library (Cambridge, Mass: Harvard University Press and London: Heinemann, 1966–1988). Cf. also Psalm 139.
4. David Burrell (b. 1933) is a Roman Catholic priest of the Congregation of the Holy Cross (*Congregatio a Sancta Cruce*).
5. Sara Grant (1922–2002) was a Roman Catholic sister of the Sacred Heart congregation (*Religieuses du Sacré Coeur de Jésus*).
6. See Burrell in the following: "From the Analogy of 'Being' to the Analogy of Being," in John P. O'Callaghan and Thomas S. Hibbs, eds., *Recovering Nature: Essays in Natural Philosophy, Ethics, and Metaphysics in Honor of Ralph McInerny* (Notre Dame, Ind.: University of Notre Dame Press, 1999), 253–66; "Creation, Metaphysics, and Ethics," *Faith and Philosophy* 18, no. 2 (2001): 204–22; "The Challenge to Medieval Christian Philosophy: Relating Creator to Creatures," in John Inglis, ed., *Medieval Philosophy and the Classical Tradition in Islam, Judaism, and Christianity* (Richmond, Va.: Curzon, 2002), 202–14; "Act of Creation with Its Theological Consequences," in Thomas Weinandy, Daniel Keating, and John Yocum, eds., *Aquinas on Doctrine: A Critical Introduction* (New York: T&T Clark, 2004), 27–44; "Maimonides, Aquinas and Ghazali:

Distinguishing God from the World," *Scottish Journal of Theology* 61, no. 3 (2008): 270–87; "Albert, Aquinas, and Dionysius," *Modern Theology* 24, no. 4 (2008): 633–51; "Creator/Creatures Relation: 'The Distinction' vs. 'Onto-Theology,'" *Faith and Philosophy* 25 (2008): 177–89, with "Reply to Cross and Hasker," 205–12; *Creation and the God of Abraham* (New York: Cambridge University Press, 2010). Most recently, Burrell spoke on Grant and non-dualism in his contribution to a celebratory conference for Prof. Janet Soskice at the University of Cambridge: "*Creation Ex Nihilo*, Divine Creation and Linguistic Creations," 2017, https://sms.cam.ac.uk/collection/2662424.

7. David Burrell, "The Christian Distinction Celebrated and Expanded," in John Drummond and James Hart, eds., *The Truthful and the Good: Essays in Honour of Robert Sokolowski* (Dordrecht: Kluwer Academic Publishers, 1996), 191–206. This also appears as Chapter 14 in Burrell 2004a.
8. Burrell is not alone in noticing that creation and redemption can often be unhelpfully opposed in Christian thought—see also, for example, Rosemary Radford Ruether, "The God of Possibilities: Immanence and Transcendence Rethought," *Concilium* 4 (2000): 45–54.
9. David B. Burrell and Elena Malits, *Original Peace: Restoring God's Creation* (Mahwah, N.J.: Paulist Press International, 1997), 1–4. Burrell calls for a "Keplerian," rather than Copernican, revolution because his whole point is that creation and redemption need to be twin foci of Christian theology, held in productive tension with one another.
10. Gregory Rocca, "Creatio Ex Nihilo and the Being of Creatures: God's Creative Act and the Transcendence-Immanence Distinction in Aquinas," in Harm Goris, Herwi Rikhof, and Henk Schoot, eds., *Divine Transcendence and Immanence in the Work of Thomas Aquinas*, (Leuven: Peeters, 2009), 3, n. 7.
11. See, for example, Burrell, "Analogy, Creation, and Theological Language," *Proceedings of the American Catholic Philosophical Association* 74 (2000): 35–52, referring to Josef Pieper, *The Silence of Saint Thomas* (New York: Pantheon, 1957). Similar references can be found in almost all of Burrell's work.
12. Sokolowski (1982).
13. Burrell in Drummond and Hart, eds. (1996), 191.
14. Burrell (2004), 243.
15. Cf. Burrell (2004): "When one of those 'things' is the creator of all the others . . . then everything else is what it is *in relation to* that One. (As Aquinas puts it so succinctly and subtly: creation consists in a relation of the creature to the creator—that is, the very being of the creature is to-be-related.)," 237 (original emphasis), quoting Aquinas, ST I.45.3.
16. This is what philosophers of religion usually refer to as "the ontological distinction" but is generally referred to by Sokolowski and Burrell simply as "the distinction."
17. Sokolowski (1982), 23. Sokolowski's emphasis on God's self-sufficiency and simplicity perhaps comes even closer to Advaita than Burrell's talk of "distinction-and-relation." In traditional Advaita, because God (*brahman*) is infinite (*ananta*), there is no place left for the world, however small, since that would *add* something to infinity, which is illogical. Hence, the world cannot exist independently of God. Malkovsky makes this point in Bradley Malkovsky, "The Personhood of Śaṁkara's 'Para Brahman,'" *The Journal of Religion* 77, no. 4 (October 1997): 555.

18. Anselm, *Proslogion* 2 in Brian Davies and G. R. Evans, eds., *Anselm of Canterbury: The Major Works Including Monologion, Proslogion, and Why God Became Man*, (Oxford: Oxford University Press, 2008), 87.
19. Sokolowski (1982), 32–33.
20. Martin G. Poulsom, *The Dialectics of Creation: Creation and the Creator in Edward Schillebeeckx and David Burrell* (London: Bloomsbury T&T Clark, 2014), 56–60. Poulsom offers a detailed analysis of these "directionality issues" that lie at the heart of Thomas's distinction between "real" and "logical" relations (a distinction that I examine in Chapter 3).
21. Conceiving of the relation between the world and God as an "external" relation between two separate entities, "results directly from having to deny that we are creatures internally related to a creator" and, according to Burrell, we should not, therefore, be surprised when this "creator alongside the universe" is seen as otiose and dispensed with—"metaphysically, for the sake of parsimony, and ethically to obviate heteronomy." Burrell (2001), 210. When Burrell talks of creatures being "internally related" to the Creator, he is making fundamentally the same point as Sokolowski—that is, we do not exist and "then" (via a specific act of salvation) *become* related to the Creator; we are related by virtue of "being" at all.
22. Burrell, (2001), 206–8.
23. Sokolowski (1982), 32–33.
24. ST I.6.2. See also ST I.3 on the simplicity of God, esp. art. 5. "Whether God is composed of genus and difference?".
25. ST I.6.2.
26. This is one reason why Aquinas is not an "onto-theologian" because there is not even a common category of "being" to which both God and creatures belong. For Thomas, God *is* Being (*esse*) itself (or even, as he suggests in other places, such as his commentary on the Neoplatonic *Liber de Causis*, "beyond Being," as the Cause of Being), whereas a particular being (*ens*) *has* being (from God). For more on this, see Chapter 4.
27. Burrell in Inglis (2002), 204.
28. Other than Sokolowski, Tanner is the contemporary theologian to whom Burrell adverts most frequently in his work on "the distinction." See, for example, *Original Peace*, 72. He mentions her in the majority of the books, chapters, and articles we have so far discussed. The main work he has in mind is Tanner's *God and Creation in Christian Theology: Tyranny or Empowerment?* (New York: Basil Blackwell, 1988).
29. Tanner (1988), 12.
30. This theological modus operandi is not peculiar to Tanner. It is an attention to the *grammar* of theology which can also be seen in Burrell and Aquinas, to name but two other theologians.
31. Tanner (1988), 46.
32. Tanner (1988), 45.
33. Tanner (1988), 47.
34. She supports her argument with a broad survey of different theological "moments" that demonstrate these rules for talk about God, not least in key figures in the early Church, like Irenaeus (ca. 125–202) and Tertullian (ca. 155–240). These figures form

particularly good case studies given that they were wrestling with many central theological questions before they became solidified into doctrinal orthodoxy. For more on this, see Norris (1965).

35. See, for example, Burrell (2008), 281–84.
36. Denys Turner, *Faith, Reason and the Existence of God* (Cambridge: Cambridge University Press, 2004), 149 (original emphasis).
37. Turner (2004), 161–62.
38. Turner (2004), 163.
39. This is why Poulsom is wary of Turner's (and others') tendency to use "difference" and "distinction" interchangeably and recommends that "distinction" is the more helpful term if we wish to maintain non-contrastivity. Cf. Poulsom (2014), 20–21.
40. Turner (2004), 213.
41. Turner (2004), 214.
42. Turner (2004), 214 (original emphasis).
43. See, for example, Dionysius's influence on Aquinas's understanding of divine ideas in Chapter 5.
44. *The Mystical Theology* 1048B; in Colm Luibheid and Paul Rorem, trans., *The Pseudo-Dionysius: The Complete Works* (Mahwah, N.J.: Paulist Press, 1987), 141. All future references will be to this edition.
45. *The Mystical Theology* 1048B
46. Turner (2004), 157.
47. Pseudo-Dionysius, *Divine Names* 817D in Luibheid (1987), 98.
48. Turner (2004), 163–64, quoting Eckhart's *Commentary on Exodus* 20.104, in Bernard McGinn, ed., *Meister Eckhart, Teacher and Preacher* (Mahwah, N.J.: Paulist Press, 1986), 79.
49. I take this phrase from Nicholas of Cusa. See Jasper Hopkins, *Nicholas of Cusa on God as Not-Other: A Translation and an Appraisal of De Li Non Aliud.* (Minneapolis: University of Minnesota, 1979). This is not simply a "rogues' gallery" of maverick thinkers who just happen to have spoken in similar terms of divinity (viz. Pseudo-Dionysius, Eriugena, Aquinas, Eckhart, and Cusa). I will later suggest—especially in Chapters 4 and 5—that it is certain Neoplatonic themes common to them that help to explain the deep resonances between these figures and the tradition of Advaita Vedānta.
50. ST I.3.
51. David B. Burrell, "Distinguishing God from the World," in Brian Davies OP, ed. *Language, Meaning and God: Essays in Honour of Herbert McCabe, OP* (London: Geoffrey Chapman, 1987), 75–91.
52. The same point could be made for the other formal divine features explored by Aquinas in the following Questions (4–11) of the *Prima Pars*, such as perfection, limitlessness, immutability, eternity, oneness, and so on. See Burrell (2008), 179–80.
53. Burrell (2003).
54. Sokolowski (1982), 31, 33.
55. For example, Burrell (2008), 179.
56. William Hasker, in "Reply to Cross and Hasker," *Faith and Philosophy* 25 (2008): 205–12. Hasker is right that Sokolowski tends to focus more on Anselm, and Burrell on Aquinas,

but these are differences in emphasis rather than mutually exclusive alternatives. Sokolowski also discusses how Thomist metaphysics help to secure "the distinction"—Sokolowski (1982), 41–46.

57. Burrell is not the only contemporary thinker to privilege Aquinas in this way, however. In a recent article, Christopher Holmes points to two theologians who "[b]oth think that Thomas's account of God's causal activity in creation is key to recognizing what distinguishes God from his creatures." Cf. Christopher R. J. Holmes, "Revisiting the God/World Difference," *Modern Theology* 34, no. 2 (April 2018): 159–76. It is especially interesting that the two figures he has in mind come from different sides of the Roman Catholic/Reformed divide—namely, Thomas Joseph White, OP, *The Incarnate Lord: A Thomistic Study in Christology* (Washington, D.C.: Catholic University of America Press, 2015) and John Webster, *Confessing God: Essays in Dogmatics II*. 2nd ed. (London: T&T Clark, 2016).
58. Simon Oliver, *Creation: A Guide for the Perplexed* (London: Bloomsbury T&T Clark, 2017), xii (my emphasis).
59. Sokolowski (1982), 107 and *passim*.
60. Though, even here, very similar expressions to Anselm's can be found in Aquinas—for example, *Quaestiones disputatae de potentia dei*, (abbreviated from here to De Pot.) Q.7, a.2 A.D.9: "But nothing that is outside the range of being can be added to being [*esse*]: for nothing is outside its range except non-being, which can be neither form nor matter."
61. Poulsom (2014), 75–78. This frequency of usage does not necessarily imply a priority of distinction over relation in terms of theological significance—as Poulsom recognizes (ibid., 90–94).
62. Burrell in Drummond and Hart, eds. (1996), 193 (my emphasis).
63. Burrell (2000).
64. Burrell (2000), 35 (my emphases).
65. Burrell (2000), 35.
66. Burrell (2000), 39 (my emphasis).
67. Poulsom (2014), 52. Cf. also Aquinas's contention that "creation is a kind of relation" in the passage cited at the head of this chapter from SCG II.18.2.
68. See the Preface to *De ente et essentia* (Maurer 1968), Thomas is paraphrasing Aristotle in his *De caelo*: see W. K. C. Guthrie, trans., *On the Heavens/Aristotle* (London: William Heinemann, 1939), Bk I, Ch. 5.
69. R. Sokolowski, "Creation and Christian Understanding," in David B. Burrell and Bernard McGinn, eds., *God and Creation: An Ecumenical Symposium* (Notre Dame, Ind.: University of Notre Dame Press, 1990), 179.
70. For a recent guide to these debates, see Edward T. Oakes, SJ, *A Theology of Grace in Six Controversies* (Grand Rapids, Mich.: W.B. Eerdmans Pub. Co, 2016). For the seminal work that first drew major attention to these issues in twentieth-century philosophical theology, see Henri de Lubac, *Le Mystère du Surnaturel* (Paris: Aubier, 1965), and, for an interesting range of articles on the controversies provoked by this book, see Serge-Thomas Bonino, ed., *Surnaturel: A Controversy at the Heart of Twentieth-Century Thomistic Thought*, translated by Robert Williams and Matthew Levering (Ave Maria, Fla: Sapientia Press of Ave Maria University, 2009).

71. Tanner (1988), 2–3.
72. Tanner (1988), 6.
73. This challenge can also be parsed the other way around: that is, of how to articulate the distinction in such a way that it doesn't become a separation, and how to articulate the relation in such a way that it doesn't collapse God into the world. This almost palindromic quality of the dilemma serves only to reinforce what I have been arguing throughout this chapter—that "distinction" and "relation" are two sides of the same coin. It is important to note that these challenges are challenges from a *Christian* point of view. As we will see in subsequent chapters, the challenge from the Advaita point of view is slightly different: namely, how to distinguish the *world* from God in order to avoid seeing the world merely as an ontological illusion. Christianity struggles, we might say, with "pantheistic monism," while Advaita leans toward "illusionistic monism."
74. Langdon Gilkey, "Creation, Being, and Nonbeing," in Burrell and McGinn (1990), 229.
75. Poulsom (2014), 41–50.
76. Burrell (1997), 74, talking of Grant.
77. Rocca, "Creatio ex nihilo" in Goris et al. (2009), 15.
78. See, for example, Burrell (2001), 208, but this crops up in nearly all of his work mentioned so far.
79. Rocca in Goris et al. (2009), 15.
80. The problem as it is conceived in Advaitic texts and thinkers—of how to account for the world at all—and the common charge that the Advaitic "solution" is to dissolve the world into a sort of verbal fiction or ontological illusion has not really been a major part of Christian theological discourse.
81. Sokolowski (1982), 26. While Sokolowski tends to refer to this as the "Christian" distinction, Burrell sees it as involving a fundamentally similar set of issues in each of the Abrahamic traditions.
82. Burrell (1993), 48.
83. Burrell in Weinandy et al. (2004), 27.
84. Burrell (1986), 2.
85. Sokolowski (1982), 34.
86. Indeed, it is Burrell's close attention to the particular faith traditions in question and their attempts to clarify founding truths of revelation that characterizes his work as belonging more properly to *philosophical theology* than to philosophy of religion, insofar as the latter might tend to treat of "theism" in the abstract and without any scriptural moorings. On this, see David B. Burrell, *Knowing the Unknowable God: Ibn-Sina, Maimonides, Aquinas* (Notre Dame, Ind.: University of Notre Dame Press, 1986), 2, and Burrell (2008b).
87. This challenge was part of a wider encounter in the Middle Ages between the heritage of classical Graeco-Roman antiquity and the doctrines of the Abrahamic faiths. For more on this, see Steven Baldner and William E. Carroll, *Aquinas on Creation: Writings on the "Sentences" of Peter Lombard, Book 2, Distinction 1, Question 1* (Toronto: Pontifical Institute of Mediaeval Studies, 1997).
88. *Metaphysics* Γ.2 and Z.1. On the question of translating *ousia* as "substance" "being" or even "reality", see Eric Perl, *Thinking Being: Introduction to Metaphysics in the*

Classical Tradition (Leiden: Brill, 2014), 82–89, and Aryeh Kosman, *The Activity of Being: An Essay on Aristotle's Ontology* (Cambridge, Mass.: Harvard University Press, 2013), ix.

89. For the fullest treatment of this question, see Edward Booth, *Aristotelian Aporetic Ontology in Islamic and Christian Thinkers* (Cambridge: Cambridge University Press, 1983).
90. Even a text that ostensibly deals with "origins," like Plato's *Timaeus*, still has the demiurge fashioning the world out of preexistent matter.
91. On this connection, see David B. Burrell, "Essence and Existence: Avicenna and Greek Philosophy," *MIDEO (Melanges Institut Dominicain d'Etudes Orientales)* 17 (1986): 53–66.
92. For a fuller treatment of Avicenna's revisions of Aristotle, see Booth (1983), 107–26.
93. Gilson, "Quasi Definitio Substantiae," in Étienne Gilson, ed., *St. Thomas Aquinas, 1274–1974: Commemorative Studies* (Toronto: Pontifical Institute of Mediaeval Studies, 1974), 126.
94. For a discussion of emanation in Al-Kindi, see Peter Adamson, *Al-Kindi* (Oxford: Oxford University Press, 2007), 57–73, and Alfred L. Ivry., *Al-Kindī's Metaphysics/a Translation of Ya'qūb Ibn Isḥāq Al-Kindī"s Treatise "On First Philosophy" (Fī Al-Falsafah Al-Ūlā) with Introduction and Commentary* (Albany: State University of New York Press, 1978).
95. Al-Ghazali, *Tahafut Al-Falasifah* in Marmura (2000). The broader assumptions underlying any perceived opposition between "emanation" and "free creation" will be tackled directly in Chapter 4.
96. Burrell (2004), xiv–xv.
97. Cf. Rudi Te Velde, *Participation and Substantiality in Thomas Aquinas* (Leiden: Brill, 1995), 102–8.
98. Burrell in Inglis, (2002), 207. This common interpretation of Avicenna, handed down by Al-Ghazali, and endorsed by Aquinas, may not, in fact, be a very fair witness to Avicenna's actual standpoint. Still, this is not a debate we can settle here, and, given that this *was* Aquinas's interpretation, whether or not it is textually accurate has little bearing on the argument of this book, which works with Aquinas. To follow the issues in detail, see Amos Bertolacci, "The Reception of Avicenna in Latin medieval culture," in Peter Adamson, ed., *Interpreting Avicenna: Critical Essays* (Cambridge: Cambridge University Press, 2013), 256–59.
99. See, for example, De Pot. 7.3 A.D.4.
100. For example, 2 Maccabees 7.28: "So I urge you, my child, to look at the sky and the earth. Consider everything you see there, and realize that God made it all from nothing, just as he made the human race."
101. Kosman (2013: vii–viii and *passim*) presents a convincing argument for translating *energeia* as "activity," rather than the more common "act," in order to underline the ongoing, verbal quality of "being." Burrell makes a similar argument in Davies, ed. (1987), 78–79.
102. For a more detailed analysis of how Thomas's notion of "participated being" undergoes development under the influence of Aristotle and Avicenna, see Te Velde (1995), 69–73.

103. Te Velde (1995), 91: "Creating does not simply mean the actualization of a possibility; creation denotes the origin of things according to their entire being, *principium totius esse.*"
104. Here we can clearly see why Burrell insists on divine simplicity as the formal feature that secures "the distinction"—cf. Burrell (1986b), 29–34. I return to the technical distinction in Aquinas between a "real" and a "logical" relation when we look in more detail at Sara Grant in Chapter 3.
105. ST I.45.4.1.
106. Burrell (2004), 217.
107. Thomas F. O'Meara, *Thomas Aquinas: Theologian* (Notre Dame, Ind.: University of Notre Dame Press, 1997), 200.
108. Burrell is not, of course, the first Aquinas scholar to have noticed these sorts of historical influences (Étienne Gilson was famously drawing attention to them as early as the 1930s), but a specific focus on the importance of figures like Avicenna for Aquinas is still quite rare in Thomist literature. A recent notable exception would be Jim Fodor and F. C. Bauerschmidt, eds., *Aquinas in Dialogue: Thomas for the Twenty-First Century* (Hoboken, N.J.: Wiley-Blackwell, 2004).
109. Burrell and Malits (1997), 79.
110. Burrell and Malits (1997) 74, and Burrell in Drummond and Hart, eds. (1996), 206.
111. Grant (2002). This was originally delivered by Grant in 1989 at Cambridge as the Teape lectures and was reprinted in 2002 with a foreword by Malkovsky.
112. Burrell and Malits (1997), 75. Burrell's characterization of monism here, namely, that the universe is "merely an expression of its originative source" is ambiguous, since such a description could be applied even to an ontologically real universe. I suspect what he has in mind, through the emphasis on the "merely," is the sort of illusionistic monism often associated with a certain (dominant) interpretation of Advaita Vedānta as acosmist. According to this reading of Advaita, the world is ultimately *illusory*. The world seems to exist only from the lower ignorance-bound perspective of people in general but not for the rare enlightened sage. I examine this interpretation of Advaita in the following chapter, but suffice it to say for now that this is a reading of (Śaṁkara's) non-dualism that is rejected by Grant and, thanks to her, also by Burrell. I am grateful to Bradley Malkovsky for helping me to think through these points more clearly.
113. Martin Ganeri, "'Thinking the Creator and Creature Together': How Rāmānuja's Account of Scriptural Meaning Encourages Unitive Language in Christian Discourse about God and the World," *Journal of Hindu-Christian Studies* 31 (2018): Article 18. Ganeri draws this phrase from his reading of Burrell.
114. He explicitly suggests "correlating relation with distinction" in order to align Sara Grant's nondualism with Sokolowski in Burrell and Malits (1997), 75, n. 6.
115. Aristotle, *Categories* 2a–b.
116. Burrell (2000), 40–41.
117. Burrell (1997), 72. This is a slightly unusual phrase, given that Vedāntic non-dualism is, linguistically, a "negative" description of Reality (viz. that it is "not-two," *a-dvaita*). Burrell perhaps has something like the following in mind: whereas Tanner tells us *not* to contrast God and world, Advaita Vedānta tell us that Reality *is* nondual.

118. Burrell (2004), xx–xxi.
119. Cf. Burrell, "The Christian Distinction" in Drummond and Hart (1996), 195, and Burrell in Weinandy (2004), 27. For more on the issues at stake at the Council of Chalcedon, and how the metaphysical options at Chalcedon might seem to mirror those we have addressed in this chapter, see Brian E. Daley, SJ, "Unpacking the Chalcedonian Formula: From Studied Ambiguity to Saving Mystery," *The Thomist* 80 (2016): 165–89. Cf. also Hans Urs Von Balthasar, *Cosmic Liturgy* (San Francisco: Ignatius Press, 2003), 63–64.
120. Turner (2004), 217.
121. I am aware that this might risk undermining the uniqueness of the incarnation by implying that the way human and divine natures are related in the person of Jesus the Christ is an instantiation of an overarching metaphysics that applies *en gros* to the relation between creatures and Creator. I will not address this here, other than to say that Grant (2002: 82–92) does seem to accept this unorthodox (according to official Roman Catholic teaching) position on Christology.
122. Burrell (2008), 182.
123. "Sara Grant carries this mode of thought [viz. non-contrastivity] a step further to make a highly suggestive connection with Sankara's *advaita*, proposing that we read Aquinas' determination that creation consists in a 'non-reciprocal relation of dependence' in creatures as a western attempt to articulate what Sankara calls 'non-duality.' For is that not what the 'non-contrastive' relation between creator and creatures comes to, in our terms: not *other*, yet not the *same* either?" Burrell in Inglis (2002), 209.
124. Burrell in Drummond and Hart, eds. (1996), 196.
125. Burrell and Malits (1997).
126. Even among scholars who work specifically on Hindu-Christian comparative themes, Sara Grant's work is not widely discussed. The main notable exceptions would be Bradley Malkovsky and Martin Ganeri: see, for example, Malkovsky's introduction to Grant's *Towards an Alternative Theology*, and Ganeri (2015), esp. 30–31. The only Christian theologian who does not work comparatively with Hinduism other than Burrell (to the best of my knowledge) to have explicitly recognized the significance of Grant is Martin Poulsom (2014), 62–63.

2. *Roman Catholic Encounters with Advaita Vedānta: Between Transcendental Illusion and Radical Contingency*

1. David Loy, *Nonduality: A Study in Comparative Philosophy*, (New Haven, Conn.: Yale University Press, 1988), 17.
2. Ganeri (2015), 4.
3. The Vedas themselves are notoriously hard to date but are generally thought to originate over centuries from ca. 1500–600 BCE with the *Upaniṣads* likely to have been composed around 900–200 BCE.
4. Examples of the first genre would be Śaṁkara's *Brahmasūtrabhāṣya* or *Gītābhāṣya*, while examples of the second genre would be his *Vivekacūḍāmaṇi* or *Upadeśasāhasrī* (though the authorship of the former is contested).

5. Two well-known "schools," which developed theistic responses to Śaṁkara's "crypto-Buddhist" (a common charge against him) non-dualism were the Śrī Vaiṣṇava tradition associated with Rāmānuja (ca. 1017–1137 CE) that came to be known as *Viśiṣṭādvaita* (non-dualism of the differentiated) Vedānta, and the *Dvaita* (dualist) Vedānta of Madhva (ca. 1238–1317 CE). For a comprehensive overview of these different interpretations of the *Upaniṣadic* revelation, see Eric J. Lott, *Vedāntic Approaches to God* (London: Macmillan, 1980).
6. Some scholars reject the traditional 788–820 dating, which emerged only in the late nineteenth century and was based on an alleged writing of Śaṁkara that is now deemed spurious. No one disagrees that Śaṁkara probably lived about thirty-two years, but he is now regularly dated as having lived "ca. 700 CE." To follow this up in more detail, see Bradley Malkovsky, *The Role of Divine Grace in the Soteriology of Śaṃkarācārya* (Leiden: Brill, 2001), 1–8.
7. For a biography of Śaṁkara, see Sudhakshina Rangaswami, ed., *The Roots of Vedānta: Selections from Śaṅkara's Writings* (New Delhi: Penguin India, 2012), 1–15.
8. For more detailed analyses of how and why Advaita Vedānta came to be the focus of the Hindu Renaissance, as well as of nineteenth- to early twentieth-century European receptions of Indian philosophical thought, see Wilhelm Halbfass, *India and Europe: An Essay in Understanding* (Albany: State University of New York Press, 1988) and Richard King, *Orientalism and Religion: Post-Colonial Theory, India and "The Mystic East,"* (New York: Routledge, 1999).
9. As suggested by the existence of at least three main schools of Vedānta and their key divergences, it is a moot point whether the *Upaniṣadic* texts should, in fact, be read in this way, but that question is beyond the scope of my discussion here.
10. *Brahma satyaṃ jagan mithyā jīvo brahmaiva nāparaḥ*. The phrase is ubiquitous in Advaitic literature, but originally comes from a text called *Bālabodhinī*. See R. Brooks, "The Meaning of 'Real' in Advaita Vedānta," *Philosophy East and West* 19 (1969), 385.
11. See E. Deutsch, *Advaita Vedānta: A Philosophical Reconstruction* (Honolulu: University of Hawaii, 1969), 47.
12. For an account of how this goal might be effected through the pedagogical techniques of Advaita, see J. G. Suthren Hirst, *Śaṃkara's Advaita Vedānta: A Way of Teaching* (Abingdon: Routledge Curzon, 2005). I provide a more nuanced textual account of different aspects of Advaita in Chapters 3–5.
13. Paul Deussen, *The System of the Vedānta* (Delhi: Oriental Reprint, 1979), 459.
14. Malkovsky (2001), 46.
15. Malkovsky (2001), 46–47.
16. Paul Hacker, "The Theory of Degrees of Reality in Advaita Vedānta," in W. Halbfass, ed., *Philology and Confrontation: Paul Hacker on Traditional and Modern Vedanta* (Albany: State University of New York Press, 1995), 137.
17. C. Ram-Prasad, *Advaita Epistemology and Metaphysics: An Outline of Indian Non-Realism* (London: Routledge, 2002), 1.
18. *Vivekacūḍāmaṇi* 230. All references will be to the critical edition of John A. Grimes, *The Vivekacūḍāmaṇi of Śaṅkarācārya Bhagavatpāda: An Introduction and Translation* (Burlington, VT: Ashgate, 2004). Hereafter, VC.
19. VC 253 (my emphasis).

20. VC 232.
21. Malkovsky (2001) mentions the following scholars who defend a "realist" reading of Advaita: D.M. Datta, R. Brooks, and J. Kattackal (cf. 47–50).
22. Uma Pandey, *Śankara: A Realist Philosopher* (Jalandhar: Kautilya Prakashan, 2015); Anantanand Rambachan, *The Advaita Worldview: God, World, and Humanity* (Albany: State University of New York Press, 2006).
23. Hacker in Halbfass (1995), 138.
24. It is important to remember that Advaita Vedānta was (and is) a living soteriological tradition and ongoing exegetical conversation. So, while it may be true to say that Śaṁkara himself would reject a subjective idealist interpretation of the empirical world, this claim may be less applicable to other thinkers in the tradition like Padmapāda (ca. 900 CE), Prakāśātman (ca. 1300 CE) and, especially, Prakāśānanda (ca. 1600 CE), as we will see in Chapter 5.
25. Cf. his *Brahma-Sūtra-Bhāṣya* II.ii.27–29 (hereafter, BSBh). All references will be to the edition translated by Swami Gambhirananda (Calcutta: Advaita Ashrama, 1977).
26. BSBh II.ii.28.
27. I return to this difference in emphasis between Christian and Advaitic theology in Chapter 5.
28. For succinct and thought-provoking analyses, see Bradley Malkovsky, "Advaita Vedānta and Christian Faith," *Journal of Ecumenical Studies* 36, nos. 3–4 (Summer–Fall 1999): 397–422, and Martin Ganeri, "Catholic Encounter with Hindus in the Twentieth Century," *New Blackfriars* 88, no. 1016 (2007): 410–32.
29. Aleaz (2008). Aleaz has also written on Eastern Christian thought in *A Convergence of Advaita Vedānta and Eastern Christian Thought* (Delhi: ISPCK, 2000) and on *The Relevance of Relation in Śaṅkara's Advaita Vedānta* (Delhi: Kant Publications, 1996). There are also studies of individual figures, for example, Teasdale (1987).
30. Ganeri (2015). See especially 14–31 for a historical overview. Ganeri traces the comparative encounter between Thomism and Advaita Vedānta back almost to the beginnings of the Western Scholastic tradition itself, to the presence in India of Franciscan and Dominican friars in the thirteenth and fourteenth centuries and, in particular, to Jesuit missionaries like Roberto de Nobili (1577–1656). On De Nobili, see also Clooney (2001), 3–7.
31. Francis X. Clooney, *The Future of Hindu-Christian Studies: A Theological Inquiry* (New York: Routledge, 2017).
32. The two major works on Upadhyay are Julius Lipner, *Brahmabandhab Upadhyay: The Life and Thought of a Revolutionary* (Delhi: Oxford University Press, 1999); and Timothy C. Tennent, *Building Christianity on Indian Foundations: The Legacy of Brahmabandhav Upadhyay* (Delhi: ISPCK, 2000).
33. *Aeterni Patris* (1879), issued by Pope Leo XIII, explicitly puts forward the Scholasticism of Aquinas as the metaphysical framework that most faithfully expresses the truths of the Catholic faith. Cf. also *Dei Filius* (1869–1870). This late nineteenth- to early twentieth-century critical revival of medieval Scholasticism (especially that of Aquinas) in European Catholic theology as a rational defense of the Catholic faith against perceived philosophical and scientific challenges to the Christian worldview became known as "Neo-Thomism" or "Neo-Scholasticism."

34. Many of the figures in the so-called Hindu Renaissance, however, become active only from 1900 onward (Swami Vivekananda is a crucial exception).
35. Lipner (1999), 116. In particular, Upadhyay was influenced by the neo-Thomism of the *Manuals of Catholic Philosophy* being produced by English Jesuits at Stonyhurst. For more on this, see Joseph Watzlawik, *Leo XIII and the New Scholasticism* (Cebu City, Philippines: University of San Carlos, 1966).
36. It was Thibaut who edited and translated the three volumes of the *Vedānta-Sūtras* (the first two with the commentaries of Śaṁkara, and the third with the commentary of Rāmānuja) for F. Max-Müller's *Sacred Books of the East* series. For more on this, see Arie L. Molendijk, *Friedrich Max Müller & the Sacred Books of the East* (Oxford: Oxford University Press, 2016), 76–77.
37. Along with Thibaut, Deussen was one of the first Europeans to translate the *Vedānta-Sūtras* (also known as the *Brahma-Sūtras*), and was particularly interested in the connections between Vedānta and Western philosophy—especially that of Plato, Kant, and Schopenhauer.
38. Lipner (1999), 189.
39. Lipner (1999), 195 (with citations from Upadhyay, "The True Doctrine of Maya," *Sophia* [February–March 1899]).
40. Tennent (2000), 268.
41. Tennent (2000), 265–66. He points out that an unbalanced focus on the "subjective delusion" type metaphor was later reinforced in the minds of many Western and Indian interpreters by eighteenth- to nineteenth-century philosophical idealisms.
42. Lipner (1999), 269.
43. Lipner (1999), 271. Hegglin taught Sanskrit at St Xavier's College in Bombay.
44. Lipner, 188.
45. Aleaz (1996), 9, 19 (n. 97), and 27–28.
46. Aleaz (1996), 28.
47. In the following section, I have deliberately chosen to focus in more detail on Dandoy because there is very little secondary literature on his work, and his essay on Advaita seems to have gone largely unnoticed even in the scholarship that focuses on the Calcutta School of Indology. Pierre Johanns's work, in contrast, has been analyzed and evaluated in detail in the excellent volume by Doyle (2006). An abbreviated version of this section on Dandoy appeared as: Daniel Soars. "Georges Dandoy SJ (1882–1962), 'The Doctrine of the Unreality of the World in the Advaita' (1919)," *Journal of Ecumenical Studies* 54 (2022). It is republished here with permission of the University of Pennsylvania Press.
48. Doyle (2006), 11.
49. Johanns alone wrote more than a hundred articles on different schools of Vedānta and analyzed their merits from a Thomist perspective. See Doyle, ibid.
50. Doyle (2006), 110. See also 130–31.
51. See Wallace's autobiography: William Wallace, *From Evangelical to Catholic by Way of the East* (Calcutta: Catholic Orphan Press, 1923) and, for an appraisal of Wallace and his influence on later figures, see Francis X. Clooney, SJ, "Alienation, Xenophilia, and Coming Home: William Wallace, SJ's *From Evangelical to Catholic by Way of the East*," *Common Knowledge* 24, no. 2 (2018): 280–90.

52. Robin Boyd, *An Introduction to Indian Christian Theology*, (New Delhi: ISPCK, 2000), 261. See, also, Joseph Mattam, "Interpreting Christ to India: A Pioneer, Pierre Johanns, SJ," *The Clergy Monthly* 37 (1973): 55.
53. Georges Dandoy, SJ, *An Essay on the Doctrine of the Unreality of the World in the Advaita* (Calcutta: Catholic Orphan Press, 1919).
54. Dandoy (1919), 1.
55. Dandoy (1919), 2.
56. Dandoy (1919), 2.
57. Dandoy (1919), 4 (original emphasis).
58. Dandoy (1919), 3.
59. Dandoy (1919), 3.
60. Dandoy (1919), 3 (original emphasis).
61. Dandoy (1919), 10.
62. Dandoy (1919), 10 (original emphasis).
63. Dandoy (1919), 16, n. 22.
64. Dandoy (1919), 21.
65. Dandoy (1919), 31.
66. Dandoy (1919), 28.
67. Dandoy (1919), 31.
68. Dandoy (1919), 34.
69. Dandoy (1919), 45.
70. Dandoy (1919), 40.
71. Dandoy (1919), 41.
72. Dandoy (1919), 62, my added parentheses.
73. Dandoy (1919), 62–63.
74. Dandoy (1919), 56.
75. Dandoy (1919), 41.
76. Dandoy (1919), 57–58.
77. Dandoy (1919), 58.
78. Dandoy (1919), 56.
79. Dandoy (1919), 57.
80. Dandoy (1919), 57.
81. Dandoy (1919), 58.
82. Dandoy (1919), 59.
83. Grant suggests that "inner cause" may be a less misleading translation of *upādānakāraṇa* than "material cause" given the connotations the latter phrase brings with it from Aristotle and the fact that Brahman is intelligible, not sensible. See Sara Grant, *Śaṅkarācārya's Concept of Relation* (Delhi: Motilal Banarsidass, 1999), 20.
84. For more on the Neo-Thomism associated with Louvain, see Doyle (2006), 51–53.
85. Johanns, "To Christ through the Vedānta," *Light of the East* 1.1 (1922): 3.
86. Doyle (2006), 64; Aleaz (2008), 113.
87. Doyle (2006), 55.
88. Doyle (2006: 188–89) specifically mentions these scholars as the main ones whom Johanns was consulting.

89. Johanns in his Synopsis of *To Christ through the Vedānta*, Part I, 22, quoted by Doyle (2006), 164–65.
90. Doyle (2006), 176–77.
91. Aleaz (2008), 118.
92. Doyle (2006), 188.
93. Doyle (2006), 179.
94. Johanns in *Light of the East*, July 1923, 3–4; here, see Doyle (2006), 180–83.
95. Doyle (2006), 183.
96. Aleaz (2008), 119.
97. In 1996, shortly before he died, De Smet initiated the publication of Johanns's articles on Vedānta, which had originally been published in *The Light of the East*. The articles were compiled in two volumes by Theo de Greeff under the title *The Writings of P. Johanns: To Christ through the Vedānta*, and published by the United Theological College, Bangalore.
98. For sensitive tributes to and biographies of De Smet, see Bradley J. Malkovsky, "In Memoriam: Richard De Smet, SJ (1916–1997)," *Journal of Hindu-Christian Studies* 10 (1997): 3–4; Julius Lipner, "Richard V. De Smet, SJ—an Appreciation," *Journal of Hindu-Christian Studies* 11 (1998): 51–54. After ordination, De Smet obtained a doctorate in 1953 from the Pontifical Gregorian University in Rome for a thesis (never formally published, but, according to Malkovsky and Lipner, widely disseminated in India) entitled "The Theological Method of Samkara." He then returned to India in 1954, and carried out research and teaching for the rest of his life at De Nobili College at the Papal Athenaeum in Pune (later known as Jnana Deepa Vidyapeeth)—see Lipner (1998), 52. For excellent critical collections of De Smet's work, see Ivo Coelho, ed., *Brahman and Person: Essays by Richard De Smet* (Delhi: Motilal Banarsidass Publishers, 2010) and *Understanding Śaṅkara* (Delhi: Motilal Banarsidass Publishers, 2013).
99. Cf. De Smet (1964), "Śaṅkara's Non-Dualism (*Advaitavāda*)" in Coelho (2013), 83–98 (also in De Smet and Neuner, eds., *Religious Hinduism: A Presentation and Appraisal,* [2nd rev. ed., St. Paul Publications, 1964], 52–62.
100. "Upadhyay's Interpretation of Śaṅkara," (1949) published for the first time in Coelho, ed. (2013), 454–62. During his studies in India and Belgium, and later, De Smet encountered many of the preeminent Roman Catholic scholars of Aquinas and Indology who would influence his academic work, including Joseph Maréchal, Pierre Scheuer, Pierre Johanns, Robert Antoine, Pierre Fallon, and Klaus Klostermaier (Lipner, 1998, 51–52).
101. Ibid. As noted earlier (fn. 43), Upadhyay's interpretation was opposed at the time by Hegglin, who contended that Śaṁkara did indeed espouse this "absurd conception of the absolute unreality of creatures," but De Smet maintains that it is Hegglin, and not Upadhyay, who misunderstood what Śaṁkara really meant.
102. Ibid. 456.
103. Ibid. 457.
104. Ibid. 458 (original emphasis).
105. De Smet, in Coelho (2013), 476.
106. De Smet, in Coelho (2013), 477. Cf. BSBh II.i.14, II.i.18, II.i.22, and II.i.26.
107. De Smet, in Coelho (2013), 458.

108. BSBh 3.2.5 (my transliteration).
109. De Smet in Coelho (2013), 458–59. For more on the importance of the perspective from which Śaṁkara is writing (i.e., that Brahman is the "measuring-rod"), see De Smet, "Śaṅkara's Non-Dualism (*Advaitavāda*)" in Coelho (2013), 84–85.
110. De Smet in Coelho (2013), 461. He takes this example from Pierre Scheuer (1872–1957), another Belgian Jesuit who was a great influence on De Smet—see Coelho, 382, n. 15.
111. De Smet in Coelho (2013), 461.
112. "A Note about Śaṅkara's Doctrine of Creation" (1949), also published for the first time in Coelho (2013), 463–84.
113. De Smet in Coelho (2013), 467. The key *Sūtra* here runs as follows: "But like what is seen in the world (creation is) a mere pastime" (*lokavattu līlākaivalyam*)—BSBh II.i.33.
114. De Smet in Coelho (2013), 467–68.
115. BSBh II.i.33.
116. De Smet in Coelho (2013), 477.
117. ST.I.45.5.
118. ST I.104.1.
119. ST I.45.3 (my emphasis). See, also, De Smet (1978), "Origin: Creation and Emanation" in Coelho (2013), 369–82 (first published in *Indian Theological Studies* 15, no. 3 [1978]: 266–279), 379.
120. Cf. also ST I.41.3, reply to obj.2: "For we can say that the creature is not the essence of God but its essence is from God" (*non est ex essentia Dei, sed est ex Deo essentia*).
121. ST I.8.1.
122. ST I.8.1 (my emphasis).
123. Cf. De Smet (1970), "Śaṅkara and Aquinas on Creation" in Coelho, ibid., 345–53 (first published in *Indian Philosophical Annual* 6 [1970]: 112–18); "Advaitavāda and Christianity" (originally published as "Does Christianity Profess Non-Dualism?" *The Clergy Monthly* 37, no. 9 [1973]: 354–57) in Coelho, 354–58; "The Correct Interpretations of the Definitions of the Absolute According to Śrī Śaṅkarācārya and Saint Thomas Aquinas," (originally published in *The Philosophical Quarterly* 27, no. 4 [1955}: 187–94) in Coelho, 326–34; "Patterns and theories of causality," *Philosophy Today* 9.2–4 (1965): 134–46.
124. ST Ia.45.1 and De Smet in Coelho (2013), 348.
125. De Smet, "Forward Steps in Śaṅkara Research" (1987), in Coelho (2013), 173–90, here 183.
126. "Origin: Creation and Emanation" in Coelho (2013), 381.

3. The Relation between the World and God in Śaṁkara and Thomas: Sara Grant's Case for a Form of Christian Non-dualism

1. Grant (2002), 5.
2. Cf. De Smet in R De Smet and J. Neuner, eds., *Religious Hinduism*, 4th ed. (Allahabad: St Pauls, 1996), 94–95.
3. Burrell, *Faith and Freedom* (2004), xx–xxi.

4. M. Ganeri, "Toward an Alternative Theology: Confessions of a Non-dualist Christian: Sara Grant RCSJ"s Contribution to Catholic Theological and Spiritual Encounter with Hinduism," 6, accessed http://publications.heythrop.ac.uk/1550/.
5. It was De Smet who encouraged Grant to focus on Śaṁkara's concept of relation for her doctoral thesis—cf. Grant (2002), 32.
6. This point is also a response to some concerns about Orientalism. Grant and her Roman Catholic predecessors are not crudely plundering the East for resources to supply Western needs. Rather, they are highlighting resonances, at a deep level, between "Western" and "Eastern" styles of conceptualizing the divine.
7. Cf. Malkovsky, "Advaita Vedanta and Christian Faith," *Journal of Ecumenical Studies* 36, no. 3–4 (Summer–Fall 1999): 397–422: "despite the assertion that Christianity may claim nonduality as part of its own tradition, the fact remains that many Christians conceive of God and creation in a dualistic sense. In this view God and world are not only regarded as distinct, but they are also taken to be *ontologically separate realities*" (422, my emphasis).
8. I am conscious that the language of "understanding" the "concept" of *advaita* may not sit easily for some readers, and am sympathetic toward those who would rather emphasize that nonduality (*advaita*) is an "experiential truth" that can only be "known" intuitively rather than grasped propositionally as a concept. Nevertheless, I think it is possible to get some measure of conceptual handle, conventionally speaking, on the metaphysics of *advaita*, which may be enough to advance our discussion—if not, perhaps, to be convinced of the truth of *advaita* in an ultimate sense.
9. My intention here is to draw out only those aspects of Grant's life that are salient to her case for a form of Christian nondualism. For a fuller biography, see her own first lecture in *Towards*, or Ganeri, "Toward an Alternative Theology—Sara Grant RSCJ's Contribution" (http://publications.heythrop.ac.uk/1550/).
10. For example, J. N. Farquhar's *The Crown of Hinduism* (1913).
11. Malkovsky in Grant (2002), ix.
12. The specific examples of works in this tradition that he mentions are: Klaus K. Klostermaier, *Hindu and Christian in Vrindaban* (London: Student Christian Movement Press, 1969); Abhishiktananda, *The Secret of Arunachala: A Christian Hermit on Shiva's Holy Mountain* (Delhi: ISPCK, 1979); Bede Griffiths, *The Marriage of East and West: A Sequel to* The Golden String (London: Fount, 1983). Other important European Christian theologian-Indologists of Grant's generation that Malkovsky refers to (whose works are less autobiographical than those mentioned previously) are Raimundo Panikkar (1918–2010), Richard De Smet, and Diana Eck (b. 1945).
13. Grant (2002), 5–6. Lecture 1 forms the first section of her book and is entitled "The Questing Beast: Mainly Autobiographical." Originally delivered as the "Teape Lectures," this lecture series was established in honor of Brooke Foss Westcott (1825–1901), who was Regius Professor of Divinity at Cambridge, Bishop of Durham, and one of the founders of the (Anglican) Cambridge Mission to India (now known as the Delhi Brotherhood Society), in 1877. In 1881, this Mission led to the founding of St. Stephen's, which would become one of Delhi University's most prestigious colleges. William Marshall Teape (1882–1944) was a student of Westcott and instituted

the lectures in 1955. It seems only fitting that I am discussing Grant's Teape Lectures alongside the possibilities of bringing Aquinas's synthesis of Graeco-Arabic philosophy and Christian revelation into conversation with Vedāntic Hinduism, given Westcott's own dream of a "new Alexandria" on the banks of the Yamuna. For more on this, see Clooney (2017), prologue.

14. Grant (2002), 6–7.
15. Grant (2002), 7 (my emphasis).
16. Grant (2002), 6, from a letter Grant wrote to *The Tablet* on July 29, 1989, rejecting the idea that the "I-Thou" paradigm offers the only appropriate language for expressing our relation to God.
17. Grant (2002), 14.
18. Grant (2002), 7.
19. Grant (2002), 9 and 17.
20. Grant (2002), 16. Unfortunately, she does not give any further indication of which aspects of Thomas's theology she found disappointing.
21. Grant (2002), 17. I will return especially in Chapters 4 and 5 to this attraction specifically to the Neoplatonic aspects of Aquinas's corpus (often mediated via Pseudo-Dionysius), not least because—I will suggest—it helps to explain why Grant was able to discern such strong resonances between Thomas's metaphysics of creation and Vedāntic non-dualism.
22. Grant (2002), 16.
23. De Smet entered the Society of Jesus in 1934 and only went to India in 1946. A similar interval applies to two of Grant's contemporaries: Henri Le Saux went to India in 1948 at the age of thirty-eight, some nineteen years after first becoming a Benedictine, and Bede Griffiths only departed for India in 1955 at the age of forty-nine, after thirteen years in various Benedictine monasteries in the UK. Other examples could be given, but the point to notice is that all of these figures were steeped—both spiritually and intellectually—in their own tradition before (and, indeed, during) their later explorations into Hinduism.
24. Grant (2002), 22.
25. She spent four years after her novitiate reading Greats at St Anne's College, Oxford. A significant personal influence that Grant acknowledges from this time was Iris Murdoch—her tutor in philosophy in her final year at Oxford (cf. 17–18).
26. Grant (2002), 29.
27. Malkovsky in Grant (2002), x.
28. In 1972 she helped to refound the ecumenical Christa Prema Seva Ashram in Pune (which had originally been started by Fr. Jack Winslow in 1929 as an Anglican community for men), and she would go on to be its spiritual director (*ācārya*) from 1977 until 1992. For more on the community and her experiences there, see her third Teape Lecture, "Theologizing from an Alternative Experience" (Grant, 2002: 59–98).
29. Grant (2002), 32.
30. Richard De Smet, *The Theological Method of Śaṅkara* (Rome: Pontifical Gregorian University, 1953).
31. Owing to the very nature of the *darśana* traditions as layer upon layer of commentaries, it is not always easy to know which "original" texts can be ascribed to any given

author, let alone one as commented upon as Śaṁkara (nor is separating the subsequent "tradition" from the "original" core a hermeneutical move that would be accepted by most orthodox Vedāntins). It is not my intention to engage in this debate here, but Grant defends the selection of Śaṁkara's texts, which she accepts as authentic in some detail in her doctoral thesis. See Grant, *Śaṅkarācārya's Concept of Relation* (Delhi: Motilal Banarsidass, 1999), 7–14.

32. Grant (1999), v.
33. Grant (1999), 12–13, and (2002), 33. Indeed, she is not convinced (on grounds of both style and content) that this is an authentic *bhāṣya* of Śaṁkara at all (and she is not alone in this scholarly judgment). Thomas E. Wood, for example, argues that it is the work of a later Advaitin trying to reconcile Advaita Vedānta with Buddhism—cf. *The* Māṇḍūkya Upaniṣad *and the* Āgama Śāstra (Honolulu: University of Hawaii Press, 1990).
34. J. J. Clarke, *Oriental Enlightenment: The Encounter between Asian and Western Thought* (London: Routledge, 1997), 61.
35. Perhaps the most obvious example of a European Idealist philosopher who was drawn to the worldview of the *Upaniṣads* as "world-negating" was Schopenhauer (1788–1860). See, for example, the preface to his magnum opus, *The World as Will and Representation* (1818). Advaita is founded on the possibility of a non-dual awareness of Brahman, which would dissolve the transcendental divide between the phenomenal and the noumenal domains—the possibility that is denied by Kant, who rejected the notion of an "intellectual intuition," but is accepted by later Idealists like Fichte (1762–1814).
36. There were also, however, Indian philosophers from around the turn of the twentieth century who began to assimilate and critically interrogate a diverse range of European "imaginations" of India, not least this presentation of Vedānta as a "world-denying" monism. For more on this complex episode in European-Indian intellectual history, see Ankur Barua, "The Absolute of Advaita and the Spirit of Hegel: Situating Vedānta on the Horizons of British Idealisms", *Journal of the Indian Council for Philosophical Research* 34, no. 1 (2017): 1–17 and Sharad Deshpande, ed., *Philosophy in Colonial India*, (New Delhi: Springer, 2015).
37. Grant (1999), v.
38. More than any other modern Śaṁkara scholar, Paul Hacker has shown the difficulty of reading Śaṁkara through the lenses of the Advaita tradition that succeeded him, starting with his immediate disciples. See Paul Hacker, "Eigentümlichkeiten der Lehre und Terminologie Śaṅkaras: Avidyā, Nāmarūpa, Māyā, Īśvara," *Zeitschrift der Deutschen Morgenländischen Gesellschaft* 100 (1950): 246–86, reprinted in English in Halbfass (1995), 57–100. This essay initiated a new phase of critical Śaṁkara scholarship. However, Hacker (as I explained in the previous chapter), believed Śaṁkara to represent illusionist non-duality, just as did the mainstream Advaita tradition after him.
39. Grant (1999), vi–vii.
40. For more on the founding of the ashram and their life there, see Jules Monchanin and Swami Abhishiktananda, *A Benedictine Ashram*, (Douglas, Isle of Man: Times Press, 1964).

41. Grant (2002), 29. Grant translated Abhishiktananda's *Rencontre de l'Hindouisme et du Christianisme* as *Hindu-Christian Meeting Point—within the Cave of the Heart* (Delhi: ISPCK, 1969).
42. Grant (2002), 29. This work was later revised and rewritten in English by Abhishiktananda and reissued as *Saccidananda: A Christian Approach to Advaitic Experience*, (Delhi: ISPCK, 1974).
43. Grant (2002), 31.
44. Grant (2002), 31.
45. Ganeri, "Toward an Alternative Theology," 7–11, and Malkovsky (1999), 415–20. For an overview of Le Saux's treatment of the issues we are discussing in this book, see Shirley Du Boulay, *The Cave of the Heart: The Life of Swami Abhishiktananda* (Maryknoll, N.Y.: Orbis Books, 2005)—esp. Chapter 8, "Christianity and Advaita: 1953–1954," Chapter 9, "Spiritual Crisis: 1955–1956," Chapter 14, "Pioneers in Dialogue: 1961–1963," and Chapter 16, "Overcoming Opposites." For a more detailed and compendious survey of his views on non-dualism, see J. Glenn Friesen, *Abhishiktananda (Henri Le Saux): Christian Nondualism and Hindu Advaita* (Calgary: Aevum Books, 2015).
46. Abhishiktananda (1969), 98.
47. Grant (1999), 26.
48. Cf. Chapter 1, 17 and 28.
49. Grant (1999), 27. All Vedāntic traditions emphasize the importance of learning or "hearing" (*śravaṇa*) the scriptures from a guru, systematically reflecting upon them (*manana*), and, crucially, the sort of deep, prayerful contemplation on them (*nididhyāsana*) that alone will lead to an intuitive understanding.
50. Grant (2002), 46 and (1999), 34–35, 71.
51. Grant (1999), 60.
52. Grant (1999), 63–65, 76–78.
53. I will expand on this notion of metaphysical "preexistence" in God in Chapter 5 when I discuss the concept of divine ideas in Christian theology.
54. *Chāndogyopaniṣadbhāṣya* VII.xxv.1 quoted in Grant (1999), 61.
55. Grant (1999), 68.
56. Grant (1999), 71.
57. Grant (1999), 68 and 73.
58. Grant (1999), 78. This is simply a different formulation of the aphorism we have already encountered—viz. "*Brahma satyaṃ jagan mithyā jīvo brahmaiva nāparaḥ.*"
59. Grant points out that this theme of the supreme self (*paramātman*) as the *svarūpa* of all beings constitutes the unifying principle of Śaṁkara's whole commentary on the *Bhagavadgītā*. Grant (1999), 107.
60. Grant (1999), 129, where Grant also points in a footnote to a text where Śaṁkara explicitly disclaims any such conformity (cf. BSBh II.ii.35).
61. Grant (1999), 88–155.
62. For a table of the frequency of usage of these different terms in the three different texts, see Grant (1999), 91.
63. There is not enough space here to reproduce and discuss all of Grant's many textual examples of different sorts of usages of *sambandha*, but these can be followed up in Grant (1999), 91–100.

64. Grant (1999), 99.
65. "a relation presupposes two distincts, and if Brahman and the world are to be related they should be regarded as distinct, but the Advaitin holds that the world is not other than Brahman . . . Brahman and the world are non-different (*ataśca kṛtnasya jagato brahma-kāryatvāt tadananyatvāt*: Br. S.B. II.i.20), and so the question of the relation between the two is an inadmissible one." S. Radhakrishnan, *History of Indian Philosophy*, II (London: Allen and Unwin, 1929), 565 ff., cited in Grant (1999), 23. As we will see later in this chapter, even Aquinas agrees that there is no "real" relation between God and the world.
66. Again, to follow up all of the textual examples, see Grant (1999), 100–2.
67. Grant (1999), 102.
68. BSBh II.ii.38
69. Grant points out that "identity" is how Thibaut normally renders *svarūpa* in his translation of the BSBh for the *Sacred Books of the East* series—see Grant (1999), 104.
70. BSBh III.ii.35, cited by Grant (1999), 104 (her emphasis).
71. BSBh I.i.6, cited by Grant (1999), 105 (her emphasis).
72. To follow up these examples, see Grant (1999), 105–9. "Self" is a common way of denoting the ultimate ground of reality in Vedānta and, as such, comes close to how a Christian theologian like Aquinas understands "God." Even more strikingly, one thinks of Eckhart, and his well-known conviction that "God's ground is my ground, and my ground is God's ground" (Sermon 5b, in *Meister Eckhart: The Essential Sermons*, 183) or even, in "The Book of Divine Consolation," where he notes: "Our Lord prayed his Father that we might become one with him and in him (John 17:11), not merely that we should be joined together," ("The Book of Divine Consolation," n.2, in *Meister Eckhart: The Essential Sermons*, 222 and 230).
73. See previous, BSBh II.ii.38.
74. Grant (1999), 128.
75. Cf. BSBh II.ii.38 (previous).
76. Grant (1999), 129.
77. Grant (1999), 150–51.
78. BSBh II.ii.38, cited by Grant (1999), 105 (her emphasis).
79. Grant (1999), 151.
80. Grant (1999), 140–45.
81. Grant (1999), 145.
82. Grant (1999), 156.
83. Grant (1999), 151.
84. Grant (1999), 151 and (2002), 42.
85. BSBh II.i.6, cited in Grant (1999), 152.
86. BSBh II.i.14, cited in Grant (1999), 152.
87. BSBh II.i.27, cited in Grant (1999), 152.
88. Grant (2002), 42. The reference is to an unspecified fourteenth-century Western mystic.
89. Malkovsky has also defended a "realist" reading of Śaṁkara and, therefore, of the need to distinguish Śaṁkara's writings from those of later illusionistic Advaitins, in

Malkovsky (1997), 541–62. See esp. 555–58 (his main focus in this article is on the nature of personhood of the Absolute).

90. Abhishiktananda (1969), 98.
91. Grant (1999), 157.
92. Grant (1999), 157–58.
93. Grant (1999), 158.
94. (Krempel 1952) For Grant's references to Krempel, see Grant (1999), 157–74 and (2002), 29.
95. Krempel (1952), 330–36.
96. Krempel (1952), 336–50.
97. Krempel (1952), 52.
98. Grant (1999), 161–65. See Aquinas, ST I.28.1.
99. Krempel (1952), 458–61.
100. Grant (1999), 165–73.
101. ST I.45.3.1, "The relation to a creature in God is not real, but it is according to reason only" (*relatio in Deo ad creaturam non est realis, sed secundum rationem tantum*).
102. Aquinas: De Pot VII.10, quoted in Grant (1999), 173. Cf. also ST I.45.3.1 "*relatio vero creaturae ad Deum est relatio realis*."
103. Grant (1999), 164.
104. Matthew R. McWhorter, "Aquinas on God's Relation to the World," *New Blackfriars* 94, no. 1049 (January 2013): 3–19 (see, esp. 9–13).
105. De Pot. 3.3. In distinction thirty of the first book of the *Sentences*, Lombard quotes Augustine's *De Trinitate*.
106. See SCG, II, Cap. XII, §913.
107. McWhorter (2013), 14. The same point could be made (at least on the kind of "realist" reading I have been defending) for Śaṁkara—cf. Malkovsky (1997), 559: "The upshot of this discussion is that *brahman's* relation to the world, far from being illusory, is a 'real' one (using the language of everyday talk), though it has no ontological effect on *brahman*."
108. Cf. Raimundo Panikkar, *The Unknown Christ of Hinduism*, rev. and enlarged (London: Darton, Longman and Todd, 1981), 104: "There is nothing independent of God. Nothing exists without being an existence, an outcome, an effect (*factus*) of God. Nothing is disconnected from him. All that is, is in, from, for, God. All beings not only proceed from God and go to God but also *are* in God" (original emphasis).
109. BSBh II.ii.17.
110. Grant (1999), 176–85.
111. Malkovsky (1997), 558–59 makes this same point.
112. Grant (1999) states boldly, "It would, therefore, seem that Śaṅkara could fully appropriate Aquinas's explanation of the relation of creator and creature, and that for all their difference of background and manner of expression they are wholly agreed that *relatio* is indeed *minime ens*, almost nothing in itself, yet providing by its very 'selflessness' the key to the mystery of *tādātmya*, by which all things have 'This' as their Self." (185).
113. Grant (1999), 185. It is important to remember here that the point that Grant (and Śaṁkara and Aquinas) are making is that the world does not affect God in a funda-

mentally *ontological* sense. This is not the same as saying that God is unaffected by the world in the sense of not *knowing* or not *caring* about it. McWhorter argues this case (against William Lane Craig) in his article (2013), 9–19.

114. Panikkar (1981), 145.
115. Panikkar (1981), 155.
116. Grant (2002), 52.
117. Grant (2002), 54.
118. Grant (2002), 53.
119. Upadhyay is an intriguing hybrid in that it would be difficult to say which of Christianity or Vedānta more clearly represented his "default" intellectual and spiritual tradition, out of which he engaged with the other as his *other*.
120. For my understanding of the historical contours of these debates, and for a nuanced discussion of the range of legitimate positions on the conceptual "intrinsicalist-extrinsicalist" spectrum, I am indebted to E. Oakes (2016), especially 1–38.
121. Not least, the fascinating question of how a notion of "grace" might be present even in Advaita. On this, see Bradley Malkovsky, *The Role of Divine Grace in the Soteriology of Śaṅkarācārya* (Leiden: Brill, 2001).
122. W. J. Hankey, "From Metaphysics to History, from Exodus to Neoplatonism, from Scholasticism to Pluralism: The Fate of Gilsonian Thomism in English-Speaking North America," *Dionysius* 16 (1998): 157–88, here, 4.
123. Brian Shanley, *The Thomist Tradition* (Dordrecht, Boston, London: Kluwer, 2002), 9.
124. Thomas F. O'Meara, *Thomas Aquinas: Theologian* (Notre Dame, Ind.: University of Notre Dame Press, 1997), 168.
125. Dandoy studied philosophy in Belgium (Namur, 1904–1905) and England (Stonyhurst, 1905–1907) as part of his Jesuit training, and then theology in St Mary's, Kurseong (1912–1916)—see Doyle (2006), 126; For a detailed survey of Belgian Thomism at the time, see Jan Van Wiele, "Neo-Thomism and the Theology of Religions: A Case Study on Belgian and U.S. Textbooks (1870–1950)," *Theological Studies* 68 (2007).
126. L. M. Gauthier in the preface to Georges Dandoy, *L'Ontologie du Vedanta: essai sur l'acosmisme de l'advaita avec commentaires de Jacques Maritain et Olivier Lacombe*, translated by Louis-Marcel Gauthier (Paris: Desclee de Brouwer et Cie., 1932), 9 (my translation). Gauthier is citing within this quotation R. Guénon, *Introduction à l'étude des doctrines hindoues* (Paris, 1921)—see 9, n. 2.
127. Maritain in Dandoy (1932), 161.
128. W. Hankey, "Denys and Aquinas: Antimodern Cold and Postmodern Hot" in Lewis Ayres and Gareth Jones, eds., *Christian Origins: Theology, Rhetoric and Community* (London: Routledge, 1998), 139–85. Here, 146–47.
129. Maritain in Dandoy (1932), 164–65.
130. Hankey in Ayres and Jones (1998), 143.
131. Hankey in Ayres and Jones (1998), 143.
132. Shanley (2002), 12.
133. Malkovsky, "In Memoriam: Richard De Smet, S.J. (1916–1997)," 3, and Malkovsky, *New Perspectives on Advaita Vedānta: Essays in Commemoration of Professor Richard De Smet, S.J.*, (Leiden: Brill, 2000), 2.
134. Shanley (2002), 13.

135. Hankey in Ayres and Jones (1998), 144–45.
136. Hankey, "From Metaphysics to History" (1998), 11–15, 22, and O'Meara (1997), 185.
137. Shanley (2002) 9.
138. Hankey, "From Metaphysics to History" (1998), 24.
139. Shanley (2002), 9.
140. Thomas compares this anonymous Arabic text (which had been falsely attributed to Aristotle) with Proclus's *Elements of Theology* and Denys's *Divine Names*. Somewhat remarkably, the first critical edition of Thomas's commentary was only produced in 1954 (the Leonine Commission had prevented it until then), by Henri-Dominique Saffrey, OP.
141. Grant (2002), 55.
142. H. Armstrong makes a similar point in his essay "Platonism" in Ian Ramsey, ed., *Prospect for Metaphysics: Essays of Metaphysical Exploration* (London: George Allen & Unwin, 1961), 93–110 (cf. esp. 97).
143. Grant (2002), 55–56 and 62–63.
144. Grant (2002), 63.

4. *Creation: "Ex Nihilo" or* "Ex Deo"*?*

1. *Ṛg Veda* 10.129.1–2, 4, 6–7.
2. Although "creation" is often used to translate *sṛṣṭi* (as in, for example, W. Doniger's authoritative version of the Ṛg Veda), I will use "world production" when discussing the Indic materials and "creation" for Christianity, lest it look like I have already settled the debate simply by using the same term in English.
3. See, for example, J. Lipner, "The Christian and Vedantic Theories of Originative Causality: A Study in Transcendence and Immanence," *Philosophy East and West* 28, no. 1 (January 1978): 53–68 or A. G. Krishna Warrier, *God in Advaita* (Simla: Indian Institute of Advanced Study, 1977), 116.
4. Ian McFarland, writes, for example, of "the radical ontological discontinuity between Creator and creature encapsulated in the doctrine of creation from nothing." McFarland, *From Nothing: A Theology of Creation* (Louisville, Ky.: Westminster John Knox Press, 2014), xii–xiii (see also 19–20). Lipner (1978) uses the same kind of language: 55, 58.
5. Śaṁkara, *Ātmabodha*, v. 63 (Nikhilānanda: 1978). The complete verse is: "Brahman is entirely different from the universe, but there exists nothing in the universe that is not Brahman. If any object in the universe other than Brahman appears to exist, it is unreal like the mirage which appears to be giving water in a desert." (*Jagadvilakṣaṇaṁ brahma brahmaṇo'nyan na kiṁcana; brahmānyad bhāti cen mithyā yathā marumarīcikā*).
6. Lipner (1978), 56.
7. Lipner (1978), 56–57.
8. Lipner (1978), 58. Cf. ST.I.28.1.ad.3.
9. Lipner (1978), 62 (my emphasis).
10. Lipner (1978), 65. Lipner suggests that the language and the metaphysics of entitative divine immanence *can* be found in the Christian tradition, but "in terms of concepts

that belong to revelative theology proper [as opposed to, I presume, philosophical theology], such as those of the Logos, the "mystical body" of Christ, sonship in Jesus, and eschatological considerations" (57).

11. In his article "Does Traditional Theism Entail Pantheism?" *American Philosophical Quarterly* 20, no. 1 (January 1983): 105–12, Robert Oakes makes the even stronger case (with which I agree) that "it is reasonable to believe an entailment of traditional theistic metaphysics to be that, necessarily, none of us exists in a condition of [metaphysical] separation-from-God" (110).
12. Wilhelm Halbfass, *On Being and What There Is: Classical Vaiśeṣika and the History of Indian Ontology* (Albany: State University of New York Press, 1992), 56. My explanation of the two different doctrines of causality in this section draws on Halbfass (1992), 56–62 and Grimes, *An Advaita Vedanta Perspective on Language*, 244–51.
13. Cf. *Vaiśeṣikasūtra* I.1.8; Halbfass uses the edition by Jambuvijaya (Baroda, 1961).
14. Surendranath Dasgupta, *A History of Indian Philosophy*, Vol. 1 (Delhi: Motilal Banarsidass, 1997), 257.
15. Halbfass (1992), 58.
16. Halbfass (1992), 57.
17. BSBh II.ii.1–10.
18. *Sāṁkhyakārikā* I.9; cited by Halbfass, 56.
19. The manifest world is explained in Sāṁkhya as the periodic evolution of an inherently dynamic and undifferentiated totality (*prakṛti*) through a process of internal modification (*pariṇāma*) and through the production within itself of a series of differentiations (*vikāra*, *vikṛti*). In other words, before its production the world already exists substantially and is pre-contained in a nonmanifest (*avyakta*) state in its cause.
20. For a detailed study of the development of the doctrine, see Gerhard May, *Creation Ex Nihilo: The Doctrine of "Creation Out of Nothing" in Early Christian Thought*. Translated by A. S. Worrall (Edinburgh: T&T Clark, 1994). For more recent overviews, see Simon Oliver, *Creation: A Guide for the Perplexed* (London: Bloomsbury T&T Clark, 2017), 36–43; Andrzej Maryniarczyk, "Philosophical Creationism: Thomas Aquinas' Metaphysics of *Creatio Ex Nihilo*," *Studia Gilsoniana* 5, no. 1 (March 2016): 217–68, esp. 221–39; or the articles in Janet Martin Soskice, ed., "Creation 'Ex Nihilo' and Modern Theology," *Modern Theology* 29, no. 2 (2013).
21. Oliver (2017), 36–38.
22. May (1994), xii.
23. May (1994), 39, suggests that the question of the creation of the world was not focused on seriously by Christian thinkers until well into the second century.
24. For example, Clement and Justin, who both accepted the existence of eternal unformed matter. Cf. Maryniarczyk (2016), 231, and May (1994), 179.
25. Some scholars would argue that these parallels between Greek and Indian thought are not coincidental, but the result of historical cross-fertilization. For a detailed examination of the issues (particularly for possible Indian influences on pre-Socratic philosophy), see Thomas McEvilley, *The Shape of Ancient Thought: Comparative Studies in Greek and Indian Philosophies* (New York: Allworth Press, 2002).
26. Theo Kobusch, *Selbstwerdung und Personalität: Spätantike Philosophie und ihr Einfluss auf die Moderne*. (Tübingen: Mohr Siebeck, 2018), 274–75. Some scholars attri-

bute these sorts of conceptual resonances to the direct influences of Christianity and Neoplatonism on each other, but I do not intend to enter into these debates here. For more on this, see R. Chiaradonna, "Plotinus' Account of Demiurgic Causation and Its Philosophical Background," in Anna Marmodoro and Brian D. Prince, eds., *Causation and Creation in Late Antiquity* (Cambridge: Cambridge University Press, 2015), 31–51, and H. Tarrant, "Platonism before Plotinus" in Lloyd P. Gerson, ed., *The Cambridge History of Philosophy in Late Antiquity*, Vol. I, online version (Cambridge: Cambridge University Press, 2011), 63–99.

27. Lipner (1978), 54 (original emphasis). I argue in Chapter 5 that the exception Lipner makes for the notion of creation existing in God as "seminal ideas" merits fuller consideration.
28. Lipner (1978), 66.
29. Halbfass (1992), 58.
30. Especially *Ṛg Veda* 10.129.1–7 and *Chāndogya* III and VI.1.4–VI.2.
31. BSBh I.iv.14–15.
32. BSBh II.i.17. "this declaration of the non-existence of the effect before creation is not meant to imply absolute non-existence."
33. BSBh I.iv.15.
34. BSBh II.i.18.
35. BSBh II.i.17.
36. See II.ii.1–10 for his refutation of the Sāṁkhya view and II.ii.11 for his refutation of Vaiśeṣika (in Greek thought-worlds, Vaiśeṣika philosophers are perhaps best likened to pre-Socratic atomists).
37. BSBh II.i.7, my emphasis.
38. Cf. *Monologion* 8.
39. ST.I.46.2.2. Cf. also, SCG II.16: *"Deus in esse res produxit ex nullo praeexistente sicut ex materia."*
40. Aquinas, *De Aeternitate Mundi.*
41. Cf. Kobusch (2018), 273: *"Die aus dem frühen Christentum stammende Formel der ‚Schöpfung aus Nichts' ist sicher als kritische Reaktion auf die platonische Vorstellung der Formung einer vorliegenden Materie zu verstehen."*
42. Cf. Te Velde (1995), 154–59, on creation ex nihilo and participation.
43. Maryniarczyk (2016), 240.
44. There are various Sanskrit terms used by Śaṁkara for this "potency": for example, *nāmarūpabījaśakti* (the potentiality belonging to name and form), *bījarūpā śaktiḥ* ("seed potency") or simply *śakti* (power). See Comans (2000), 241 and 248.
45. Lipner (1978), 54.
46. Aquinas, *De Aeternitate Mundi.*
47. We saw in Chapter 1 that this error was the potentially misleading consequence of Avicenna's language of "possible existence." It is true, for Aquinas, that there is a *conceptual distinction* between "essence" and "existence," but this does not entail a *separation*, as if essences could "be" without existence.
48. Lipner (1978), 54.
49. Cf. Gavin Hyman, "Augustine on the "Nihil": An Interrogation," *Journal for Culture and Religious Theory* 9, no. 1 (Winter 2008): 35–49—here, 41: "the doctrine of *creatio*

ex nihilo depends on the 'nihil' being conceived literally as nothing, as no form of substance or quasi-substance, and as having no ontological referent whatsoever."

50. Oliver (2017), 36.
51. ST.I.45.2, ad.1.
52. ST.I.2.3. Cf. also SCG II.34.6. "some people say that created things must always have existed; in so saying they contradict the Catholic faith, which affirms that *nothing besides God* has always existed [*nihil praeter Deum semper fuisse*], but that all things, save the one eternal God, have had a beginning" (my emphasis).
53. ST.I.45.1, ad.3.
54. BSBh I.iv.23. The Sanskrit *kāraṇa*, which is the word most frequently used by Śaṁkara in the passages I am discussing simply means "cause," but the Aristotelian terms for different styles of causation are often used in English editions, perhaps because the first Western translators of Śaṁkara worked with them as conceptual bridgeheads between Grecian and Indic worlds.
55. It should be noted that the nature of this relationship is ontological, not temporal; religious Hindus across all Vedāntic traditions tend to see empirical reality as beginningless (even if particular forms within it clearly do come into and pass out of existence).
56. Lott (1980), 16. Cf. also BSBh I.iv.14, Ch.VI.ii.1–3, *Aitareya Up*.I.i.1.
57. BSBh I.iv.23
58. BSBh II.i.4
59. See previously on BSBh I.iv.14.
60. BSBh II.i.24. Cf. also passages like "He wished, "let me be many, let me be born" (*Taittirīya Up*.II.v.2, Ch. VI.ii.3).
61. A. G. Krishna Warrier, *God in Advaita* (Simla: Indian Institute of Advanced Study, 1977), 95–96, makes this same point.
62. BSBh II.i.4.
63. BSBh III.ii.11, *Bṛhadāraṇyaka* IV.iv.25.
64. BSBh II.i.26.
65. BSBh II.i.13.
66. M. Comans, *The Method of Early Advaita Vedānta—A Study of Gauḍapāda, Śaṅkara, Sureśvara and Padmapāda* (Motilal Banarsidass, Delhi: 2000), 193.
67. BSBh II.i.26.
68. BSBh II.i.7.
69. BSBh I.iv.26 and BSBh II.i.4 above.
70. BSBh II.i.9.
71. BSBh II.i.14. The final sentence runs as follows: *tasmāt-kāraṇāt-paramārthato" nanyatvaṃ vyatirekeṇa-abhāvaḥ kāryasya-avagamyate*. This is the verse we saw earlier referred to by Grant.
72. Ch.VI.viii.7.
73. Parts of the argument in this chapter also appear in Daniel Soars, "Creation in Aquinas: Ex Nihilo or Ex Deo?" *New Blackfriars* 102, no. 1102 (November 2021): 950–966.
74. L. Gilkey, "Creation, Being, and Nonbeing" in Burrell and McGinn, eds., *God and Creation: An Ecumenical Symposium* (Notre Dame, Ind.: University of Notre Dame Press, 1990), 226. See also McFarland (2014), 19 n. 65.

75. One significant way in which Christian articulations of creation differ from (neo)Platonist, Islamic, Jewish (and Vedāntic) conceptions is due to the emergence of Trinitarian theology. See McFarland (2014), xiii, 86, and *passim*.
76. Rudi te Velde, "God and the Language of Participation," in Harm Goris, Herwi Rikhof, and Henk Schoot, eds., *Divine Transcendence and Immanence in the Work of Thomas Aquinas*, (Leuven: Peeters, 2009), 20.
77. Oliver (2017), 48, 62, 72.
78. Kobusch (2018), 277, describes this question of whether creation is "out of God" or "out of nothing" as, at first sight, one of the key differences between Neoplatonic and early Christian understandings of creation. He argues, however, (as I do) that the prima facie difference between creation *ex deo* and creation ex nihilo dissolves under closer scrutiny.
79. ST I.3.8.
80. De Smet, "Śaṅkara and Aquinas on Creation"—first published in *Indian Philosophical Annual* 6 (1970): 112–118—in Coelho (2013), 347.
81. See, for example, ST.I.13.11 where Aquinas approvingly cites St. John Damascene (De Fide Orth. i): "HE WHO IS, is the principal of all names applied to God; for comprehending all in itself, it contains existence itself as an infinite and indeterminate sea of substance."
82. Battista Mondin, *The Principle of Analogy in Protestant and Catholic Theology*, 2nd ed. (The Hague: Martinus Nijhoff, 1968), 86; Oliver (2017), 52; for a detailed history of the doctrine, see Philipp W. Rosemann, *Omne Agens Agit Sibi Simile: A "Repetition" of Scholastic Metaphysics*, (Leuven: Leuven University Press, 1996).
83. Etienne Gilson, *L"Esprit de la Philosophie Médiévale* (Paris: Vrin, 1989), 97. For instances of this principle in Aquinas, see, for example: *In III Sent.* 23.3.1.1; De Pot. 2.2; SCG II.21.8; ST I.5.3, 45.6.
84. *Commentum in IV libros Sententiarum*, lib. IV, dist.1, qu.1, art.4, ad 4: "*quia omne agens agit sibi simile, ideo effectus agentis oportet quod aliquo modo sit in agente.*"
85. ST I.19.4: "*Secundum hoc enim effectus procedunt a causa agente, secundum quod praeexistunt in ea, quia omne agens agit sibi simile.*"
86. ST I.4.2: "*Effectus praeexistit virtute in causa agente.*"
87. See Te Velde (1995), 92–93 for how this notion of causal participation in Thomas is influenced by Pseudo-Dionysius (especially his *Divine Names*). On the role of the *omne agens* principle in Aquinas, see 98–99.
88. Lipner (1978), 58.
89. Cf. De Smet in Coelho (2013), 332. "Anyone, therefore, who resorts to analogy (or *lakṣaṇā*) in order to know God, implies by the very fact some ontological community between creatures and God. St Thomas established this ontological community on the fact that God is the supreme and total Cause upon which all other beings depend entirely in their very being."
90. Mondin (1968), 93. See also *In I Sent.* 3.1.3, SCG I.29, ST I.4.2.
91. Warrier (1977), 98, makes the point that Aristotle was also a *satkāryavādin* as he believed that matter can only become what it has the inherent potential to be: for example, the oak is implicitly already in the acorn.

92. For Johanns, see Aleaz (2008), 115 and Doyle (2006), 50, n. 26.
93. P. Johanns, "To Christ through the Vedānta," *Light of the East* III, no.4 (January 1925): 4 (cited in Aleaz, 115).
94. Doyle worries that Johanns and others are trying to impose an alien notion of causality (*creatio ex nihilo*) onto Vedāntic philosophy, but I would argue that this notion of causality is only alien at the level of doctrinal specificities (e.g., that creation, in Christianity, is through the Trinitarian God), and not fundamental metaphysics. See Doyle (2006), 190.
95. De Smet, "Categories of Indian Philosophy and communication of the Gospel," *Religion and Society* x, no.3 (September 1963): 26, cited in Aleaz, 74–75.
96. De Smet, "Origin: Creation and Emanation"—first published in *Indian Theological Studies* 15, no. 3 (1978): 266–79, cited here in Coelho (2013), 372.
97. See, also, De Smet, "Śaṅkara and Aquinas on Creation" in Coelho, 347.
98. Steven E. Baldner and William E. Carroll, *Aquinas on Creation* (Toronto: Pontifical Institute of Mediaeval Studies Press, 1997), 12–13, 22.
99. For a concise overview of different metaphors of emanation in Neoplatonist and Christian thinkers, see Stephen Gersh, *From Iamblichus to Eriugena: An Investigation of the Prehistory and Evolution of the Pseudo-Dionysian Tradition* (Leiden: Brill, 1978), 17–27. For Plotinus's influence on medieval Arabic philosophers, see Adamson (2002).
100. Burrell in Drummond and Hart (1996), 196–98.
101. Ibid., 198–206.
102. Burrell in Kerr (2003), 75–83, here, 76–77.
103. Cf. SCG II.18.2–3. "For creation is not a change, but the very dependency of the created act of being upon the principle from which it is produced. And thus, creation is a kind of relation."
104. Burrell (2004a), xv.
105. ST.I.45.1.
106. De Pot. 7.2.
107. Damascene, quoted by Aquinas in ST.I.13.11.
108. Śaṁkara, too, insists that the production of the world is an intentional (though ultimately motiveless) act: BSBh II.i.11 and II.iii.7.
109. Burrell and McFarland make this point in greater detail. See Burrell in Weinandy et al. (2004), 40–42, and McFarland (2014), 86. For a full treatment of the issues involved, see G. Emery, *La Trinité Créatrice: Trinité et Création dans les Commentaires aux Sentences de Thomas d'Aquin et de ses Précurseurs Albert le Grand et Bonaventure* (Paris: J. Vrin, 1995).
110. ST.I.45.6 (see Article 7 of the same question also).
111. Cf. Kobusch (2018), 277: "*Das Christentum kennt zwar auch den Unterschied zwischen dem göttlichen Hervorbringen aus Nichts und dem Hervorbringen 'aus sich selbst,' aber dieser Unterschied markiert die Grenze zwischen dem 'Erschaffen' der Welt und der 'Zeugung' des Sohnes. So ist nach den christlichen Autoren die Zeugung ein selbstursprüngliches Hervorbringen eines Gleichwesentlichen, während die Schöpfung aus Nichts ein Hervorbringen ‚von außen her'* (exôthen) *darstellt.*"

112. Romans 11.36.
113. Aquinas, *Super Romanos* 11.5.
114. ST.I.13.5 (my emphasis).
115. Burrell in Weinandy et al. (2004), 36. The citations within the quotation are from Te Velde (1995), 94.
116. De Pot.7.2 (see previous).
117. Burrell, *Faith and Freedom* (2004), xv–xvi.
118. Commentary on *LdC* Prop. 4. Aquinas also cites Pseudo-Dionysius (*Divine Names*, V) in support of his commentary. All references are to the following version: Vincent A. Guagliardo, Charles R. Hess, and Richard C. Taylor, trans., *Commentary on the Book of Causes/St. Thomas Aquinas* (Washington, D.C.: Catholic University of America Press, 1996).
119. Aquinas, Commentary on *LdC* Prop. 10 in Guagliardo et al. (1996), 76. See also Prop. 18: "the first being is at rest and the cause of causes. If it gives being to all things, then it gives it to them by way of creation. And the first life gives life to those which are under it, not by way of creation, but by way of form," and ST.I.4.2.
120. Aquinas, Commentary on *LdC* Prop. 3 in Guagliardo et al. (1996), 23, (citing *Divine Names*, V.4).
121. Aquinas, Commentary on *LdC* Prop. 12 in Guagliardo et al. (1996), 90. See also Prop. 24 (Guagliardo, 137).
122. Warrier (1977), 107, agrees with De Smet and Grant that even Advaita does not affirm absolute identity between effect and cause, but the *absence of difference* between the two.
123. *Divine Names* V, cited by Aquinas in *ST*.I.4.2. resp.
124. See the Introduction by Guagliardo (1996) for further thematic resonances (xxx–xxxi).
125. His *Commentary on the Book of Causes* was one of Aquinas's last works (1272) and written while he was still busy with the ST and his commentaries on Aristotle (Guagliardo, 1996, ix.)
126. He was also, no doubt, influenced by the fact that his teacher had written a commentary on the LdC. See Therese Bonin, *Creation as Emanation: The Origin of Diversity in Albert the Great's* On the Causes and the Procession of the Universe (Notre Dame, Ind.: University of Notre Dame Press, 2001).
127. Aquinas, Commentary on *LdC* Prop. 6 in Guagliardo et al. (1996), 51–52.
128. Burrell in Kerr (2003), 77.
129. Burrell in Inglis (2002), 209.
130. In the Chalcedonian Creed, the phrases "without confusion, without change" are usually understood as being directed against the Monophysite denial (associated with Eutyches) of two distinct natures (human and divine) in Christ.
131. The phrases "without separation, without division" are supposed to have been directed against Nestorianism, which was understood as having claimed that the divine nature of Christ and the human nature of Christ are not simply two natures but are, in fact, two persons.
132. Cf. Warrier (1977), 108: "The truth is that there is no conceivable analogy available to elucidate the doctrine of anything whatsoever being produced by an immutable, timeless entity."

5. *How Real Is the World? Being and Nothingness in Śaṁkara and Thomas*

1. Malkovsky (editor's introduction) in Grant (2002), xvi.
2. *De ente et essentia*, ca. 4.
3. Cf. Warrier (1977), 107.
4. Richard King, "Brahman and the World: Immanence and Transcendence in Advaita Vedānta. A Comparative Perspective," *The Scottish Journal of Religious Studies* XII, no. 2 (Autumn 1991): 107–27, here 112.
5. King (1991), 112.
6. Matt. 10.29–30, John 10:2–15.
7. BSBh I. Preamble. For a fuller explanation of precisely how this "superimposition" functions, see T. M. P. Mahadevan, *Superimposition in Advaita Vedānta* (New Delhi: Sterling, 1985), 1–17.
8. One of the reasons Grimes thinks the *Vivekacūḍāmaṇi* can be attributed to Śaṁkara (in spite of a lack of scholarly consensus) is precisely the fact that "*avidyā*" occurs more frequently in the text than "*māyā*" (Hacker argues that Śaṁkara did not distinguish between these two terms as later Advaitins did), and that it is used to mean not first and foremost some kind of metaphysical entity, but a description of a state of being and affliction of one's psyche. He freely admits, however, that there are counterexamples (e.g., v.110), as indeed there are in the BSBh—cf. the verse from the preamble mentioned previously, which talks of "unreal nescience" as the "*material cause*" of superimposition; though, on some accounts, this translation as "material cause" is to be traced to Padmapāda and not Śaṁkara: E. A. Solomon, *Avidyā—A Problem of Truth and Reality* (Ahmedabad: Gujarat University, 1969) 267.
9. *Vedāntasāra*, translated by Swami Nikhilananda (Advaita Ashrama, Calcutta: 1978), v. 55 (my emphasis).
10. These terms are not identical, but more or less synonymous, for Śaṁkara. See Warrier (1977), 87; Mahadevan (1985), 33–36; Comans (2000), 248.
11. Thomas O'Neil, *Maya in Sankara: Measuring the Immeasurable* (Delhi: Motilal Banarsidass, 1980), 92–93 and 193–96. His supposed "doctrine" of *māyā* was the main reason why Śaṁkara was criticized as a "crypto-Buddhist." For further examples of this "quasi-substantializing" tendency in later Advaita, see Barua (2015), 44–64.
12. Hacker, "Distinctive Features of the Doctrine and Terminology of Sankara: Avidyā, Nāmarūpa, Māyā, Īśvara" in Halbfass (1995), 78.
13. Rambachan (2006), 73.
14. Pandey (2015), 14. Cf. also Srinivasa Rao, "Two 'Myths' in Advaita," *Journal of Indian Philosophy* 24 (1996): 265–79.
15. As Hacker points out, we should not be surprised by this conflation of terms because "It is inherent in the nature of monistic-illusionistic thought that these three concepts [*avidyā, māyā, nāmarūpa*], which are supposed to explain or at least allude to the transition from a purely spiritual Reality to an 'untrue' material state, should tend to coincide." Hacker in Halbfass (1995), 82.
16. Alston (2004), 119–20. The term *nāmarūpa* also appears in the *Upaniṣads*—for example, Br.Up. 1.4.7 and Ch.Up. 6.3.2 and 8.14.1.

17. BSBh 1.4.2 and Comans (2000), 240.
18. US 1.18. See also Ch.Up.Bh. 8.14.1.
19. For textual examples of this distinction between "un-unfolded" (*avyākṛte*) and "unfolded" (*vyākṛte*) *nāmarūpe*, see Hacker in Halbfass (1995), 67–77 and Alston (1983), 119–26. A good example is BSBh 1.2.22.
20. Hacker in Halbfass (1995), 70.
21. Comans (2000), 244–45.
22. Br.Up.Bh. 3.5.1 in Swami Madhavananda, trans., *The Bṛhadāraṇyaka Upaniṣad with the Commentary of Sankaracarya* (Calcutta: Advaita Ashrama, 1975). See also Warrier (1977), 94. The relationship between the concepts of *nāmarūpa* and *avidyā* in Śaṁkara is a subtle one. Comans agrees with Hacker that "what later Advaitins have done is to discard the concept of the unmanifest *nāmarūpa* and attribute its capacities directly to *avidyā*. Thus, *avidyā* is said to be the material cause (*upādāna*) and indeterminable (*anirvācya*), terms which in Śaṅkara's works apply only to the *avyākṛtanāmarūpa*." Comans (2000), 248.
23. Comans (2000), 241–43.
24. Br.Up.Bh. 2.4.10. See also US 1.19.
25. O'Neil (1980), 150.
26. Ṛg Veda 10.129. Obviously, talk of states "prior" to the origin of the world must be taken metaphorically, but the ontological conundrum of how something comes from nothing remains (except that it is not a conundrum for Advaitins!).
27. Hacker in Halbfass (1995), 141.
28. Hacker in Halbfass (1995), 143.
29. The following section relates to the exception we saw (Chapter 4, fn. 27) Lipner make for the existence of "seminal Ideas" in God as one sense in which the world exists prior to its creation. Parts of what follows also appear in Soars, D. "Divine Ideas and the Dependent Nature of Creation," *Medieval Mystical Theology* 30, no. 1 (2021): 47–58.
30. I draw on the following for my understanding of the role of divine Ideas in Aquinas: John F. Wippel, *Thomas Aquinas on the Divine Ideas* (Toronto: Pontifical Institute of Mediaeval Studies, 1993); Vivian Boland, *Ideas in God According to Saint Thomas Aquinas* (New York: E.J. Brill, 1996); Gregory T. Doolan, *Aquinas on the Divine Ideas as Exemplar Causes* (Washington, D.C.: The Catholic University of America Press, 2014). For the relevant passages in Thomas, see, for example, *Commentary on Sentences*, d.36, q.2, a.1. (What is an "Idea"?); De ver. q.3; ST I, q.15 and q.44.
31. Although the kind of "priority" I have in mind in these discussions is of an ontological and not temporal nature, it should be pointed out that Aquinas also accepted (on the basis of scripture) that the world had an origin in time (ST.I.46.2)—a position that Śaṁkara would not share.
32. I only offer a brief synopsis of the intellectual history of the divine Ideas insofar as it helps to clarify the place of divine Ideas in Aquinas. For a fuller historical treatment, see Boland (1996) and W. Norris Clarke, "The Problem of the Reality and Multiplicity of Divine Ideas in Christian Neoplatonism," in Clarke, *The Creative Retrieval of Saint Thomas Aquinas: Essays in Thomistic Philosophy, New and Old*, (New York: Fordham University Press, 2009), 66–89.

33. For example, *Republic* 476a–479d, 509d–511d, and 596b–597d. See also *Phaedrus* 247c and *Sophist* 240b–248a.
34. *Timaeus* 27c–47e. The Forms in Plato are, therefore, in H. Wolfson's phrase, "extradeical." See Harry A. Wolfson, "Extradeical and Intradeical Interpretations of Platonic Ideas." *Journal of the History of Ideas* 22, no. 1 (1961): 3–32.
35. Perl (2014), 33.
36. Armstrong in Ramsey (1961), 99. Cf. *Phaedo* 65d13–e2.
37. Cf. Armstrong (ibid.), 108–9. Interestingly, Grant (1999, 14–15) accuses Aristotle of "gravely misunderstanding" Plato on the relation of Forms to particulars, almost certainly because of "the lack of any term to express adequately the notion of immanence-in-transcendence that was not fatally colored with spatial implications."
38. Perl (2014), 25.
39. Boland (1996), 22 and 28–33. Some scholars claim that this hermeneutical move of placing the Ideas in a divine mind is already present in Plato himself (e.g., Perl, 2014, 62–64), but the generally accepted view is that this was a reasonable development of Plato's philosophy but not one made explicitly until sometime later in the Platonic tradition (Boland, 1996, 21).
40. Boland (1996), 31–33.
41. Platonist thinkers themselves would see their philosophy not as a development, but rather as a faithful continuation, of Plato's systematic vision, but Boland suggests that identifying the Ideas with the divine mind is "certainly the most important aspect of Plotinus' departure from middle Platonist metaphysics." Boland (1996), 58.
42. Armstrong in Ramsey (1961), 110.
43. *Ennead* 5.9.5.22–23.
44. *Ennead* 5.9.8.1–3.
45. *Metaphysics* Λ.9.
46. Boland (1996), 65 (my emphasis).
47. Augustine, *De diversis quaestionibus*, 46. Augustine was heir to the Platonism of Philo via the Alexandrians Clement (150–ca. 215 CE) and Origen (184–253 CE). See Norris Clarke (2009, 72) and Boland (1996, 38–47). Boland suggests that Augustine's choice of the particular term *rationes* was probably the result of Stoic influence.
48. Boland (1996), 67 and 86.
49. Boland (1996), 88.
50. *The Divine Names*, 824c.
51. Boland (1996), 103 and 146.
52. Boland (1996), 137–8.
53. ST.I.15.1: "It is necessary to suppose Ideas in the divine mind. For the Greek word *Idea* is in Latin 'forma.' Hence by Ideas are understood the forms of things, existing apart from the things themselves."
54. Boland (1996), 323.
55. ST.I.15.1, reply to objection 1.
56. Gregory T. Doolan, "Aquinas on the Divine Ideas and the Really Real," *Nova et Vetera* 13, no. 4 (2015): 1059–91. Here, 1059–60.
57. *Quaestiones de quodlibet* 8, a.2.
58. Doolan (2014), 82.

59. Doolan (2014), 104.
60. This is a phrase I take from a short article by Raimon Panikkar, "Nine Ways Not to Talk about God," *Cross Currents* 47, no. 2 (1997).
61. Boland (1996), 249 and 258–59.
62. ST Ia.4.3, ad. 3. "The likeness [*similitudo*] of creatures to God is not affirmed on account of agreement in form according to the formality of the same genus or species, but solely according to analogy [*secundum analogiam tantum*], inasmuch as God is essential being [*ens per essentiam*], whereas other things are beings by participation [*per participationem*]."
63. Boland (1996), 209 and 234. See also De ver. 3.2.
64. Burrell discusses the divine Ideas in Weinandy et al. (2004), 36. See also Te Velde (1995), 113 and 255–56.
65. ST.I.15.2. As Te Velde (1995, 113) puts it, "The Ideas should not be seen as so many 'mental pictures' in God's mind representing the possible essences of things. Their multiplicity does not stand apart from the one essence."
66. Cf. Te Velde (1995), 93: "Creatures do not result from a differentiation of the divine essence in many parts, but they are the many partial 'similitudes' into which the similitude of God's essence is distinguished and multiplied."
67. *Republic* 597a.
68. Clarke (2009), 86–87.
69. *Gauḍapādakārikā* 2.34. Edited and translated by R. D. Karmarkar (Poona: Bhandarkar Oriental Research Institute), 1953.
70. Comans puts this point particularly clearly: "Ultimately (*paramārthataḥ*), according to Vedānta, there are not two realities: Brahman existing over and against a real universe. In the final analysis, the universe is an appearance (*māyayā*) of Brahman; it is an appearance in and of pure Awareness itself, and since the real and its appearance do not constitute two realities, the truth is therefore non-duality (*advaita*)." Comans (2000), 66.
71. Richard Brooks, "The Meaning of 'Real' in Advaita Vedānta," *Philosophy East and West* 19, no. 4 (October 1969): 385–98, here, 385.
72. As I have already noted, all of this is grounded in the theme found in the *Upaniṣads*—that ultimate reality does not change. See also, for example, BG 2.16: "Of the nonexistent there is no coming to be; of the existent, there is no ceasing to be," and *Gauḍapādakārikā* 2.6.
73. This conclusion is logically implicit in the Advaitins' foundational belief that reality (Brahman) has an unchanging intrinsic nature. Barua points out how Madhyamika Buddhists like Nāgārjuna share the same premise (that intrinsic nature is by definition unchangeable) but, because of their diametrically opposed starting point (their belief in dependent co-arising, or *pratītyasamutpāda*) arrive at the opposite conclusion: namely, that change is all, and there is no such thing as perduring substantiality. For more on this, see Barua (2015), 48.
74. BGBh. 2.16
75. Deutsch coins the term "subratable" (my emphasis) to describe the same concept. See Eliot Deutsch, Advaita *Vedanta: A Philosophical Reconstruction* (Honolulu: East-West Center Press, 1973).

76. Brooks (1969), 388–89.
77. Ch.Up. 6.1.2–6.
78. BGBh. 2.16.
79. BGBh. 2.16.
80. It would be interesting to follow up this Idea of a "twofold cognition" in conversation with Aquinas's notion of *esse commune*, since it is not entirely clear what it would mean to be conscious of "existence" as such, as opposed to the existence of *this* particular pot (nor *can* it be entirely clear in empirical terms; only the *jīvanmukta*, through intuitive awareness, is (super-)conscious of pure existence; in conventional terms, it would mean that when we see gold bracelets our cognitive gaze remains "fixated" on the gold and not on the bracelets). For Aquinas's thoughts on this, see Te Velde (1995), 184–200.
81. Just as with the proverbial rope snake or magician's conjuring trick, no one perceives the rope *and* the snake or the trick *and* the sleight of hand at the same time.
82. Though, even here, it would be more accurate to speak of epistemic levels in our *understanding* of reality, than ontic levels of reality as such because the notion itself only holds from within the standpoint of ignorance.
83. Cf. Br.Up. II.iv.14: "Through what should one know That owing to which all this is known—through what, O Maitreyī, should one know the Knower?"
84. Pandey (2015), 178 and Brooks (1969), 393.
85. BSBh II.i.14 (my emphases). See also II.i.16.
86. Even though, strictly speaking, from this perspective there would be no awareness even of the mistaken perception of duality.
87. Cf. Grimes's Introduction to the VC (2004), 31. He uses the analogy of the appearance of the sun moving across the sky (from the "relative" point of view) in contrast to the earth moving around the sun (from the "absolute" point of view) to illustrate this idea.
88. Hacker in Halbfass (1995), 138. Cf. also BSBh I.i.11.
89. Cf. Warrier (1977), 128: "The conclusion seems inevitable that the question, is the world an illusion? is both imprecise and misleading. It raises the further question, to whom? No answer that does not specify the nature of the inquirer can make sense. To the perfected saint there is no world [distinct from God] at all, but only God; to the Advaitic dialectician the world may be [conventionally] accountable as an illusion; to the naïve worldling it is the sole reality."
90. See Grant (1999), 187–89, for her discussion of the later Advaita tradition.
91. Cf. Hacker in Halbfass (1995), 138.
92. Barua (2015), 45. My emphasis, because it is important not to forget that this is indeed only a *conceptual* spectrum (as Barua recognizes); that is to say that *all* Advaitins, if pushed, would have to say that it is ultimately impossible to talk about the reality or unreality of the world as if it were some-one-*thing* other than Brahman. Indeed, it is more likely that they would remain silent on this question than say anything at all.
93. For a detailed explanation of and comparison between the *Vivaraṇa* and the *Bhāmatī* schools, see O'Neil, (1980), 97–102.
94. The school takes its name from the title of Vācaspati Miśra's commentary on Śaṁkara's BSBh.

95. Both images—of the empirical self as a "reflection" of the Self and as "containing" the Self—can be found in Śaṁkara (see, e.g., *Vivekacūḍāmaṇi* 220 and 289 for the contrast).
96. Barua (2015), 22. Cf. also Alston (1983), 60–61.
97. Prakāśānanda, of course, would not think that we have departed at all from Śaṁkara. Not all scholars of Vedānta emphasize the difference between Śaṁkara and later Advaitins as much as Hacker and others have. Clooney, notably, stresses the continuity of the Advåita tradition and reads Śaṁkara in the light of later commentaries on his work. See Francis X. Clooney, *Theology after Vedānta* (Albany: State University of New York Press, 1993), 21–22.
98. Pandey (2015, 14), for example, claims that: "Much harm is also done to Sankara by the post-Advaitins . . . These scholars of post-Sankara era developed his philosophy in such a way, even Sankara would have been reluctant to accept." See also O'Neil (1980), 193–96.
99. R. W. Perrett: *An Introduction to Indian Philosophy* (Cambridge: Cambridge University Press, 2016), 182–83.
100. Brooks (1969), 391.
101. De Smet, "Origin: Creation and Emanation" (first published in *Indian Theological Studies* 15, no. 3 (1978): 266–79). Here, cited in Coelho (2013), 377.
102. Cf. De Smet (1964/1968), "Śaṅkara's Non-Dualism (*Advaitavāda*)," cited in Coelho (2013), 85.
103. De Smet in Coelho (2013), 93–94.
104. Hyman (2008, 46) talks, for example, of how "Augustine's image is of a world precariously balanced between God (being) and the "nihil" (non-being), precisely because the world is created *by* God (being) *out of* the 'nihil' (non-being)"—original emphasis.
105. Cf. Aleaz (1996), 19–20.
106. Doyle (2006), 163.
107. Johanns, cited in Doyle (2006), 164–65.
108. De Smet in Coelho (2013), 94.
109. Pope John XXII condemned twenty-six propositions drawn from Eckhart's works on March 27, 1329, in a Bull entitled "In agro dominico." See E. Colledge and B. McGinn, *Meister Eckhart: The Essential Sermons, Commentaries, Treatises, and Defense* (London: SPCK, 1981), 80.
110. From "In agro dominico" in Colledge and McGinn (1981), 80. McGinn points out that this language of the unreality of the world occurs throughout Eckhart's Latin and German works. See McGinn, "Do Christian Platonists Really Believe in Creation?" in David B. Burrell and Bernard McGinn, eds., *God and Creation: An Ecumenical Symposium* (Notre Dame, Ind.: University of Notre Dame Press, 1990), 197–219 (esp. 200). See also Anastasia Wendlinder, *Speaking of God in Thomas Aquinas and Meister Eckhart: Beyond Analogy* (Abingdon: Taylor & Francis, 2014), 10 and *passim.*
111. Selections from Eckhart's Defense in Colledge and McGinn (1981), 75.
112. Burrell, "Analogy" (2000), 43. It is important to note that Burrell refers here specifically to "Thomism" as opposed to Thomas Aquinas himself.
113. King (1991), 112.
114. Ch.Up. 3.14.1.

115. *Republic* 514a–520a.
116. King (1991), 123–24. Interestingly, C.S. Lewis makes a fundamentally similar point in a paper (originally a sermon) entitled "Transposition"—see C.S. Lewis, *They Asked for a Paper* (London: Geoffrey Bles, 1962), 166–83.
117. Grant (2002), 53.
118. McGinn in Burrell and McGinn (1990), 214. McGinn specifically has Eriugena and Eckhart in mind here, however, not Thomas.
119. Doolan (2015), 1061–62.
120. Zachary Hayes speaking of Eckhart in response to McGinn's "Do Christian Platonists Really Believe in Creation?" in Burrell and McGinn (1990), 220–25 (here, 221). Hayes shows (222) how Bonaventure says something similar.
121. Hayes, ibid. (my emphasis).
122. Hayes, ibid.
123. Cf. Hayes in Burrell and McGinn (1990), 224.
124. I take this phrase from Anantanand Rambachan, *Accomplishing the Accomplished: The Vedas as a Source of Valid Knowledge in Śaṅkara* (Honolulu: University of Hawaii Press, 1991).
125. Hayes in Burrell and McGinn, 225.
126. Hayes, ibid., 223.
127. Hayes, ibid., 225.
128. The concept of participation in Aquinas has attracted considerable scholarly attention since the second half of the twentieth century, and I cannot do justice to the details here. For seminal studies, see L. B. Geiger, *La participation dans la philosophie de saint Thomas d'Aquin* (Montreal: Institut d'Etudes Médiévales, 1952); C. Fabro, *Participation et Causalité selon S. Thomas d'Aquin* (Louvain: Publications Universitaires, 1961) and "The Intensive Hermeneutics of Thomistic Philosophy: The Notion of Participation" in *Review of Metaphysics* 27 (1974): 449–91; J. F. Wippel, "Thomas Aquinas and Participation" in *Studies in Medieval Philosophy* (Washington, D.C.: Catholic University of America Press, 1984), 117–58.
129. Doolan (2015), 1071.
130. Doolan (2015), ibid., quoting ST Ia.18.4, ad 3. See also *Commentary on the Metaphysics* III 3.356.
131. Doolan, ibid., 1073, quoting *Commentary on the Sentences* I, q. 36, a. 1.3, ad 2.
132. Doolan, ibid., 1074, quoting *De veritate* q. 4, a. 6, ad. 1.
133. "*Et sic sunt in Deo per proprias rationes, quae non sunt aliud in Deo ab essentia divina. Unde res, prout sic in Deo sunt, sunt essentia divina.*" (ST Ia.18.4, ad 1). Cf. also Doolan, ibid., 1084–85.
134. Doolan, ibid., 1079–82 discusses the relation between ontological and logical truth in Aquinas in some detail.
135. Doolan, ibid., 1075.
136. ST Ia.18.4.
137. Doolan, ibid., 1078, quoting ST Ia.18.4.ad.3. Cf. also, 1082: "the *esse* of a divine Idea, ontologically considered, is nothing other than the immaterial, uncreated *esse* of God. The divine Idea of Man, therefore, cannot be called 'a man' because the *esse* of a man is not that of God."

138. De ver. q.3, a.8.
139. Boland (1996), 325.
140. Boland (1996), 331.
141. ST I.15.2.
142. ST I.44.3.
143. De ver. q. 2, a. 3 A.D. 18. Cf. also Te Velde (1995:183), "Something particular and finite, considered in isolation from the universal and the infinite, will immediately dissolve into nothing."
144. Aquinas defines participation in his commentary on Boethius's *De Hebdomadibus* as follows: "*Est autem participare quasi partem capere* [to take a part of something]; *et ideo quando aliquid particulariter recipit id quod alterum pertinet universaliter* [when something has in a particular way what belongs to another universally], *dicitur participare illud.*" *In de hebd.*, lect.2, n.24.
145. ST.I.3, ad.2.
146. Te Velde (1995), 281.
147. Te Velde (1995), 106 (my emphasis).
148. Hyman (2008, 44, fn. 27) argues that Augustine's understanding of the "nihil" is similarly ontologically ambiguous: "when speaking of the role the concept of the 'nihil' plays within Augustine's writings as falling between nothing and something, I am . . . suggesting that it is neither unequivocally nothing nor unequivocally something. The 'nihil,' it seems, is between nothing and something in the sense that it escapes that very opposition rather than falling at a mid-point between the two."
149. BSBh 2.1.14.
150. ST I.41.3.2.
151. Rudi te Velde, "God and the Language of Participation," in Goris et al. (2009) 19–36—here, 19. L. Gilkey makes a similar point in "Creation, Being, and Nonbeing" in Burrell and McGinn (1990), 226–40: "Creation is neither a part of God, *de Deo*; nor is the ground of its reality separated from God: *ex materia.* It is of God and so absolutely dependent; and yet it is also real and self-constituting. This is an almost fiercely paradoxical set of relations" (238).
152. Certain contemporary Advaita scholars are attempting to address this imbalance and to show that a devaluing of the world is not a necessary implication of the Advaita worldview. See, for example, Anantanand Rambachan, *A Hindu Theology of Liberation: Not-Two Is Not One* (Albany: State University of New York Press, 2015).
153. Wendlinder (2014), 10–11, and Burrell, "Analogy" (2000), 42.
154. H. Nicholson suggests that it is the "denial of intrinsic being to created reality [which] marks the essential difference between Eckhart's ontology and Thomas's," in Nicholson, *Comparative Theology and the Problem of Religious Rivalry* (Oxford: Oxford University Press, 2011), 164.
155. Burrell, "Analogy" (2000), 44.
156. Norris Clarke (2009), 85–87.
157. Indeed, Boland goes so far as to say that "[t]he intelligibility and value of the created order derive ultimately from the divine Ideas." Boland (1996), 6.

Conclusion

1. Grant (2002), 37.
2. Grant (2002), 1.
3. Grant (2002), 33–36.
4. Malkovsky in Grant (2002), xvii.
5. Grant (2002), 2.
6. Ibid.
7. For example, Job 19:26, Luke 23:39–43, SCG IV.84.3, 7–8.
8. Cf. Psalm 90:3–6.
9. 1 Corinthians 15:28, Acts 17:28.
10. Rowan Williams discusses the "non-competitive" nature of divine and human agency in an interesting article on Augustine. See "'Good for Nothing?' Augustine on Creation." *Augustinian Studies* 25 (1994), 9–24 (esp. 19).
11. Tanner (1988), 105. In 106–19, she examines various factors that might influence which "side" of the rules gets emphasized, such as the particular philosophical milieu, the theological method, the specific topics and issues, or even practical concerns to do with what sorts of behavior the theologian wishes to encourage or discourage.
12. Ch.Up.Bh. XII.i and VII.xvii.i, cited in Grant (1999), 29.
13. Cf. Luke 9:3, Mark 6:8.
14. Luke 22:35.
15. For two recent overviews, see J. Lipner, "Comparative Theology in the Academic Study of Religion: An Inquiry." *Interreligious Relations*, no. 6 (July 2019); S. Mark Heim, "Comparative Theology at Twenty-Five: The End of the Beginning." *Modern Theology* 35, no. 1 (January 2019). Heim offers a "stock-check" on the state of the discipline via four works: Francis X. Clooney and Klaus Von Stosch, eds., *How to Do Comparative Theology* (New York: Fordham University Press, 2018); Michelle Voss Roberts, *Comparing Faithfully: Insights for Systematic Theological Reflection* (New York: Fordham University Press, 2016); Mara Brecht and Reid B. Locklin, eds., *Comparative Theology in the Millennial Classroom: Hybrid Identities, Negotiated Boundaries* (New York: Routledge, Taylor and Francis Group, 2016); Francis X. Clooney and John Berthrong, eds., *European Perspectives on the New Comparative Theology* (Basel: MDPI, 2014). In the same vein, we might also think of two works that both came out in 2010—one written by Clooney—*Comparative Theology: Deep Learning across Religious Borders* (Chichester: Wiley-Blackwell, 2010), and the other a collection of essays (many by Clooney's former students) edited by him: *The New Comparative Theology: Interreligious Insights from the next Generation* (London: T&T Clark, 2010).
16. Francis X. Clooney, *Theology after Vedānta: An Experiment in Comparative Theology*, (Albany: State University of New York Press, 1993).
17. I take the concept of "slow reading" from Francis X. Clooney's recent work, *Reading the Hindu and Christian Classics: Why and How Deep Learning Still Matters* (Charlottesville: University of Virginia Press, 2019).
18. Catherine Cornille, *Meaning and Method in Comparative Theology* (Hoboken, N.J.: John Wiley & Sons, 2020).

19. Ibid., 121–24.
20. Cf. Nicholson (2011), 198.
21. Swami Dayananda Saraswati, *Introduction to Vedanta: Understanding the Fundamental Problem* (Delhi: Vision Books, 2016).
22. Cornille (2020), 105.
23. Ibid., 116–21 and 124–29.
24. Acts 17:28
25. See David Tracy, "Comparative Theology," in *Encyclopaedia of Religion* (New York: Macmillan 1987), 446–55.
26. Michelle Voss Roberts, *Comparing Faithfully: Insights for Systematic Theological Reflection* (New York: Fordham University Press, 2016).
27. Cornille (2020), 151.
28. Swami Dayananda (2016), 104 and 107.
29. Matthew 10:39 and 16:25, Mark 8:35, Luke 9:24, John 12:25.
30. Galatians 2:20.
31. From a Sanskrit mantra attributed to Śaṁkara, called *Nirvana Shatakam*.
32. John 10:30.
33. *manobuddhyahaṃkāra cittāni nāhaṃ na ca śrotrajihve na ca ghrāṇanetre.*
34. *ahaṃnirvikalpo nirākārarūpo vibhutvācca sarvatra sarveṃdriyāṇaṃ na cāsaṇgatam naiva muktir na meyaḥ cidānandarūpaḥ śivo'ham śivo'ham.*

"For of him, and through him, and to him, are all things: to whom be glory for ever. Amen"

—ROMANS 11.36 (King James Bible)

"That from which these beings are born; on which, once born, they live; and into which they pass upon death—seek to perceive that! That is brahman!"

—TAITTIRĪYA UPANIṢAD III.1.1 (Olivelle)

BIBLIOGRAPHY

Śaṁkara and Other Primary Texts

Doniger, Wendy, trans. 1981. *The Rig Veda*. London: Penguin.

Grimes, John A. 2004. *The Vivekacūḍāmaṇi of Śaṅkarācārya Bhagavatpāda: An Introduction and Translation*. Aldershot: Ashgate.

Karmarkar, R. D. 1953. *Gauḍapādakārikā*. Poona: Bhandarkar Oriental Research Institute.

Olivelle, Patrick, trans. 1996. *Upanisads*. Oxford: Oxford University Press.

Radhakrishnan, S. 1963. The *Bhagavadgītā* with an introductory essay, Sanskrit text, English translation and notes. London: George Allen & Unwin.

Sengaku Mayeda. 2006. *Śaṅkara's Upadeśasāhasrī*. Delhi: Motilal Banarsidass.

Swami Madhavananda. 1975. *The Bṛhadāraṇyaka Upaniṣad with the Commentary of Śaṅkarācārya*. Calcutta: Advaita Ashrama.

Swami Nikhilānanda. 1978. *Sadānanda's Vedāntasāra*. Calcutta: Advaita Ashrama.

Swami Nikhilānanda. 1978. *Self-knowledge: An English Translation of Śaṅkarācārya's Ātmabodha with Notes, Comments and Introduction by Swami Nikhilānanda*. Madras: Sri Ramakrishna Math.

Swami Gambhirananda. 1983. *Chāndogya Upaniṣad: With the Commentary of Śrī Śaṅkarācārya*. Kolkata: Advaita Ashrama.

Swami Gambhirananda. 2016. *Brahma Sūtra Bhāṣya of Śaṅkarācārya*, 13th ed. Kolkata: Advaita Ashrama.

Aquinas

Anderson, James F. 1975. *Saint Thomas Aquinas, Summa Contra Gentiles—Book Two: Creation*. Notre Dame, Ind.: University of Notre Dame Press.

Fathers of the English Dominican Province. 1948. *St Thomas Aquinas, Summa Theologica*. London: Benziger Brothers.

Fathers of the English Dominican Province. 1952. *St Thomas Aquinas, Quaestiones Disputatae de Potentia Dei (On the Power of God)*. Westminster, Md.: The Newman Press.

Guagliardo, Vincent A., Charles R. Hess, and Richard C. Taylor, trans. 1996. *Commentary on the Book of Causes/St. Thomas Aquinas.* Washington, D.C.: Catholic University of America Press.

Maurer, Armand. 1968. *On Being and Essence/St. Thomas Aquinas*, 2nd rev. ed. Toronto: Pontifical Institute of Mediaeval Studies.

Miller, Robert T. 1997. *St Thomas Aquinas, De aeternitate mundi* (after the Leonine edition of Aquinas's works, Vol. 43 *Sancti Thomae De Aquino Opera Omnia* 85–89). Rome, 1976.

Mulligan, R. W., James V. McGlynn, and R. W. Schmidt. 1952–1954. *St Thomas Aquinas, Questiones Disputatae de Veritate.* Chicago: Henry Regnery Company.

Other Works

Abhishiktananda. 1979. *The Secret of Arunachala: A Christian Hermit on Shiva's Holy Mountain.* Delhi: ISPCK.

———. 1969. *Hindu-Christian Meeting Point—within the Cave of the Heart.* Translated by Sara Grant. Delhi: ISPCK.

———. 1974. *Saccidānanda: A Christian Approach to Advaitic Experience.* 1st English ed. Delhi: ISPCK-LPH.

Adamson, Peter. 2002. *The Arabic Plotinus: A Philosophical Study of the "Theology of Aristotle."* London: Duckworth.

———. 2007. *Al-Kindi.* Great Medieval Thinkers. Oxford: Oxford University Press.

———. 2013. *Interpreting Avicenna: Critical Essays.* Cambridge: Cambridge University Press.

Aleaz, K. P. 1996. *The Relevance of Relation in Sankara's Advaita Vedanta.* Kant Publications, Delhi.

———. 2000. *A Convergence of Advaita Vedanta and Eastern Christian Thought.* Delhi: ISPCK.

———. 2008. *Christian Thought Through Advaita Vedanta.* Reprint of 1996 edition. Delhi: ISPCK.

Aristotle. 2004. *Metaphysics.* Translated by Hugh Lawson-Tancred. London: Penguin.

Augustine. 1973. *City of God* and *On Christian Doctrine.* Translated by M. Dods and J. F. Shaw. Michigan: Grand Rapids.

Ayres, Lewis, and Gareth Jones, eds. 1998. *Christian Origins: Theology, Rhetoric and Community.* New York: Routledge.

Baldner, Steven Earl, and William E. Carroll. 1997. *Aquinas on Creation: Writings on the "Sentences" of Peter Lombard, Book 2, Distinction 1, Question 1.* Toronto: Pontifical Institute of Mediaeval Studies.

Barua, Ankur. 2015. "Classical Advaitic Definitions of 'Substance' and the Unreality of the World." *Journal of Hindu Studies* 8, no. 1: 44–64.

———. 2016. "'The Absolute of Advaita and the Spirit of Hegel: Situating Vedānta on the Horizons of British Idealisms.'" *Journal of the Indian Council for Philosophical Research* 34: 1–17.

Boland, Vivian. 1996. *Ideas in God According to Saint Thomas Aquinas.* New York: E.J. Brill.

Bonin, Therese. 2001. *Creation as Emanation: The Origin of Diversity in Albert the Great's* On the Causes and the Procession of the Universe. Notre Dame, Ind.: University of Notre Dame Press.

Bonino, Serge-Thomas, ed. 2009. *Surnaturel: A Controversy at the Heart of Twentieth-Century Thomistic Thought.* Translated by Robert Williams and Matthew Levering. Ave Maria, Fla.: Sapientia Press of Ave Maria University.

Booth, Edward. 1983. *Aristotelian Aporetic Ontology in Islamic and Christian Thinkers.* Cambridge: Cambridge University Press.

Bourgeault, Cynthia. 2016. *The Heart of Centering Prayer: Nondual Christianity in Theory and Practice.* Boulder, Colo: Shambhala.

———. 2007. "Beatrice Bruteau's 'Prayer and Identity': An Introduction with Text and Commentary." *Sewanee Theological Review* 50, no. 3: 385–407.

Boyd, Robin. 2000. *An Introduction to Indian Christian Theology*, rev. ed. New Delhi: ISPCK.

Brooks, Richard. 1969. "The Meaning of 'Real' in Advaita Vedanta." *Philosophy East and West* 19, no. 4: 385–98.

Burrell, David B. 1986a. "Essence and Existence: Avicenna and Greek Philosophy." *MIDEO (Melanges Institut Dominicain d'Etudes Orientales)* 17: 53–66.

———. 1986b. *Knowing the Unknowable God: Ibn-Sina, Maimonides, Aquinas.* Notre Dame, Ind.: University of Notre Dame Press.

———. 1993. *Freedom and Creation in Three Traditions.* Notre Dame, Ind.: University of Notre Dame Press.

———. 2000. "Analogy, Creation, and Theological Language." *Proceedings of the American Catholic Philosophical Association* 74: 35–52.

———. 2001. "Creation, Metaphysics, and Ethics." *Faith and Philosophy* 18, no. 2: 204–22.

———. 2004. *Faith and Freedom: An Interfaith Perspective.* Oxford: John Wiley & Sons.

———. 2008a. "Albert, Aquinas, and Dionysius." *Modern Theology* 24, no. 4: 633–51.

———. 2008b. "Creator/Creatures Relation: 'the Distinction' vs. 'Onto-Theology.'" *Faith and Philosophy* 25: 177–89.

———. 2008c. "Maimonides, Aquinas and Ghazali: Distinguishing God from the World." *Scottish Journal of Theology* 61, no. 3: 270–87.

———. 2010. *Creation and the God of Abraham.* New York: Cambridge University Press.

———. 2017. *Creation Ex Nihilo.* Divine Creation and Linguistic Creations. https://sms.cam.ac.uk/collection/2662424.

Burrell, David B., and Bernard McGinn, eds. 1990. *God and Creation: An Ecumenical Symposium.* Notre Dame, Ind.: University of Notre Dame Press.

Burrell, David B., and Elena Malits. 1997. *Original Peace: Restoring God's Creation.* Mahwah, N.J.: Paulist Press International.

Cabezon, Jose Ignacio. 1998. *Scholasticism: Cross-Cultural and Comparative Perspectives.* Albany: State University of New York Press.

Charlton, James. 2014. *Non-Dualism in Eckhart, Julian of Norwich and Traherne*, reprint ed. New York. Bloomsbury Academic.

Clarke, J. J. 1997. *Oriental Enlightenment: The Encounter between Asian and Western Thought.* London: Routledge.

Clarke, W. Norris. 2001. *The One and the Many: A Contemporary Thomistic Metaphysics.* Notre Dame, Ind.: University of Notre Dame Press.

———. 2009. *The Creative Retrieval of Saint Thomas Aquinas: Essays in Thomistic Philosophy, New and Old.* New York: Fordham University Press.

Clayton, Philip. 1998. "The Case for Christian Panentheism." *Dialog: A Journal of Theology* 37, no. 3: 201–8.

———. 1999. "The Panentheistic Turn in Christian Theology." *Dialog* 38: 289–93.

———. 2000. *The Problem of God in Modern Thought.* Grand Rapids, Mich.: Eerdmans Publishing Company.

Clooney, Francis X. 2017. *The Future of Hindu-Christian Studies: A Theological Inquiry.* Routledge Hindu Studies. New York: Routledge.

———. 2018. "Alienation, Xenophilia, and Coming Home: William Wallace, SJ's *From Evangelical to Catholic by Way of the East.*" *Common Knowledge* 24, no. 2: 280–90.

———. 1993. *Theology after Vedānta: An Experiment in Comparative Theology.* Albany: State University of New York Press.

———. 2001. *Hindu God, Christian God: How Reason Helps Break down the Boundaries between Religions.* New York: Oxford University Press.

———. 2010. *Comparative Theology: Deep Learning across Religious Borders.* Chichester: Wiley-Blackwell.

Coelho, Ivo, ed. 2010. *Brahman and Person: Essays by Richard De Smet.* Delhi: Motilal Banarsidass Publishers.

Coelho, Ivo, ed. 2013. *Understanding Sankara.* Delhi: Motilal Banarsidass Publishers.

Colledge, Edmund, and Bernard McGinn. 1981. *Meister Eckhart: The Essential Sermons, Commentaries, Treatises, and Defense.* London: SPCK.

Comans, Michael. 2000. *The Method of Early Advaita Vedānta: A Study of Gauḍapāda, Śaṅkara, Sureśvara, and Padmapāda.* Delhi: Motilal Banarsidass Publishers.

Cooper, John W. 2007. *Panentheism: The Other God of the Philosophers.* Westmont, Ill.: Intervarsity Press.

Cornille, Catherine. 2020. *Meaning and Method in Comparative Theology.* Hoboken, N.J.: John Wiley & Sons.

Coward, Harold G. 1989. *Hindu-Christian Dialogue: Perspectives and Encounters.* Faith Meets Faith Series. Maryknoll, N.Y.: Orbis Books.

Daley, Brian E. 2016. "Unpacking the Chalcedonian Formula: From Studied Ambiguity to Saving Mystery." *The Thomist* 80: 165–89.

Dandoy, Georges. 1919. *An Essay on the Doctrine of the Unreality of the World in the Advaita.* Calcutta: Catholic Orphan Press (Reprinted from the *Catholic Herald* of India).

———. 1932. *L'Ontologie Du Vedanta: Essai Sur L'Acosmisme de L'Advaita Avec Commentaires de Jacques Maritain et Olivier Lacombe.* Translated by Gauthier Louis-Marcel. Paris: Desclee de Brouwer et Cie.

Dasgupta, Surendranath. 1997. *A History of Indian Philosophy.* Vol. 1. Delhi: Motilal Banarsidass.

Davies, Brian, ed. 1987. *Language, Meaning and God: Essays in Honour of Herbert McCabe, O.P.* London: Geoffrey Chapman.

Davies, Brian, and G. R. Evans, eds. 2008. *Anselm of Canterbury: The Major Works Including Monologion, Proslogion, and Why God Became Man*. Oxford World's Classics. Oxford: Oxford University Press.

De Smet, R., and J. Neuner, eds. 1996. *Religious Hinduism*, 4th ed. Allahabad: St Pauls.

De Smet, Richard, and Bradley J. Malkovsky. 2000. *New Perspectives on Advaita Vedānta: Essays in Commemoration of Professor Richard De Smet, S.J.* Leiden: Brill.

Deshpande, Sharad, ed. 2015. *Philosophy in Colonial India*. New Delhi: Springer.

Deussen, Paul. and Charles Johnston. 1979. *The System of the Vedānta*. Delhi: Oriental Reprint.

Doolan, Gregory T. 2014. *Aquinas on the Divine Ideas as Exemplar Causes*. Washington, D.C.: Catholic University of America Press.

———. 2015. "Aquinas on the Divine Ideas and the Really Real." *Nova et Vetera* 13, no. 4: 1059–91.

Doyle, Sean. 2006. *Synthesizing the Vedanta: The Theology of Pierre Johanns S.J.* Vol. 32. Religions and Discourse. Bern: Peter Lang.

Drummond, John, and James Hart, eds. 1996. *The Truthful and the Good: Essays in Honour of Robert Sokolowski*. Dordrecht: Kluwer Academic Publishers.

Du Boulay, Shirley. 2005. *The Cave of the Heart: The Life of Swami Abhishiktananda*. Maryknoll, N.Y.: Orbis Books.

Fabro, Cornelio. 1961. *Participation et Causalité selon S. Thomas d'Aquin*. Louvain: Publications Universitaires.

———. 1974. "The Intensive Hermeneutics of Thomistic Philosophy: The Notion of Participation." *Review of Metaphysics* 27: 449–91.

Fodor, Jim, and F. C. Bauerschmidt, eds. 2004. *Aquinas in Dialogue: Thomas for the Twenty-First Century*. Malden, Mass.: Wiley-Blackwell.

Friesen, J. Glenn. 2015. *Abhishiktananda (Henri Le Saux): Christian Nondualism and Hindu Advaita*. Calgary: Aevum Books.

Ganeri, Martin. "Toward an Alternative Theology: Confessions of a Non-Dualist Christian—Sara Grant RSCJ"s Contribution to Catholic Theological and Spiritual Encounter with Hinduism." http://publications.heythrop.ac.uk/1550/.

———. 2007. "Catholic Encounter with Hindus in the Twentieth Century." *New Blackfriars* 88, no. 1016: 410–32.

———. 2015. *Indian Thought and Western Theism: The Vedānta of Rāmānuja*. New York: Routledge.

———. 2018. "'Thinking the Creator and Creature Together': How Rāmānuja's Account of Scriptural Meaning Encourages Unitive Language in Christian Discourse about God and the World." *Journal of Hindu-Christian Studies* 31: Article 18.

Geiger, L.-B. 1952. *La participation dans la philosophie de saint Thomas d'Aquin*. Montreal: Institut d'Etudes Médiévales.

Gersh, Stephen. 1978. *From Iamblichus to Eriugena: An Investigation of the Prehistory and Evolution of the Pseudo-Dionysian Tradition*. Leiden: Brill.

Gerson, Lloyd P., ed. 2011. *The Cambridge History of Philosophy in Late Antiquity*. Online. Vol. I. Cambridge: Cambridge University Press.

Gilson, Étienne, ed. 1974. *St. Thomas Aquinas, 1274–1974: Commemorative Studies*. Toronto: Pontifical Institute of Mediaeval Studies.

———. 1989. *L'esprit de la Philosophie Médiévale*. Paris: Vrin.

Goris, Harm, Herwi Rikhof, and Henk Schoot, eds. 2009. *Divine Transcendence and Immanence in the Work of Thomas Aquinas*. Publications of the Thomas Instituut Te Utrecht. Leuven: Peeters.

Grant, Sara. 1999. *Śaṅkarācārya"s Concept of Relation*. Delhi: Motilal Banarsidass.

———. 2002. *Towards an Alternative Theology: Confessions of a Non-Dualist Christian*. Notre Dame, Ind.: University of Notre Dame Press.

Gregorios, Paulos. 2002. *Neoplatonism and Indian Philosophy*. Albany: State University of New York Press.

Griffiths, Bede. 1983. *The Marriage of East and West: A Sequel to the Golden String*. London: Fount.

Griffiths, Bede. 1985. "Transcending Dualism: An Eastern Approach to the Semitic Religions," *Cistercian Studies* XX: 73–87.

Guthrie, W. K. C., trans. 1939. *On the Heavens/Aristotle*. London: William Heinemann.

Hacker, Paul. 1950. "Eigentümlichkeiten der Lehre und Terminologie Śaṅkaras: *Avidyā, Nāmarūpa, Māyā, Īśvara*." *Zeitschrift der Deutschen Morgenländischen Gesellschaft* 100: 246–86.

Hacker, Paul, and Wilhelm Halbfass. 1995. *Philology and Confrontation: Paul Hacker on Traditional and Modern Vedānta*. Albany: State University of New York Press.

Halbfass, Wilhelm. 1988. *India and Europe: An Essay in Understanding*. Albany: State University of New York Press.

———. 1992. *On Being and What There Is: Classical Vaiśeṣika and the History of Indian Ontology*. Albany: State University of New York Press.

Hankey, W. J. 1998. "From Metaphysics to History, from Exodus to Neoplatonism, from Scholasticism to Pluralism: The Fate of Gilsonian Thomism in English-Speaking North America." *Dionysius* 16: 157–88.

Harris, R. Baine. ed. 1981. *Neoplatonism and Indian Thought*. Albany: State University of New York Press.

Hart, David Bentley. 2013. *The Experience of God: Being, Consciousness, Bliss*. New Haven, Conn.: Yale University Press

Heim, S. Mark. 2019. "Comparative Theology at Twenty-Five: The End of the Beginning." *Modern Theology* 35, no. 1: 163–80.

Holmes, Christopher R. J. 2018. "Revisiting the God/World Difference." *Modern Theology* 34, no. 2 (April): 159–76.

Hopkins, Jasper. 1979. *Nicholas of Cusa on God as Not-Other: A Translation and an Appraisal of De Li Non Aliud*. Minneapolis: University of Minnesota.

Hyman, Gavin. 2008. "Augustine on the 'Nihil': An Interrogation." *Journal for Culture and Religious Theory* 9, no. 1: 35–49.

Inglis, John. ed. 2002. *Medieval Philosophy and the Classical Tradition in Islam, Judaism, and Christianity*. London: Curzon.

Ivry, Alfred, L. 1978. *Al-Kindī's Metaphysics/a Translation of Yaʿqūb Ibn Isḥāq al-Kindī's Treatise "On First Philosophy" (Fī al-Falsafah al-Ūlā) with Introduction and Commentary*. Albany: State University of New York Press.

Keller, Catherine. 2008. *On the Mystery: Discerning Divinity in Process*. Minneapolis, Minn.: Fortress Press.

Kerr, Fergus ed. 2003. *Contemplating Aquinas: On the Varieties of Interpretation*. London: SCM Press.
King, Richard. 1991. "Brahman and the World: Immanence and Transcendence in Advaita Vedānta. A Comparative Perspective." *The Scottish Journal of Religious Studies* XII, no. 2: 107–27.
———. 1999. *Orientalism and Religion: Post-Colonial Theory, India and "The Mystic East."* London: Routledge.
Klostermaier, Klaus K., 1969. *Hindu and Christian in Vrindaban;* London: Student Christian Movement Press.
Kobusch, Theo. 2018. *Selbstwerdung und Personalität: Spätantike Philosophie und ihr Einfluss auf die Moderne*. Tübingen: Mohr Siebeck.
Kosman, Aryeh. 2013. *The Activity of Being: An Essay on Aristotle's Ontology*. Cambridge, Mass.: Harvard University Press.
Krempel, A. 1952. *La Doctrine de la Relation chez Saint Thomas*. Paris: J. Vrin.
Kretzmann, Norman. 2002. *The Metaphysics of Creation: Aquinas's Natural Theology in Summa Contra Gentiles II*. Oxford: OUP.
Lewis, C. S. 1962. *They Asked for a Paper*. London: Geoffrey Bles.
Lipner, Julius J. 1978. "The Christian and Vedāntic Theories of Originative Causality: A Study in Transcendence and Immanence." *Philosophy East and West* 28, no. 1: 53–68.
———. 1998. "Richard V. De Smet, S.J.—An Appreciation." *Journal of Hindu-Christian Studies* 11 (January): Article 13, 51–54.
———. 1999. *Brahmabandhab Upadhyay: The Life and Thought of a Revolutionary*. Oxford: Oxford University Press.
Lossky, Vladimir. 1973. *Théologie Négative et Connaissance de Dieu chez Maître Eckhart*. Paris: Vrin.
Lott, Eric J. 1980. *Vedāntic Approaches to God*. Library of Philosophy and Religion. London: Macmillan.
Loy, David. 1988. *Nonduality: A Study in Comparative Philosophy*. New Haven, Conn.: Yale University Press.
Lubac, Henri de. 1965. *Le Mystère du Surnaturel*. Paris: Aubier.
Luibheid, Colm, and Paul Rorem, trans. 1987. *The Pseudo-Dionysius: The Complete Works*. Mahwah, N.J.: Paulist Press.
Mahadevan, T. M. P. 1985. *Superimposition in Advaita Vedānta*. New Delhi: Sterling.
Malkovsky, Bradley. 1997. "In Memoriam: Richard De Smet, S.J. (1916–1997)." *Journal of Hindu-Christian Studies* 10: Article 5, 3–4.
———. 1997. "The Personhood of Śaṁkara's 'Para Brahman.'" *The Journal of Religion* 77 (4): 541–62.
———. 1999. "Advaita Vedānta and Christian Faith." *Journal of Ecumenical Studies* 36, nos. 3–4: 397–422.
———. ed. 2000. *New Perspectives on Advaita Vedānta: Essays in Commemoration of Professor Richard De Smet, S.J.* Leiden: Brill.
———. 2001. *The Role of Divine Grace in the Soteriology of Śaṅkarācārya*. Leiden: Brill.
Marmodoro, Anna, and Brian D. Prince, eds. 2015. *Causation and Creation in Late Antiquity*. Cambridge: Cambridge University Press.

Marmura, Michael E. 2000. *The Incoherence of the Philosophers: Tahafut Al-Falasifah: A Parallel English-Arabic Text*. Provo, Utah: Brigham Young University Press.

Maryniarczyk, Andrzej. 2016. "Philosophical Creationism: Thomas Aquinas' Metaphysics of Creatio Ex Nihilo." *Studia Gilsoniana* 5, no. 1: 217–68.

Mattam, Joseph. 1973. "Interpreting Christ to India: A Pioneer, Pierre Johanns, S.J." *The Clergy Monthly*, 37: 55.

May, Gerhard. 1994. *Creation Ex Nihilo: The Doctrine of "Creation out of Nothing" in Early Christian Thought*. Translated by A. S. Worrall. Edinburgh: T&T Clark.

McEvilley, Thomas. 2002. *The Shape of Ancient Thought: Comparative Studies in Greek and Indian Philosophies*. New York: Allworth Press.

McFague, Sallie. 1987. *Models of God*. Philadelphia: Fortress Press.

McFarland, Ian A. 2014. *From Nothing: A Theology of Creation*. Louisville, Ky.: Westminster John Knox Press.

McGinn, Bernard, ed. 1986. *Meister Eckhart, Teacher and Preacher*. New York: Paulist Press.

McWhorter, Matthew R. 2013. "Aquinas on God's Relation to the World." *New Blackfriars* 94, no. 1049: 3–19.

Molendijk, Arie L. 2016. *Friedrich Max Müller & the Sacred Books of the East*. Oxford: OUP.

Monchanin, Jules, and Swami Abhishiktananda. 1964. *A Benedictine Ashram*, rev. ed. Douglas, Isle of Man: Times Press.

Mondin, Battista. 1968. *The Principle of Analogy in Protestant and Catholic Theology*, 2nd ed. The Hague: Martinus Nijhoff.

Nicholson, Hugh. 2011. *Comparative Theology and the Problem of Religious Rivalry*. Oxford: Oxford University Press.

Norris, Richard A. 1965. *God and World in Early Christian Theology*. New York: Seabury Press.

O'Callaghan, John P., and Thomas S. Hibbs, eds. 1999. *Recovering Nature: Essays in Natural Philosophy, Ethics, and Metaphysics in Honor of Ralph McInerny*. Notre Dame, Ind.: University of Notre Dame Press.

Oakes, Edward T. 2016. *A Theology of Grace in Six Controversies*. Grand Rapids, Mich.: W.B. Eerdmans Pub. Co.

Oakes, Robert. 1983. "Does Traditional Theism Entail Pantheism?" *American Philosophical Quarterly* 20, no. 1: 105–12.

Oliver, Simon. 2017. *Creation: A Guide for the Perplexed*. London: Bloomsbury T&T Clark.

O'Meara, Thomas F. 1997. *Thomas Aquinas: Theologian*. Notre Dame, Ind.: University of Notre Dame Press.

O'Neil, L. Thomas. 1980. *Māyā in Śaṅkara: Measuring the Immeasurable*. Delhi: Motilal Banarsidass.

Otto, Rudolf. 1932. *Mysticism East and West: A Comparative Analysis of the Nature of Mysticism*. London: Macmillan and Co.

Panikkar, Raimundo. 1981. *The Unknown Christ of Hinduism*, rev. and enlarged. London: Darton, Longman and Todd.

———. 1997. "Nine Ways Not to Talk about God." *Cross Currents* 47, no. 2.

Perl, Eric. 2014. *Thinking Being: Introduction to Metaphysics in the Classical Tradition.* Leiden: Brill.

Perrett, R. W. 2016. *An Introduction to Indian Philosophy.* Cambridge: Cambridge University Press.

Pieper, Josef. 1957. *The Silence of Saint Thomas.* New York: Pantheon.

Plotinus and A. H. Armstrong. 1966–1988. *Enneads.* Loeb Classical Library. Cambridge, Mass.: Harvard University Press.

Poulsom, Martin G. 2014. *The Dialectics of Creation: Creation and the Creator in Edward Schillebeeckx and David Burrell.* London: Bloomsbury T&T Clark.

Ram-Prasad, Chakravarthi. 2002. *Advaita Epistemology and Metaphysics: An Outline of Indian Non-Realism.* London: Routledge.

Rambachan, Anantanand. 1991. *Accomplishing the Accomplished: The Vedas as a Source of Valid Knowledge in Sankara.* Honolulu: University of Hawaii Press.

———. 2015. *A Hindu Theology of Liberation: Not-Two Is Not One.* Albany: State University of New York Press.

Ramsey, Ian, ed. 1961. *Prospect for Metaphysics: Essays of Metaphysical Exploration.* London: George Allen & Unwin.

Rangaswami, Sudhakshina, ed. 2012. *The Roots of Vedānta: Selections from Śaṅkara's Writings.* New Delhi: Penguin India.

Rao, Srinivasa. 1996. "Two 'Myths' in Advaita." *Journal of Indian Philosophy* 24: 265–79.

Rosemann, Philipp W. 1996. *Omne Agens Agit Sibi Simile: A "Repetition" of Scholastic Metaphysics.* Leuven: Leuven University Press.

Ruether, Rosemary Radford. 2000. "The God of Possibilities: Immanence and Transcendence Rethought." *Concilium* (2000/2004): 45–54.

Saraswati, Swami Dayananda. *Introduction to Vedanta.* Delhi: Vision Books, 2016.

Shanley, Brian. 2002. *The Thomist Tradition.* Dordrecht, The Netherlands: Kluwer.

Shortt, Rupert. 2016. *God Is No Thing: Coherent Christianity.* London: C. Hurst & Co.

Sokolowski, Robert. 1982. *The God of Faith and Reason.* Notre Dame, Ind.: University of Notre Dame Press.

Solomon, E. A. 1969. *Avidyā—A Problem of Truth and Reality.* Ahmedabad: Gujarat University.

Soskice, Janet Martin, ed. 2013. "Creation 'Ex Nihilo' and Modern Theology." *Modern Theology* 29, no. 2.

Staal, J. F. 1961. *Advaita and Neoplatonism: A Critical Study in Comparative Philosophy.* Madras: University of Madras.

Suthren Hirst, J. G. 2005. *Śaṁkara's Advaita Vedānta: A Way of Teaching.* Abingdon: Routledge Curzon.

Tanner, Kathryn. 1988. *God and Creation in Christian Theology: Tyranny or Empowerment?* Oxford: Basil Blackwell.

Te Velde, Rudi. 1995. *Participation and Substantiality in Thomas Aquinas.* Leiden: Brill.

Teasdale, Wayne Robert. 1987. *Toward a Christian Vedānta: The Encounter of Hinduism and Christianity According to Bede Griffiths.* Bangalore: Asian Trading Corp.

Tennent, Timothy C. 2000. *Building Christianity on Indian Foundations: The Legacy of Brahmabandhav Upadhyay.* Delhi: ISPCK.

Thatamanil, John J. 2006. *The Immanent Divine: God, Creation and the Human Predicament*. Minneapolis, Minn.: Augsburg Fortress.

———. 2009. "Ecstasy and Nonduality: On Comparing Varieties of Immanence." *Journal of Hindu-Christian Studies* 22 (January): 19–24.

Turner, Denys. 2004. *Faith, Reason and the Existence of God*. Cambridge: Cambridge University Press.

Un moine d'Occident. 1982. *Doctrine de la Non-Dualité (Advaita-Vāda) et Christianisme: Jalons pour un accord doctrinal entre l'Église et le Vedānta*. Paris: Dervy-Livres.

Van Wiele, Jan. 2007. "Neo-Thomism and the Theology of Religions: A Case Study on Belgian and U.S. Textbooks (1870–1950)." *Theological Studies* 68: 780–807.

Vanhoozer, Kevin J. 1999. "A Christian Case for Panentheism? The Case Remains Unproven." *Dialog: A Journal of Theology* 38, no. 4: 281–85.

Von Balthasar, Hans Urs. 2003. *Cosmic Liturgy*. San Francisco: Ignatius Press.

Von Brück, Michael. 1986. *The Unity of Reality: God, God-Experience, and Meditation in the Hindu-Christian Dialogue*. Mahwah, N.J.: Paulist Press.

Voss Roberts, Michelle. 2010. *Dualities: A Theology of Difference*. Louisville, Ky.: Westminster John Knox Press.

Warrier, A. G. Krishna. 1977. *God in Advaita*. Simla: Indian Institute of Advanced Study.

Wallace, William. 1923. *From Evangelical to Catholic by Way of the East*. Calcutta: Catholic Orphan Press.

Watzlawik, Joseph. 1966. *Leo XIII and the New Scholasticism*. Cebu City, Philippines: University of San Carlos.

Webster, John. 2016. *Confessing God: Essays in Dogmatics II*, 2nd ed. London: T&T Clark.

Weinandy, T., D. Keating, and J. Yocum, eds. 2004. *Aquinas on Doctrine: A Critical Introduction*. London: T&T Clark.

Wendlinder, Anastasia. 2014. *Speaking of God in Thomas Aquinas and Meister Eckhart: Beyond Analogy*. London: Taylor & Francis.

White, Thomas Joseph. 2015. *The Incarnate Lord: A Thomistic Study in Christology*. Washington, D.C.: Catholic University of America Press.

Williams, Rowan. 1994. "'Good for Nothing'? Augustine on Creation," *Augustinian Studies* 25: 9–24.

Wippel, John F. 1984. "Thomas Aquinas and Participation" in *Studies in Medieval Philosophy*. Washington, D.C.: Catholic University of America Press: 117–158.

———. 1993. *Thomas Aquinas on the Divine Ideas*. Toronto: Pontifical Institute of Mediaeval Studies.

———. 2000. *The Metaphysical Thought of Thomas Aquinas: From Finite Being to Uncreated Being*. Washington, D.C.: Catholic University of America Press.

Wolfson, Harry A. 1961. "Extradeical and Intradeical Interpretations of Platonic Ideas." *Journal of the History of Ideas* 22, no. 1: 3–32.

INDEX

Daniel Soars teaches in the Divinity Department at Eton College and is book reviews editor for the *Journal of Hindu–Christian Studies*.

Comparative Theology / *Thinking Across Traditions*

SERIES EDITORS

Loye Ashton and John Thatamanil

Hyo-Dong Lee, *Spirit, Qi, and the Multitude: A Comparative Theology for the Democracy of Creation*

Michelle Voss Roberts, *Tastes of the Divine: Hindu and Christian Theologies of Emotion*

Michelle Voss Roberts (ed.), *Comparing Faithfully: Insights for Systematic Theological Reflection*

Francis X. Clooney, S.J., and Klaus von Stosch (eds.), *How to Do Comparative Theology*

F. Dominic Longo, *Spiritual Grammar: Genre and the Saintly Subject in Islam and Christianity*

S. Mark Heim, *Crucified Wisdom: Theological Reflection on Christ and the Bodhisattva*

Martha L. Moore-Keish and Christian T. Collins Winn (eds.), *Karl Barth and Comparative Theology*

John J. Thatamanil, *Circling the Elephant: A Comparative Theology of Religious Diversity*

Catherine Cornille (ed.), *Atonement and Comparative Theology: The Cross in Dialogue with Other Religions*

Daniel Soars, *The World and God Are Not-Two: A Hindu–Christian Conversation*

CPSIA information can be obtained
at www.ICGtesting.com
Printed in the USA
JSHW011353170323
39100JS00001B/10

9 781531 502058